Town Planning in

Making Contemporary Britain Series

General Editor: Anthony Seldon
Consultant Editor: Peter Hennessy

Forthcoming

British Industry since 1945
Margaret Ackrill

British Foreign Policy since 1945
Anthony Adamthwaite

The Conservative Party since 1945
John Barnes

Sport in Britain since 1945
Richard Holt and Tony Mason

Class and Inequality in Britain
since 1945
Paul Keating

Parliament since 1945
Philip Norton

British Youth Cultures since 1945
William Osgerby

Terrorism since 1945
Paul Wilkinson

Local Government since 1945
Ken Young and Nirmala Rao

* Indicates title now out of print.

The series *Making Contemporary Britain* is essential reading
for students, as well as providing masterly overviews for the
general reader. Each book in the series puts the central
themes and problems of the specific topic into clear focus.
The studies are written by leading authorities in their field,
who integrate the latest research into the text but at the same
time present the material in a clear, ordered fashion which
can be read with value by those with no prior knowledge of
the subject.

THE INSTITUTE OF CONTEMPORARY
BRITISH HISTORY

Senate House
Malet Street
London WC1H 7HU

Town Planning in Britain since 1900

The Rise and Fall of the Planning Ideal

Gordon E. Cherry

First published 1996

Blackwell Publishers Ltd
108 Cowley Road
Oxford OX4 1JF

Blackwell Publishers Inc.
238 Main Street
Cambridge, Massachusetts 02142
USA

British Library Cataloguing in Publication Data
A CIP catalogue record for this book is available from the British Library.

Library of Congress Cataloging-in-Publication Data
Cherry, Gordon Emanuel.
    Town planning in Britain since 1900 : the rise and fall of the planning ideal / Gordon E. Cherry.
        p.   cm. — (Making contemporary Britain)
    Includes bibliographical references and index
    ISBN 0–631–19993–4. — ISBN 0–631–19994–2 (pbk.)
    1. City planning (Great Britain)—History—20th century.   2. Urban policy—Great Britain—History—20th century.   I. Title.
II. Series.
HT169.G7C4598   1996
307.1′2′09410904—dc20   96-8105
                                                                CIP

Typeset in 10 on 12pt Ehrhardt
by Grahame & Grahame Editorial, Brighton, East Sussex

Printed in Great Britain by Hartnolls Limited, Bodmin, Cornwall
This book is printed on acid-free paper

Contents

Series Editor's Preface

The Institute of Contemporary British History's series *Making Contemporary Britain* is aimed directly at students and at others interested in learning more about topics in post-war British history. In the series, authors are less attempting to break new ground than presenting clear and balanced overviews of the state of knowledge on each of the topics.

The ICBH was founded in October 1986 with the objective of promoting the study of British history since 1945 at every level. To that end, it publishes books and a quarterly journal, *Contemporary Record*; it organizes seminars and conferences for school students, undergraduates, researchers and teachers of post-war history; and it runs a number of research programmes and other activities.

A central theme of the ICBH's work is that post-war history is too often neglected in British schools, institutes of higher education and beyond. The ICBH acknowledges the validity of the arguments against the study of recent history, notably the problems of bias, of overly subjective teaching and writing, and the difficulties of perspective. But it believes that the values of studying post-war history outweigh the drawbacks, and that the health and future of a liberal democracy require that its citizens know more about the most recent past of their country than the limited knowledge possessed by British citizens, young and old, today. Indeed, the ICBH believes that the dangers of political indoctrination are higher where the young are *not* informed of the recent past.

This book is an exciting addition for the series. Not ony does it branch into an area, town planning, which is new, but it also covers the whole period from 1900 and thus has a larger reach and can assess events in greater historical context than other books. It is very much hoped that it will appeal not just to those studying courses in building town planning but also to those reading history, politics and economics, as the subject is an often overlooked dimension of those fields.

Gordon Cherry was a distinguished academic and author. He embarked on this project with tremendous enthusiasm and managed to complete the book very shortly before he died.

Anthony Seldon

Acknowledgements

Since my retirement from the University of Birmingham a few years ago my interests have turned to the professional aspects of town planning today. I have been helped by two aspects of planning work. One has been with regard to Examinations in Public organized by the Department of the Environment (DoE). They have given me an insight into present-day planning problems and I thank the DoE for this opportunity, and also the colleagues with whom I worked at Humberside, the Lake District, Buckinghamshire, and the early stages of Glamorgan.

These new aspects have been guided by some of my well-tuned historical observations and this *Town Planning in Britain since 1900* is the result of these historical forces. My strongest indebtedness is to the International Planning History Society (IPHS), whose members have been at the forefront of planning history: I must remember them at all times. My thanks also to the British Academy for expenses towards a conference in Hong Kong in 1994 which enabled me to gain experience of a major gathering in this field.

In retirement years it is a privilege to have such supports to one's academic pursuits. I am grateful to the School of Geography for having me as an Honorary Research Fellow; equally to the Institute for Advanced Research in the Humanities for their Honorary Fellowship.

For the last three years my attention has been drawn to Poland. In a Know How Fund project I have had the privilege of being one of a team of experts led by F. J. C. Amos. I worked on this project with Llewelyn Davies and in particular three of their planning consultants, David Walters, Patrick Clarke, Michael Mattingley and, especially, Graham Tomlinson. I must also mention Dr Zygmund Ziobrowski of the Institute of Physical Planning and Municipal Economy, who was the co-ordinator in Poland.

I thank Dr Peter Catterall, from the Institute of Contemporary History, for suggesting the idea for the book, and Tessa Harvey of Blackwell Publishers for help in making it come to fruition.

To my wife, Margaret, who has borne the greater burden: all praise for having typed the manuscript, having done so with patience and, she tells me, with pleasure.

Gordon E. Cherry
University of Birmingham
December 1995

To

Members of the

INTERNATIONAL PLANNING HISTORY SOCIETY

and the comradeship they always bring

1 The Collectivist Advance

During the nineteenth century the state in the form of both central and local government came to play an increasingly interventionist role in the social affairs of the country and to engage widely in matters of urban regulation. New units of local government were set up and by the time of the Edwardian era they came to be major players, discharging an array of municipal services. During the early years of the twentieth century town planning was one of an expanding range of functions for which they were responsible. The outreach of the state, in its various forms and changing ways, now constitutes a key element in the economic, social and political history of the country. In respect of the subject of this book – town planning – it provides an indispensable backcloth for any understanding of its adoption and subsequent development.

The evolutionary processes whereby the tentacles of state governance were extended during the nineteenth century were slow to take either shape or effect. It required at least 50 years from the 1830s to the 1880s for local government structures to emerge in a form which we would regard today as modern. It took the whole of the second half of the century for action on housing to reach a point whereby it could be seen as the beginnings of a coherent social welfare programme. Likewise with forms of urban regulation: these spanned many decades in their development and it was the Edwardian period before the action taken by energetic and ambitious cities, bolstered by the general scope of national objectives, produced an urban environment which we could regard as suitably improved.

The shift towards interventionism and an engagement in local affairs was gradual. Injustices perpetrated by property owners against the property-less (as in harmful conditions in factories and mines) were only slowly corrected as religious and political sentiment came to emphasize the responsibility of property rather than its rights. But assumptions by the middle classes as to moral duties in public service gained ground in the complex terrain of societal change, as described by Perkin (1989). The rise of professional society in England from the last quarter of the nineteenth century coincided with the period when the growth of London and the major industrial centres threw up problems of urban administration, the scale and complexity of which had never before been confronted. Britain industrialized and urbanized earlier than any other country in the western world during the nineteenth century.

Social, economic and environmental regulation had previously been the responsibility of a variety of different bodies. Medieval guilds maintained schools or alms houses, craft guilds supervised trading practices and labour conditions, and the church and charities provided facilities in health, welfare and education. But by the beginning of the nineteenth century the primary role was occupied by the chartered boroughs with their array of privileges and rights. Through their charters these towns had a corporate identity in the name of Mayor and Council. With growth in the size of towns becoming a significant feature in the new manufacturing areas from the middle of the eighteenth century onwards, most corporate boroughs established a body of Town (or Improvement) Commissioners to regulate their affairs. Influential town residents, acting as commissioners, sought to attain certain objectives. Particularly after 1760 and up to the 1830s, as many as 300 Improvement Commissions were appointed throughout the country, undertaking tasks such as opening up new streets, building bridges, paving, lighting or drainage works. Around the beginning of the nineteenth century, therefore, the growing towns were managed only by the sporadic action of a variety of independent bodies, regulation conducted on an ad hoc piecemeal basis.

Birmingham may be cited as an example (Cherry, 1994). In the middle of the eighteenth century the population of the town was around the 25,000 mark, and growing. It still had a manorial court, though the parish was the principal institution to supervise local affairs. It took over a century before the elements of a local government system, of the kind we would recognize today, were in place. Five Improvement Acts for Birmingham between 1769 and 1828 established new arrangements for dealing with the issues of the growing town. The commissioners had duties in cleansing and lighting, but these widened to include the maintenance of a force of watchmen and the improvement of market facilities. Ultimately the commissioners had ad hoc powers over streets, markets, scavenging, the Poor Law, highways and public order. The town received its Charter in 1838 (after the Municipal Corporations Act, 1835, repealed the old municipal charters) and municipal government, based on an elected council extended to a wider area than that exercised by the commissioners. For some years the new Council operated in parallel with the Improvement Commissioners and it was not until 1852 that the commissioners' duties were transferred to the Council. A system of governance which met the needs of an eighteenth-century town was finally replaced by one that could cope with the complexities of a growing city.

Local Government

In July 1833 a commission of 22 members was appointed to investigate conditions in the old corporations. Their report in 1835 was dismissive of the existing system of oligarchic corporate organization. The ensuing Municipal Corporations Act, 1835, abolished all previous charters and placed the constitution and power of the new municipal corporations on a simple uniform basis, elected from a popular franchise restricted to those with significant property qualifications, of above two and a half years' standing. A total of 178 reformed cities and boroughs came into existence in November 1835 (Vine, 1879). London was excluded, different arrangements applying to the capital, and so too were many of the growing towns of the Midlands and the North. But the populous towns which were excluded could be granted charters if application were made: this is how Birmingham received its Charter of Incorporation in 1838. By 1860 over twenty places had been added to the original 178 towns which enjoyed municipal incorporation. By 1901 there were 313 municipal boroughs.

A new pattern of local government emerged slowly, to match the new geography and population distribution of the country (Cherry, 1988). It was accompanied by a restructuring of government departments, which involved the setting up of the Local Government Board in 1871. It took over four separate elements: the Local Government Act Office, the Registrar General's Office, the Medical Department of the Privy Council and the Poor Law Board. The President of the Board became in effect the minister for local government. The next change for local administration was provided by the Public Health Act, 1875, which created over 700 Urban Sanitary Authorities. Meanwhile London had its Metropolitan Board of Works and Metropolitan Sanitary Authorities. Scotland's administrative map rested on Police Authorities.

A further modification for England and Wales came with the Local Government Act, 1888, which created County Boroughs with powers equal to and independent of the County Councils. The remainder (municipal boroughs and urban sanitary districts) were subject to the jurisdiction of the County Council. The intention behind the Act was that the administrative counties would be a unifying instrument of authority, combining rural and urban services, with shared costs. Only ten cities of more than 150,000 population (Birmingham, Bradford, Bristol, Hull, Leeds, Liverpool, Manchester, Newcastle, Nottingham and Sheffield) would be excluded from this arrangement and be granted practical autonomy: these were the County Boroughs. In fact 61 towns and cities of more that 50,000 population were granted this status, and the number had reached 81 by 1914. The seeds of a twentieth-century dispute between urban and rural power had been sown. In 1894 the Local Government Act gave a more orderly pattern to the district councils of England, through the creation of a patchwork of urban and rural districts, and revived the old village vestries by creating parish councils, but twentieth-century local government was heavily weighted towards the strength of the urban revenue base and the political influence of the large city authorities.

London stood apart from this system. The City Corporation governed the 673 acres (roughly a square mile) which made up the commercial heart; its constitution, privileges and procedures were ancient survivals. The Metropolitan Board of Works, with 46 appointed members, was the primary unit of administration for the bulk of the built up area; created in 1855 it had done good work in controlling main drainage and implementing the building acts, but its relationships with the vestries and district boards were not easy, and it ended its life with charges of corruption pressed against key officials. The Local Government Act 1888 created the London County Council in its place, with 118 directly elected councillors; the vestries were retained until 1899 when metropolitan borough councils replaced them. The powers of the LCC were further restricted through the existence of other central bodies operating within its area; these included the Metropolitan Water Board, the Metropolitan Asylums Board, the Central Unemployed Body, Thames Conservancy, Metropolitan Police, and of course the City Corporation – a list added to in 1908 with the setting up of the Port of London Authority.

Thus during the last 65 years of the nineteenth century the country's system of local government was fundamentally recast. The new pattern, the essentials of which have endured throughout the twentieth century, both reflected the interests of local, independent communities and provided fresh conduits for the exercise of state intervention. The precise definition of local and national interests remained elusive in a process whereby Britain became a much governed nation.

As the new units of local government were established the role of the full-time official grew in importance. By the late nineteenth century a number of town clerks had made their names and the larger towns had appointed key officers on a full-time basis – Medical Officers of Health, surveyors, treasurers and sanitary inspectors, bolstered by a growing local government salaried staff ranging from school attendance officers and school teachers to rent collectors, librarians, accountants and a public works labour force including street cleaners, gas workers and tramway men. The trade union NALGO, the National Association of Local Government Officers, was founded in 1905.

By the end of the century the larger councils had become multipurpose authorities, well resourced and demonstrably capable of being very effective units of organization. A former fragmentation of local government was replaced by a unifying corporate existence. Sanitary authorities were taken over by town councils; a former separation of boards of guardians and school boards from town councils ended when education and welfare services were added to the council's functions. They became local states whereby public sector authority was increasingly exercised over their communities. An uncertain relationship evolved between local and central powers and responsibilities. Certain functions were imposed upon local councils by Parliament, but many more were made permissible. In any event they could seek additional powers through private Acts of Parliament.

During the last third of the nineteenth century the larger urban authorities witnessed the emergence of popular politics and the creation of party machines. Legislation in 1869 effectively tripled the (male) electorate, from 717,000 in 1832 to 2,226,000, by adjusting voting qualifications (still dependent on rate paying). New opportunities for the manipulation of power were presented. The affairs of the Birmingham Liberal Association, founded in 1865, provide an extreme example of what could be done. It formed itself into a caucus with ward branches and fought the 1868 general election with great efficiency.

Joseph Chamberlain entered public life in Birmingham via the National Educational League and used his Unitarian connections to the full, but the party machine of the Liberal Party caucus was his political power base. Great things indeed were done in his mayoralty, 1873–6: municipalization of two private gas companies, and the Birmingham Water Works Company, and the launching of the Improvement Scheme to clear a central area of insanitary housing and replace it with an imposing boulevard (Corporation Street). His harnessing of municipal capitalism to the affairs of Birmingham transformed the city.

Social Welfare

The new local authorities became the agencies through which the various elements of social welfare programmes were ultimately delivered. Education and housing provide two examples.

By the 1840s, after many years of unresolved opposition between the Anglican Church and the Dissenting Churches, forces working for the extension of state control in education were gaining the upper hand. Voluntaryism would never be enough in a national educational system, where higher standards in educational attainment were increasingly regarded as crucial in an advanced industrial nation. Following the recommendations of a Royal Commission (1858–61) chaired by the Duke of Newcastle, rationalization of government grants in 1862 to two (a central grant based on attendance and a local grant financed from rates based on pupil achievements) confirmed the state's role in education. Within eight years the Education Act, 1870, established in principle the right of every child to some form of schooling. (The Scottish Education Act, coming two years later in 1872, differed from its English counterpart by imposing compulsory education on all children.) W. E. Forster, Vice-President of Education in Gladstone's first ministry, had conducted surveys in four large towns, finding less than 10 per cent of their population in schools. Estimates of literacy at the time suggest that 80 per cent of men and 70 per cent of women had some ability to read (rather than to write). The Act provided for School Boards to be established where there was proven need; these could provide non-denominational elementary schools financed out of the rates, voluntary schools existing side by side. By 1880 one child in six attended a Board School; by 1900 the proportion had risen to more than half (54 per cent). Further legislation in 1880 made attendance compulsory for children aged between five and ten. Meanwhile the minimum age for school-leaving was progressively raised: age 10 in 1876, 11 in 1893, 12 in 1899, and in 1900 School Boards were permitted to raise the age to 14.

Local authorities were progressively drawn into a major area of provision and control. In 1903 they were enabled to make by-laws licensing street trading by children aged over 11 years. More importantly, in 1902 the School Boards (2,560 in total) were abolished and the county councils, boroughs with populations in excess of 10,000, and urban districts with populations over 20,000, were made education authorities. In 1906 they were empowered to provide meals for elementary pupils by voluntary contributions or a halfpenny rate. School medical services began in 1907 and school clinics were established from 1912.

The provision of housing was another area of state intervention, operated through local authorities. A number of provincial centres had flirted with municipal housing, with various degrees of enthusiasm, but the first programme for its systematic provision belongs to London (Beattie, 1980). The 'Progressive' Administrations of the LCC, 1889–92 and 1892–5, formed by alliances of Liberals and early socialists, took advantage of the Housing of the Working Classes Act, 1890. Parts I and II of the Act facilitated rebuilding on cleared sites and Part III allowed authorities to undertake further rehousing without first clearing the slums. Within the LCC's Architects' Department a Housing of the Working Classes Branch was set up and a Works Department was formed as an alternative to the use of private contractors. The earliest schemes used Parts I and II of the 1890 Act: they were for blocks of flats on cleared sites in Limehouse and Poplar, and the largest comprised 19 blocks of dwellings at the Boundary Street redevelopment area in Bethnal Green. The Progressives, returned to office in 1898 after three years in opposition, proceeded to implement Part III of the Act in the Millbank Estate, Westminster.

These inner-city estates were expensive because of high land costs. Much cheaper land could be obtained in the suburbs, now serviced by municipal tramways. The LCC bought land for the development of cottage estates at Tooting (Totterdown Fields), Croydon (Norbury), Tottenham (White Hart Lane) and East Acton (Old Oak); they were all started before 1914, and the estate at Tooting was completed by this time.

Some authorities which had been lukewarm if not resistant to the principle of building municipal houses, either to replace demolished slum properties or to build for general need, responded with greater enthusiasm to the notion of encouraging building development in the suburbs. Birmingham went further than most down this line, perhaps satisfying its position of hostility to municipal housing. There had been no replacement housing in the Corporation Street scheme, but model schemes at Ryder Street (22 dwellings) and Lawrence Street (82 dwellings) were undertaken in 1890 and 1891 respectively. A further scheme in Milk Street in 1898 provided 64 flats in two-storey balcony access form. The Housing of the Working Classes Act, 1900, extended to provincial boroughs the powers given to London in 1890, but Birmingham preferred a different route. As described further in chapter 2, Councillor J. S. Nettlefold, chairman of a newly-formed Housing Committee, took a decided stance against the very principle of municipal house building. Instead he favoured purchasing suburban land, making it available for housing by private individuals and Public Utility Building Societies at low densities, ensuring an ample supply of open space and community facilities. The local council would benefit from a rise in land values which would be returned to ratepayers. There would be no municipal landlord for the houses; Birmingham preferred an indirect enabling role in garden suburb style for the resolution of its housing problem.

The two examples of education and housing readily suggest that British politicians did not act on social questions until they became serious. The same applied to a range of other examples. Reformist pressure was instrumental in the setting up of a Children's Employment Commission, the Reports of which in the 1860s led to legislation averting abuse, bringing noxious trades under control and raising standards in workshop conditions. Similarly it was only after a long struggle that legislation was introduced to regulate safety in coal mines. The state was slow to act in making provision for medical facilities in the form of doctors and hospitals; these were left to the poor law guardians, to doctors and philanthropists, and compulsory vaccination for children, introduced in 1853, was contested by those who saw it as an intrusion into civil liberties. The state began its role as quality guardian of the nation's food supplied to the public with a series of Adulteration of Food Acts, the first as early as 1860. The relief of poverty was likewise a long-running problem, tackled hesitatingly and slowly. Boards of Guardians operating within the Poor Law Act, 1834, exercised discretion, and in London, especially, outdoor relief was being given on a large scale by the 1860s. But the treatment of poverty and the particular problem of the able-bodied poor required national arrangements, not dependency on local circumstances, and it was not until the Edwardian period that this particular nettle was grasped.

The general inclination in all these matters was towards a minimum of state action with regard to social welfare. There was resistance to the taxation that would be necessary to implement the action demanded by social policy, and there was a residual suspicion of patronage and corruption likely to be found in state bureaucracies. Although in the Conservative Party, under the leadership of Benjamin Disraeli, the paternalist concern for the less fortunate remained in evidence, the sentiment of Gladstonian Liberalism was unequivocally for minimal state action. Nonetheless progress on the welfare front since the middle of the nineteenth century had been made and by the beginning of the last quarter the aggregate effect was considerable. Conditions of working and living were now generally accepted as a proper responsibility of government. New Liberal Governments after the fall of Balfour in 1906, first under Campbell-Bannerman and then Asquith, gave additional impetus to state intervention. The introduction of old-age pensions in 1908 for persons over the age of 70, of a contributory national insurance and unemployment insurance scheme in 1911, and of rudimentary forms of health insurance before 1914, all operating alongside the traditional poor law system marked a pattern of social welfare provision on which later generations would build. The Victorian predilection for charities, voluntaryism and self-help philanthropy was increasingly challenged. Fraser (1973) observes that 'the efficacy of private charity was the main Victorian bulwark against a totally collectivist approach. Once charity was found to be ultimately inadequate to meet the pressures placed upon it, then the floodgates opened and the collectivist tide flowed in' (p. 114).

Urban Regulation

Mounting concern over the health of towns and the need to secure sanitary improvements for the poorly housed dominated much of the nineteenth century; it obliged successive governments to promote measures whereby elements within the urban environment were controlled and regulated to ever higher standards. The cholera epidemics of 1831–3 and 1848–9, and those of declining virulence in 1853–4 and 1866–7, finally revealed the disease as water-borne. Effective sanitation to remove waste, cleanse polluted subsoil and provide pure drinking water was essential if this particular ravage was to be overcome. Another killer disease was typhoid, also spread by the intake of contaminated food and drink. Typhus was spread by the faeces of the body louse, and therefore was prevalent in conditions of overcrowding. Tuberculosis thrived where undernourishment, squalor and lack of ventilation were prevalent. Health, housing, sanitation and the incidence of poverty were interrelated, as the Poor Law Commission's (1842) *Report on the Sanitary Condition of the Labouring Population of Great Britain* revealed. Actually there were three Reports, two being Local Reports and one a General Report written by the secretary to the Commissioners, Edwin Chadwick. His damning findings were to breathe life into the public health movement which dominated urban reform for the next half century. The links between insanitation, overcrowding and disease were demonstrated; the remedies (drainage, removal of refuse and improvements in water supply) were pointed out.

Lord Morpeth's Public Health Bill was enacted in 1848 though not before some convoluted stages in the political process. But it became the first in a long line of measures of similar title. The 1848 Act was permissive, and did not apply to Scotland (or London which had its own Metropolitan Commission on Sewers), but it established the basic principles of sanitary improvement. A new Central Board was set up (its functions later transferred to the Privy Council), and Local Boards of Health were established. The tide of central and local government intervention now flowed strongly. From 1855 Medical Officers of Health were compulsory in London, though not elsewhere. The Local Government Board Act, 1871, established a new Government Department (of that name) which took over all the powers of duties of the Poor Law Board, the Privy Council and the Home Office relating to public health and sanitation. The Public Health Act, 1875, established a comprehensive administrative service for public health for the whole country. During the last quarter of the nineteenth century the sanitary conditions of British towns and cities were significantly improved. Abundant water supplies were provided, the larger cities in the Midlands and the North going far afield to upland reservoirs in Wales, the Lake District and the Pennines, and urban areas were systematically sewered and drained.

A related aspect of state intervention in the environment was in respect of Building Regulations (Gaskell, 1983). London's regulations were codified in the London Building Act, 1774 and for many years these provided a model for provincial towns during the time of Improvement Commissions and the chaotic, overlapping jurisdiction of local vestries and ad hoc bodies. In due time the Metropolitan Building Act, 1844 greatly extended the range of London building regulations, introducing controls relating to street widths and spaces at the rear of buildings, drainage, heights of buildings and structural safeguards. For the provinces the cumbersome procedure whereby individual localities needed separate acts to control buildings, streets and drainage, was resolved by the Town Improvement Clauses Act, 1847 which introduced a measure of co-ordination such as with regard to standard street widths and methods of building construction. The Public Health Act, 1848, broke further new ground by establishing national standards to be observed by local authorities. It stipulated the submission of plans for buildings, streets and drainage before operational work began. The act was permissive and it required the Local Government Act, 1858, to introduce significant building control powers. A Local Government Act Office was set up within the Home Office and a so-called 'Form of by-laws' was issued in an attempt to establish a set of nationwide guidelines covering street widths and space around buildings. All major towns proceeded to issue by-laws under the 1848 and 1858 Acts.

The problems caused by the frailty of the permissive legislation, constant evasion of local controls, legal difficulties regarding enforcement and the limitations of the 'Form of by-laws' were overcome by legislation in the 1870s. The Public Health Act, 1872, established sanitary authorities across the whole country, with obligatory powers. The Public Health Act, 1875, consolidated and codified all previous sanitary legislation. In 1877 the Local Government Board (established in 1871) published its Model by-laws – permissive, but in the event speedily established as standard local authority practices. By the mid-1880s most municipalities had issued new by-laws and the late Victorian city became almost synonymous with the 'by-law house' and 'by-law street'. An imposed environmental uniformity and a regulated order of space in the new suburbs affected street widths, space standards to the front and rear of houses, regulation room sizes and externally opening windows and detailed sanitary arrangements. For some time London remained outside the national legislation, but caught up with the Building Act, 1894. It had taken 50 years for an effective system of public control over the constituent elements of built form to be put in place through a blend of central and local powers.

Regulation also extended to the question of insanitary housing. From the 1860s local authorities were given increasing power to undertake clearance schemes to close or demolish houses which were insanitary or of faulty construction to the point that they were unfit or unsafe for habitation. The sanctity of private property rights was progressively invaded by the action of compulsory purchase of dwellings and land, but the bridgehead of the state's incursion into an area of individual responsibility was hard-fought and took some time to secure. In 1866 William Torrens, a back-bench MP, introduced a bill providing for compulsory powers of demolition or repair over unfit properties, and also for the building of replacement dwellings. Fierce opposition resulted in the replacement clause being dropped when the bill was reintroduced the following year. When the bill was enacted in 1868 as the Artizans' and Labourers' Dwellings Act the powers granted to local authorities to secure improvement by repair or demolition were limited because there were no provisions for compensation.

But the principle of enforced housing fitness had been established. Home Secretary R. A. Cross introduced his Artizans' Dwellings Bill in 1875, and it reached the statute book as the Artizans' and Labourers' Dwellings Improvement Act in the same year with much less opposition than with the Torrens Bill. The 1868 Act had dealt with single properties, but the 1875 Act was concerned with whole areas of unfit properties. The legislation remained permissive and the compensation clauses worked to the benefit of propertied interests, but the principle of state action to secure the comprehensive renewal of insanitary districts and to engage in subsequent rehousing would guide public action for the next hundred years. Local authorities would be the agent for the removal of the slums and their replacement by new working class dwellings. Not that local authorities had freedom of action to be the rehousing agency – they could only undertake this function with central government approval and even then any dwellings built had to be sold within ten years. Moreover, political attitudes to compensation over property and public expenditure proved resistant to any enthusiastic take-up by local authorities, and Cross's Act failed to generate effective schemes of urban renewal. The one exception was Birmingham where Joseph Chamberlain used the act in the Corporation Street project, but even here there was no replacement housing. Other central area projects had different origins, typically local acts. London was the most successful example of implementing the Cross Act, with the Peabody Trust active in replacing the old rookeries with their apartment blocks (Yelling, 1986).

Measures of urban regulation also extended to the opening of parks and to securing improvements in the quality of air and water. Satisfactory community health meant access to open space, fresh air and sunlight. The Metropolitan Board of Works pursued a programme of municipal parks for London; in the provinces the major cities eagerly took advantage of local philanthropy to bolster their own plans for parks. The health lobby attacked smoke pollution and lent weight to the pressure exerted by the National Smoke Abatement Society for action to be taken against pollution from industrial and domestic sources. The alkali industry, its fumes particularly noxious and damaging to property, was brought under some control by a succession of Alkali Acts; the first, in 1863, established an Inspectorate. Effective legislation was slow to come in respect of river pollution. Once again the issues were public costs and private responsibilities. The River Pollution Prevention Act, 1876, allowed the Local Government Board to establish joint committees to co-ordinate local action along stretches of rivers.

Another area of the public environment, roads, also fell to local authority responsibility by the end of the nineteenth century. Since Tudor times the duty to maintain roads had fallen on parishes but from the late seventeenth century this duty had existed alongside Turnpike Trusts, which were authorized to charge tolls on stage-coach routes in return for measures of improvement and modernization. Railways ruined their business anyway, but the trusts failed to keep the roads in good repair. Following a critical Select Committee report in 1864, they were dissolved when they came to apply for renewal of contracts. London was freed of tolls in 1871; trusts in the rest of the country were eliminated by 1895. The roads were at first transferred to parishes or highway districts with a modest grant-in-aid to cover costs of road maintenance. In 1888 county councils were made responsible for main roads; secondary roads were maintained by non-county boroughs and urban and rural district councils. Rising expenditure was a contentious burden for ratepayers – a problem only partially resolved in 1909 when the budget of that year introduced vehicle licenses and a petrol duty, the funds to assist with the cost of road improvements. It was only a matter of time before a new central authority was set up: a Ministry of Transport was founded in 1919.

Municipal Services

Up to the middle of the nineteenth century, although there had been some investment in gas and water supply, local councils' priorities were essentially public order, street maintenance and lighting, the provision of basic sanitary services and perhaps the improvement of market trading and (where appropriate) the development of dock facilities. During the second half of the century the relative emphasis switched to an expansion of municipal trading and engagement in public utilities.

The increased pace of municipalization in water supply was the first indication of a change in priorities. Chadwick's *Sanitary Report* in 1842 dismissed the performance of private companies in water supply; only in six instances in the fifty largest towns could the arrangements be described as good.

Legislation in 1847–8 permitted municipalities to establish their own water companies, though a number had already done so through private bills. But municipalities had to prove company failure or mismanagement before authority was given, and local authority assumption of water supply was relatively slow to take effect. In 1914 one-third of the population of England and Wales had its water supplied by private companies; the majority of the county boroughs and municipal boroughs, but fewer than half the urban districts managed their own waterworks.

Interest in the municipalization of gas had different origins. Arguments for the purchase of waterworks centred on health; the acquisition of a gasworks was undertaken for municipal profit. Local councils expressed concern at the disruption to public highways from the laying of services, but it was the de facto monopoly conditions enjoyed by the private gas companies that aroused pecuniary interest. Nine municipalities assumed control of their gas supply before 1850; in the next 50 years a further 172 did so, with the 1870s and 1890s prominent during this period. Northern and midland towns were well-represented, but London and several large cities (Bristol, Liverpool, Newcastle and Sheffield) remained the province of private companies. By the turn of the century local authority gas sales comprised more than one-third (37 per cent) of the total.

Domestic enjoyment of gas expanded hugely around the end of the century, the invention of the gas mantle and the slot machine encouraging its more widespread use. But another private monopoly, electricity, expanded from the 1890s. Municipal undertakings were quick to gain a foothold, in part in order to protect their own gas holdings, and the slow progress recorded in the early years of the electricity supply industry was due at least in some measure to the narrow outlook of the municipal sector, which viewed its supply role limited to within local authority boundaries.

Municipal undertakings also extended to transport – for which, initially, read tramways. The Tramway Act, 1870 sought to license private companies to run tram systems; municipalities might build and lease them, but not operate them. However, they might purchase private systems after 21 years, which from the 1890s onwards many local authorities proceeded to do. In 1905, 161 out of 276 systems were local authority owned and run – increasingly from locally generated municipal electricity services.

The municipalization of essential services (water, gas, electricity and transport) had been underpinned by arguments which held that it was a sound way to achieve efficiency and economy. But by the Edwardian period the scale of indebtedness by local councils fuelled controversy over alleged wastefulness.

As Waller (1983) puts it: 'Once thought "practical progress", Municipal Socialism now seemed a rake's progress as debts increased faster than amortization' (p. 307). Experiments in and certain extensions to municipalization would continue, but by 1914 a 50-year period of expansion was coming to an end. Other forms of municipal management were in sight.

During the last quarter of the nineteenth century social collectivism advanced on a number of fronts. We have chosen to concentrate on two. It has been demonstrated that the state assumed a responsibility to establish the rules in the contest between labour and employees. Equally, a general obligation had also been adopted on such social questions as caring for the poor, promoting public health, improving housing conditions and providing elementary education. Most of the cost of this involvement in social action fell on industry or the local authorities, and the interventionist role of the latter was curtailed through popular resistance to higher taxes.

Additionally we have examined the extension of some of the functions of local government. To begin with, much rested on the outcome of specific local initiatives, but by the close of the Victorian era and into the Edwardian period a clear shift of balance could be seen whereby the power of the centre grew in relation to the local periphery. But a reliable and powerful structure of local government had been set in place, which over the next century would share with central government the dual system of checks and balances and shared responsibilities which is so different from the centralist and federalist regimes in other countries.

These various elements have been portrayed as factors in the early outreach of the state. They are far from comprehensive, and they have been selected for their pertinence for what follows. The objective is to chart the rise and fall of planning in the twentieth century, and in so doing focus on developments in town planning within that context. The argument is that by 1900 important building blocks were in place as a result of certain nineteenth-century developments which permitted, indeed encouraged, further state advances to be made. As Checkland (1983) put it, 'As the old century ended and the new one began, the two great political parties and the emergent new one were being increasingly pressed by a miscellany of proposals towards the adoption of a consistent and to some degree comprehensive view of the welfare responsibilities of the state' (p. 227). The term 'welfare' can be interpreted liberally, to embrace economic, social and environmental measures. It is those elements of planning with which we are most concerned.

2 The Birth of Town Planning

During the years on either side of the turn of the century, say from 1885–1915, or more centrally 1895–1910, the building blocks of town planning were put in place. There were various guises. It was an activity which promoted housing development of a particular kind; it was a social movement which captured the reformist aspirations of a broad following in regard to city life; a university discipline, taught for the first time; a function of government, resting on the provision of new statutory powers; and it was a professional organization, founded to advance the art and science of a new activity and to secure the association of those engaged in it. The very term 'town planning' can be dated: 1906 was the year when it first came into usage.

The act of conscious town building, whereby the constituent elements of urban form were shaped in accordance with some deliberate design principles, has extended over millennia, and is to be found in all our urban histories. Town planning, however, was different, resting as it did on notions of an extension of public control over private interests in land and property. Without precise definition, even in British statute, a new activity in urban affairs took root within a remarkably short period, around a set of key propositions. Around that core it built up a corpus of knowledge and secured a place in political and institutional structures then current. Both in its origins and in its subsequent development, town planning remains inexplicable outside the socio-political context of its time.

This chapter seeks to examine the origins of British town planning and suggest what it came to stand for. There were a number of interconnecting threads. The late nineteenth century, across the western world, was noted for its commitment to philanthropy and philanthropic experiments particularly with regard to housing, and it provided a number of practical forerunners for the town planning movement. By the close of the Victorian period, a collective experience of living in cities had been gained; and as the experience was judged unfavourable by elements of the increasingly professionalized middle classes, there were pressures for reform to tackle the worst of the urban excesses prejudicial to an acceptable quality of life. This is where town planning came to focus: the amelioration of urban living conditions, in accordance with certain precepts of design and layout, so as to provide for health, beauty and convenience. Innovations in other countries were shared amongst an international brotherhood; the conference network was all important in exchange and transference of ideas and practice.

In these contexts a uniquely British model for future urban living was promoted – the garden city expounded by Ebenezer Howard; only two were ever built in Britain but it had many imitators, including the derivative garden suburb. Inherent in both was another firmly British design tradition – low density housing and the rudiments of cottage-style architecture. In 1909 the first British town planning legislation was enacted and statutory town planning became a new function of local government. In 1914 an independent profession of town planning was founded. By this time the basic elements of town planning had been established: new forms of architecture, a new approach to roads and transport, a recognition of the constituent features of land use, notions of the comprehensive management of urban space for the public good, and visions of a midwife role for creating cities of the future. We must now unravel the various threads.

Philanthropy

Charitable giving of personal wealth to relieve the poor, or to support worthy causes such as education or hospitals, has long been the source of public welfare. During the nineteenth century the scale of personal philanthropy was not only greatly extended as wealth increased, but it was directed to a wider range of outlets, including those concerned with the quality of social life in cities. In Britain, reformist zeal for improved housing, the provision of parks and arrangements for local community facilities attracted philanthropic money. In the years around the turn of the century this sort of activity peaked in a welter of initiatives. At the same time, as huge personal fortunes were amassed in the United

States, an enlarged form of 'wholesale philanthropy' appeared with the likes of J. D. Rockefeller and Andrew Carnegie who institutionalized their fund-giving to objectives broadly defined as social progress and civilization (Meller, 1995). Philanthropy came to be associated with some of the early stirrings of the town planning movement in two particular ways: housing and community affairs, and the building of model settlements.

If we confine our attention to the second half of the century, a starting point is the Columbia Square housing development by Miss Burdett Coutts in Bethnal Green, London – four five-storey blocks arranged around a central open space built between 1859 and 1862. The architect was Henry Derbishire, who would go on to build the early estates for the Peabody Trust. This Trust was founded in 1862 by George Peabody, a wealthy American banker who had settled in this country. An original donation of £150,000 was augmented by a further £200,000 in 1866 and another £150,000 at the time of his death a few years later. Half a million pounds 130 years ago might be equated to £25 million at today's prices. By 1870, 400 families had been housed, but their most extensive work was reserved for the 1880s. A number of societies in London over the previous 20 years or so had developed model housing projects and commercial companies followed suit, building working class housing at a modest return – 5 per cent philanthropy as Tarn (1973) describes it. One prominent body was the Improved Industrial Dwellings Co., founded by Sir Sydney Waterlow, which was building houses from 1863; one of the largest was the Artizans', Labourers' and General Dwelling Co., operating from 1868. By the mid-1880s the 28 associations active in London were estimated to be housing more than 32,000 people, and the scale of the involvement would increase markedly over the next quarter of a century. By comparison, model housing schemes in other cities were slow to catch on.

One element in the provision of improved housing was the role of management, given prominence through the work of Octavia Hill. In 1864 she purchased a group of houses known as Paradise Place, Marylebone, notorious both for their condition and inhabitants. Her management style, described later in her book *Homes of the London Poor* (1883), was personal involvement with the tenantry: frequent visits, insistence on prompt payment of rents and a determination to ensure cleanliness in common areas such as stairs and landings. With evidence of self-help, improvements would be made to the dwellings, in so far as the rents allowed. Together with a band of other women workers she proceeded to buy up the leases of slum property and, supported by influential and wealthy friends, effectively became a housing manageress of tenants on the lowest of incomes and living in poor conditions. She was soon appointed by the Ecclesiastical Commissioners to manage the bulk of their properties in Southwark. This emphasis on direct involvement with householders may also be seen with the numerous co-operative housekeeping ventures which were started at this time, in attempts to improve working-class living conditions (Pearson, 1988).

Octavia Hill was a member of the Charity Organisation Society, founded in 1869. This influential body, wedded to the individualism of the free labour market, argued against further extension of state intervention in matters of slum housing, seeing more benefit in traditional paternalism underpinned by philanthropy as a means of rescuing the deserving poor. A development of this philosophy could be seen in the Settlement House movement of the 1880s, a product of the reformed Universities of Oxford and Cambridge, in which the beginnings of organized social work may be seen. Canon Samuel Barnett founded Toynbee Hall in Whitechapel, East London in 1885; from his St Jude's Vicarage he had already been engaged in promoting housing schemes for the poor. One visitor was the American, Jane Addams; on returning to Chicago from a continental tour she established her own Settlement at Hull House, Halstead Street in 1889.

Philanthropy took another route, applying the objective of improved housing and the notion of housing management undertaken to meet a variety of social aims, to the building of whole townships. There were plenty of examples where factory owners with a social conscience involved themselves with schemes in which the boundary line between philanthropy and business acumen was hard to draw. In mid-century (nearly 50 years after Robert Owen's scheme at New Lanark by the Falls of Clyde) the Quaker, John Grubb Richardson, built a settlement adjoining a mill at Bessbrook, Newry, Northern Ireland in 1845. Around the same time the Halifax area of Yorkshire was the setting for Edward Ackroyd's model village at Ackroyden. In the 1850s Bromborough Pool on the south bank of the Mersey estuary provided the location for company housing for Price's Patent Candle Co.

The third quarter of the nineteenth century (1851 to 1876 to be precise) saw the building of a virtually self-contained industrial village:

Saltaire, near Bradford. Titus Salt amassed a personal fortune as a manufacturer processing alpaca wool in his five Bradford mills. He was mayor when in the summer of 1849 an epidemic of cholera ravaged the area, but his concern for ill-health was also matched by his anxieties about the moral state of the town, which environmental and social measures would help to remedy (Reynolds, 1976). It so happened that the time had come to invest considerably in plant and machinery for his mills. A new site for a replacement factory was required. His solution was to leave the town, build a new mill and found his own industrial settlement. The result was a new six-storey mill, called the Palace of Industry, the largest plant of its kind in Europe when it was opened in 1853, built close to the River Aire to the north west of Bradford and adjoining the Leeds–Liverpool canal and a railway. Immediately to the south he laid out a compact village for 775 houses, for which he provided a range of facilities: a hospital, school, park, baths and public washhouse, an institute, shops, almshouses and a Congregational church.

The gridiron of streets and the sturdy, stone-fronted terraces at Saltaire had been completed for only 12 years when William Hesketh Lever began his industrial village at Port Sunlight. Lever was a successful wholesale grocer, expanding the family firm beyond the confines of his native Bolton (Hubbard and Shippobottom, 1988). He began to specialize in the marketing of soap, under the registered name 'Sunlight'; previously made by various manufacturers, in 1885 he began to make it independently in leased premises at Warrington. Expanding trade necessitated new premises and in 1888 he began the construction of new works at Port Sunlight, only a little distance from Bromborough Pool (see above) on the Mersey Estuary. The Warrington plant was progressively abandoned.

Industrial relocation was one common thread between Salt and Lever, in that requirements for a new plant gave rise to the opportunity to develop a workers' estate adjoining. But Port Sunlight would appear very differently from Saltaire, having the benefit not only of a developer who had a personal interest in building styles, but also of a certain timeliness in that it could reflect recent advances made in domestic architecture. For example the flexibility of the Queen Anne revivalist style had been successfully demonstrated at Bedford Park in West London in an estate begun in 1876. Port Sunlight was inaugurated in 1888; the factory was completed in 1889 and in the period to 1897 the original village in the south-western corner of a later expanded community was developed in an ensemble of cottages, shops and public buildings. By 1914 the bulk of the estate of 890 houses had been completed to provide a classic layout of picturesque groupings, with stylistic variety and varying materials. A wealth of public buildings appeared, the cost of many met by Lever himself.

The workers' model settlement, the product of a benevolent paternalism, became a form of development widely emulated in Britain and other countries in Europe, and in the United States. Lever's Port Sunlight was followed by Cadbury's Bournville. The chocolate manufactury of George and Richard Cadbury outgrew its central Birmingham site and in 1879 new premises were built on a 15-acre site in rolling countryside four miles to the south-west; it was called Bournville after the small local stream and in deference to a French-sounding brand name for the product. The factory enterprise went from strength to strength and the Cadbury brothers were able to engage in their social experiment of building a 'village in a garden'. The first houses dated from 1895 and it was not long before an estate took shape, its groups of cottage-style houses in tree-lined streets markedly different from the by-law terraces of the neighbouring districts. Houses of style and individuality, ample gardens, abundant open space and the provision of a wealth of community facilities came to mark the new residential environment. By 1900, on an endowed site of 330 acres, there were already more than 300 dwellings and George Cadbury (Richard by then having died) launched the Bournville Village Trust. The rest is twentieth-century history (Hillman, 1994); suffice to say that Bournville made an important mark on the early town planning movement.

Another Quaker chocolate magnate, Joseph Rowntree, followed in this tradition. Purchasing 150 acres adjacent to the firm's factory in 1901, New Earswick was laid out, the basic features of informality and cottage architecture established by 1914 (see also p. 12). Rowntree followed Cadbury in having his estate governed by a trust. In Hull, a different model was followed: Sir James Reckitt in 1907 formed a private company to build a model village to house his own workmen. A variant was corporate philanthropy whereby a group of people succeeded in raising money to buy land, and set up a trust to develop an estate. Hampstead Garden Suburb owes its origins to this practice. Henrietta Barnett (wife of Canon Barnett of Whitechapel) and her colleagues succeeded in raising more than £100,000 to buy a 256-acre site and founded the Hampstead Garden Suburb Trust in 1907.

A distinctive and internationally famous development unfolded (see also p. 23).

The Experience of Living in Cities

Towards the end of the nineteenth century, across the western world, a keen interest was being shown in cities, and speculation was rife about city life and alternative forms of urban environments. The founding fathers of the social sciences did their early work in this period: Frederic le Play, Herbert Spencer, Charles Booth, Emile Durkheim, Karl Marx, Georges Sorel, Georg Simmel, Beatrice and Sidney Webb, L. T. Hobhouse and others. They sought rules of explanation and proffered theories. Meanwhile everyday experiences of urban life were expressed by doctors, clergymen, diarists, novelists, propagandists and politicians, and by and large they communicated a widely-shared view that city conditions left much to be desired (Lees, 1985). The situation was conducive to reform. The irony was that the worst of the earlier experiences had gone; by the end of the century cities were healthier and many of the rookeries and areas of decrepit housing had been removed. But this was not enough and from a number of sources new approaches to housing provision were being urged, in a way that would radically change city life. The activity which emerged as town planning took root in this fertile soil.

Throughout the century, in fact, escapist element groups on the fringes of society sought new arrangements in alternative communities so that they might distance themselves from the urban and industrial product of the Industrial Revolution (Hardy, 1979). The utopian idealism (itself going back many centuries) also surfaced in a purely imaginary form: in 1849, James Silk Buckingham, an MP, proposed the building of a model town (suitably called Victoria) designed in the manner of concentric squares, to accommodate 10,000 people. His book *National Evils and Practical Remedies* described how the box-like layout of the town would have eight radial avenues; the names were instructive – Peace, Concord, Fortitude, Charity, Hope, Faith, Justice and Unity. Even in mid-century then there was an alternative, however implausible, to the haphazard, imperfect town building of the time; it would have a consciously designed form and the declared social values of its community would be at variance from those of current society. Buckingham's work captured a reformist visionary dream and harnessed it to an idealized process of town building. These were the very elements at the close of the century which would resurface very powerfully and be captured by an embryonic town planning movement.

In the meantime there had been at least one indication of another feature which the early twentieth century would adopt with enthusiasm – the promise of scientific technological progress allied to urban design. Sir Benjamin Ward Richardson (1876) postulated a model city where disease would be banished; he called his 'city of health' Hygeia, where 100,000 people could live at low densities in an environment of controlled cleanliness. The potential for science to underpin new forms of urban living was recognized quite early on.

But the reformist movements secured their immediate strength from some very practical concerns. Town planning gained an identity as a response to certain pressing problems of the day which spoke of deep dissatisfactions with the late-Victorian city. It would thrive because it stood for reform and change in everyday living experiences, not because of an association with abstract futures, however appealing utopian idealism might be. The urgent issue was undoubtedly housing, and it was in this area that British town planning would take on its early defining characteristic. Long-standing pressure for improvements to working-class housing, together with demands for the improvement of sanitary arrangements, had secured discernible results. During the final quarter of the nineteenth century progressive by-law adoption would have a beneficial consequence for new housing stock, and incremental advances alone would suggest that the worst was over. But a late-Victorian housing crisis was in the making. Overcrowding in central London had worsened as the supply of working-class accommodation actually declined, and rents remained high. Alternative housing for the poor was scarcely available and in any case they were obliged to remain living in their traditional districts which were near to the range of casual work in warehouses, markets and docks. The Royal Commission on the Housing of the Working Classes (1884–5), chaired by Sir Charles Dilke, received voluminous evidence of the triple problems of the time: poverty, squalor and bad housing.

The 1880s and 1890s proved a remarkable period for sharp comment about the deteriorating housing situation and the prevalent abject social conditions in particular districts of London and some other cities. Popular opinions were shaped from a number of sources: evangelical reports, social enquiries, and investigative journalism, the most obvious. The result was a heightened interest in the possibilities of social reform, particularly measures which led to improved housing and associated environmental conditions. In Britain, if not necessarily in other parts of the world, the origins of town planning would rest squarely in this context and would take on its early defining characteristics as a solution to the complex nature of the late-Victorian housing crisis.

Evangelically-inspired tracts were widely read and hugely influential. *The Bitter Cry of Outcast London* was a 20-page pamphlet written by the Rev. W. C. Preston (1883), a Congregationalist, as 'an inquiry into the condition of the abject poor'. One of his targets, the evil of drink, was shared by General William Booth (1890), founder of the Salvation Army. In his book, *In Darkest England and the Way Out*, drink was the common denominator of the country's social ills, manifested in poverty, homelessness, vice and crime. He advocated planned emigration from the overcrowded city to colonies, either overseas or at home in the form of farm colonies in the countryside.

The plight of the poor attracted growing concern, but there was ignorance as to the actual numbers involved. The *Pall Mall Gazette* in 1885 serialized the results of a survey undertaken by the Social Democratic Foundation; the leader of the SDF, F. D. Hyndman, suggested that one-quarter of Londoners lived in conditions of abject poverty. Charles Booth repudiated this claim and promised to conduct his own survey by means of an inquiry which employed the latest statistical techniques used by social scientists. Booth, Liverpool born, founded and managed a large and prosperous shipping line, and he had other business interests. But in his spare time, often in the evenings and late at night, the gigantic labours of his survey work were undertaken. The result was the publication of 17 volumes of *Life and Labour of the People in London* between 1889 and 1903 in which he reported on the living conditions, homes, environments, work and conditions of work of the people, first of East London and then the rest of the city. Booth had misjudged the SDF's estimate of the extent of poverty, and concluded that nearly 35 per cent of the working class population of East London could be classified as 'poor', and that poverty, far from being sharply concentrated in the East End, was much more widely distributed throughout London as a whole than had previously been thought.

Factual data revealed the state of poverty and deprivation in other parts of the country. Seebohm Rowntree (1901) calculated that in York nearly the same proportion of the population as in London was living in poverty (28.8 per cent as opposed to 30.7 per cent).

In Manchester and Salford in 1904 there were upwards of 212,000 people in a state of poverty, 75,000 of whom experienced severe poverty, according to a survey by Marr (1904), the secretary of a local 'Citizens Association for the Improvement of the Unwholesome Dwellings and Surroundings of the People'. Later commentators have remarked on the huge concentrations of disadvantaged populations elsewhere at that time: Glasgow had the most heavily populated city centre in Europe in 1914 (Checkland, 1981) and Dublin was the worst housed and unhealthiest city in the British Isles (Aalen, 1987).

Investigative journalism came into its own at a time of increasing readership levels. The popular journalist George Sims published articles in the *Pictorial World* (June 1883) on 'How the Poor Live'. Newspapers in Birmingham and Manchester reported adversely on local conditions. The most graphic work was that of Jack London (1903): the story of his experiences living amongst the people of East London was published in the American periodical *Wilshire's Magazine* and appeared as a book, *The People of the Abyss*.

These examples, which typified a plethora of impressionistic accounts of working–class life described from the outside, served to focus concern on a number of key environmental issues. One was the unacceptable levels of overcrowding which obtained in parts of inner London and certain cities elsewhere. The 1901 census indicated that 16 per cent of the population of the Administrative County of London were living in overcrowded conditions (then defined as more than two persons per room). Some metropolitan boroughs, particularly those in East London, recorded much higher figures with around one third of the population overcrowded. Elsewhere in England the Newcastle and Sunderland areas were black spots; in Scotland all the major cities recorded very high rates.

Overcrowding reflected the number of persons per dwelling. Another measure of concentration was density, expressed in terms of the number of persons per unit area of land. London recorded many boroughs with average densities in excess of 100 persons per acre; the very highest were in Stepney, Bethnal Green, Finsbury, Shoreditch and Southwark, where the range extended (in that order) from 169 to 182 persons per acre. In the rest of the country average urban densities were much lower; Liverpool for example stood at 52 persons per acre. But there were some highly localized concentrations, as in the North Everton district of Liverpool where 54,000 people were living at a density of 178 to the acre.

These experiences increasingly suggested to late-Victorian society that the urban product of the nineteenth century, however extensive the sanitary improvements and however successful the new by-law arrangements had been, still provided an unnatural setting for human life. The argument that in big cities man must deteriorate physically, mentally and morally, was advanced by the American observer Henry George (1884) in his influential book *Social Problems*, and was taken up by many others. There was a fear that a puny and ill-developed urban race was being raised, evidence of which was adduced from statistics provided by army recruiting stations at the time of the Boer War: between 1893 and 1902, 35 per cent of all men medically examined for enlistment were rejected as medically unfit (Wohl, 1983). The spectre of race degeneration was fed by the facts of stunted growth and physical decline; medical inspection of school children from the inner wards of cities recorded smaller heights and lower weights than for children at school elsewhere. An official government inquiry was appointed; the Inter-Departmental Committee on Physical Deterioration reported in 1904. The debate widened into 'eugenics' (Francis Galton's term); the Eugenics Society dated from 1907 and there was overlapping membership between town planning and eugenist groups (Garside, 1988). The aim was to improve racial quality through eliminating unfitness, including the prevention of reproduction.

The late-Victorian urban crisis was reflected in long-standing problems concerning housing (particularly the provision of housing at rents the working class could afford), poverty and health. Sporadic outbreaks of social protest by the casual labouring class of 'outcast London' (Jones, 1971) reflected the wider issues involved – class structure and the locus of economic power. The middle classes felt threatened and turned to a variety of reform movements in the search for assurances about a safer future. Improvements to housing fitness and standards of accommodation, better health for an urban population conferred through availability of fresh air and sunlight, and better arrangements for the removal of waste and provision of pure water, were high priorities for those urging solutions to the late-nineteenth-century experience of living in cities.

The British Solution

By the early years of the twentieth century various formative influences were coming together in a way which created conditions conducive to change. The time was ripe for novel advances to be made.

The issues were really threefold. First, it had been established that large numbers of people could not be accommodated in the vast urban concentrations of *fin-de-siècle* Britain without the consequences of ill-health and physical degeneration manifest to an unacceptable extent. London's size was exceptional (at 4.5 million, its population established it as a world giant), but the country had a network of medium-sized provincial cities where the same concerns were expressed. Moreover, the older districts of the inner areas of these cities contained populations which were living on the margins of poverty and destitution. Secondly, it was feared that the pace of incremental reform was too slow to effect much change in the foreseeable future; therefore new alternatives were needed. Philanthropy could only do so much; new house building outside the arrangements of the model dwellings companies was unlikely to be sufficient to meet the needs of the poor; and municipal house building (even in London where some progress had been made) seemed unlikely to secure political blessing. Meanwhile the stock of old and decrepit houses remained, progress on closure and demolition was slow, not least because of compensation problems. Thirdly, there was the question of land values. London's experience had already shown that redevelopment would be an extremely costly means of rehousing, while land on the outskirts was much cheaper. The exploitation of the suburban periphery was held to be the key. It had two major benefits: it offered the possibility of providing land on which cheaper houses could be built, and it had the attributes of healthiness where houses could be built in conditions of space, fresh air and sunlight. The British model for twentieth-century urban development took shape: low density housing built in the form of garden suburbs, with an extreme variant being that of the garden city.

This solution provided many answers to pressing problems. It addressed the question of land reform, a potentially explosive issue for land- and property-owning classes. The recently founded Land Nationalization Society was securing a following; Henry George (1880) in his book *Progress and Poverty* had advocated a new tax on land values; and Liberal Party politics seized on taxation as a stick to beat the interests of landed property. But the garden suburb/garden city objective, which would have the effect of releasing large blocks of land into the housing market, did not threaten anyone and avoided the need for municipalities to engage in house building themselves. It also directly addressed the worrying question of urban ill-health.

To be effective, the model could only be implemented by a new approach to housing design and layout. The ambience of the by-law terrace, minimum street widths and regulated space standards was replaced by one of cottage-style architecture, roads varied in type, and an overall setting of informality, gardens and greenery. These design principles were already in evidence at Bournville where the architect William Alexander Harvey was building George Cadbury's garden village, but the seminal influence proved to be Raymond Unwin often working in collaboration with his cousin by marriage, Barry Parker.

Unwin's work has been exhaustively examined in biographies by Jackson (1985) and particularly Miller (1992). The importance of his contributions to twentieth-century architecture and town planning can scarcely be exaggerated. Between 1895 and 1901 Unwin and Parker gained their initial experience of house design and construction, a period culminating in the publication of their jointly-authored book *The Art of Building a Home* (1901). After that, his work was seen in a major project at New Earswick (Rowntree's model village) where he prepared the layout and combined with Parker on cottage design to achieve a low density estate with shops, hall and school, a prototype for much that would follow in this genre. Hampstead, however, was his celebrated creation (Green, 1977). He was chosen by Mrs (later Dame) Henrietta Barnett to layout a garden suburb on a tract of land adjoining Hampstead Heath. The development was inaugurated in 1907 following the enactment of a Private Member's Bill; the Hampstead Garden Suburb Act, 1906, gave immunity from the restrictive by-laws of Hendon Urban District and allowed the use of culs-de-sac and closes in an open, picturesque layout. Edwin Lutyens was appointed as an additional consultant, working with Unwin to create an internationally renowned estate.

From about this time garden suburbs made their appearance up and down the country as the fashion for the new style of architecture and low density layouts caught on. These developments were largely the product of public utility societies, which were a specialist form of combined limited dividend company and Friendly Society; in a 'co-partnership' ideal, tenants controlled both their own society and their houses (Skilleter, 1993). The Co-partnership Tenants Housing Council, founded in 1903, comprised a number of constituent societies; their tenant shareholders bought shares and through their investment became house owners in a collective enterprise. It is intriguing to note that the Executive Committee included Ebenezer Howard, Raymond

Unwin, W. H. Lever and George Cadbury. In 1907 the central Federation was Co-partnership Tenants Ltd, chaired by Henry Vivian MP; their architect was G. Lister Sutcliffe, assisted by Unwin as consultant.

The pioneer co-partnership organization was Ealing Tenants Ltd, registered in 1901. Their first houses differed little from standard by-law types, but subsequent development undertaken after 1907 reflected the Unwinesque tradition of grouped dwellings and communal spaces. This new suburban form was replicated in more than forty schemes before 1914 (Birchall, 1995). The schemes began ambitiously enough and were widely dispersed geographically in Hertfordshire (Knebworth), Leicester, Cardiff, Sevenoaks, Stoke, Wolverhampton, Birmingham (Harborne), Liverpool and Manchester. Yet there was a huge gap between intentions and achievements. Fewer than 3,500 houses were actually built in co-partnership schemes before 1914, and even allowing for a similar figure in other public utility societies, the overall total was considerably less than that built by local authorities (at a time when most councils were not building at all).

Meanwhile another variant was being pursued in resolution of the late-Victorian housing crisis: this involved schemes to resettle large numbers of London's overcrowded population in the rural areas beyond the fringes of the metropolis. Decentralization as a means of housing the London poor had already been advanced (Marshall, 1884) on the grounds of economic advantage, and countryside colonies had appeared in General William Booth's scheme of things. In the early 1900s actual schemes of farm resettlement in Essex were undertaken, but these were quite overtaken by a carefully worked out proposal initiated by a practical experiment, for a collection of garden cities.

The source of this scheme was Ebenezer Howard, a parliamentary shorthand writer who moved in earnest debating circles in the London of his day. He has become something of a folk hero in town planning circles, examined biographically (Beevers, 1988), revered unquestioningly (Macfadyen, 1933) and the association which he founded fully researched (Hardy, 1991a and b). In his book, *Tomorrow; a peaceful path to real reform*, Howard (1898) envisaged a constellation of small towns of 30,000 population as satellites to a parent city; they would be surrounded by an agricultural belt and developed on land held in common. The intended strategy was that territorial expansion of the parent city would cease and the surplus population would be redirected to the satellites (garden cities) beyond. As one satellite reached its target size, another would be started;

a constellation would constitute 'Social City'. Cheap land would result in cheaper housing, and community ownership of the site would enable profits to be returned to the people. Overall it was a solution directed to the problems of both urban and rural areas, and the appropriate terminology found expression in the revision of Howard's book, retitled *Garden Cities of Tomorrow* (1902).

The scheme attracted attention and enthusiasts were recruited to membership of a Garden City Association, founded in 1900, chaired by the barrister and former Liberal MP Ralph Neville. A Pioneer Company was registered in 1902. Howard was Managing Director, and the Secretary was Thomas Adams, a Lowland Scot making his way in London as a freelance journalist. The Association proved a successful proselytizing organization. Annual conferences were arranged – at Bournville in 1901 and Port Sunlight in 1902 – and membership surged to the 1,500 mark.

An actual development project began in 1904. The Pioneer Company was liquidated and the First Garden City Company was founded. A land holding was purchased at Letchworth (Hertfordshire) for the building of a garden city. A plan prepared by Unwin and Parker was accepted; in practice the former dealt with matters relating to layout while the latter undertook detailed design control. Locationally the scheme reflected the strategy for population dispersal; in design terms Letchworth provided an early test-case for working up the principles of informality of layout and cottage-style architecture. The domestic work of Parker and Unwin was extensive; some of their assistants moved into independent practice; and outside this circle Courtenay Crickmer contributed to the overall tradition (Miller, 1989). Adams was appointed secretary of the development company, holding the post until 1905. He soon left the GCA to work independently as an estate designer, largely of garden suburbs; his biographer (Simpson, 1985) asserts that he became the first man to earn his living solely from town planning work.

In 1909 the Association became the Garden Cities and Town Planning Association. Other Garden City Associations were established in many other parts of the world as translations of Howard's book, and interpretations of his ideals appeared in a number of countries in Europe (France, Germany, Belgium and Russia) and also Japan. In 1913 the International Garden Cities and Town Planning Association was set up, the first President, appropriately, was Ebenezer Howard. For much of the rest of the century the garden city and its derivatives have appeared repeatedly in strategic planning circles throughout the world (Ward, 1992).

The International Dimension

Britain was not the only country to experience the expanding towns of the industrial age, where the accommodation of low paid manual workers proved a persistent problem. Britain's response was shaped by historical precedent in the form of long-standing attempts to deal with the legacy of unfit housing, to improve the building stock and to secure access to it for those in need. The response was also forged through political and social institutions characteristic of late-Victorian Britain. The context for the response in other countries was similarly moulded by history and socio-political circumstances. Town Planning (or to give the equivalents, 'Stadteplanung' in Germany, 'urbanisme' in France and 'city planning' in America) began as, and remains, an essentially cultural reaction to a set of urban housing and environmental questions.

In Germany a particularly advanced form of planning emerged through the work of urban administrations which inherited a pre-industrial framework of intervention, readily adapted to meet new needs. There was a general power to lay out new streets around the existing built-up areas; a process of controlled town building, town extension planning, came to be known as 'Stadtebau' (Sutcliffe, 1981). This feature of German local government was made even more distinctive by the marked professionalization of public life (occurring much earlier and more strongly than in Britain) whereby salaried officials were appointed to positions of some power and influence. Meanwhile Germany's much vaunted system of technical education spawned other professionals in high schools and universities: a cadre of trained people emerged and a corpus of knowledge was established. A comprehensive urban planning technique was secured by the turn of the century, which served the German institution of public competition very well. Plans for a number of German towns were prepared at this time. No wonder some British observers, for example Horsfall (1904), were envious of 'the German example'.

By comparison, the situation in France was very different, and the notion of urban planning had little to sustain it during the early years of the century. France had shared in the nineteenth century an urban revolution much less than Britain, Belgium and Germany, and while Paris and a host of provincial cities were no strangers to housing and environmental problems, the legislature was dominated by rural representatives. Urban problems were accorded less importance than they deserved. Louis Napoleon's Prefect of the Seine, Georges Haussmann, had emphasized improvements of street communications in his schemes of public investment in Paris, and housing matters were largely ignored, so much so that by the turn of the century there was virtually no progress to record regarding slum clearance and rehousing. The ingredients for planning, present in both Britain and Germany, were absent in France, and although there was some quickening of a social reform movement, and while Lyon amongst French provincial cities acquired a reputation in local town planning affairs, the country had to experience war-time bombardment before town planning was seriously considered nationally.

Britain drifted into town planning, German cities had it thrust upon them, and France was simply reluctant. The United States was different again. US cities for the most part did not generate the range of environmental and housing problems of the kind which attracted schemes of public intervention in Europe, so that a housing reform movement lagged behind that of Britain quite markedly. The grid street plan produced an efficient circulation system, so the public control of the planning of new streets was not a major issue. Instead, city beautification was more important, to which the urban park movement contributed strongly. The World's Columbian Exhibition held in Chicago in 1893, celebrating the 400th anniversary of the discovery of the continent, enlivened the campaign for the conscious development of urban beauty and culture with a beaux-arts set piece, which impressed Americans and Europeans alike. Daniel Burnham was Director of Works and he went on to become one of the primary figures in the development of city planning in America. His Chicago Plan of 1909 took the notion of comprehensive planning further than anywhere else in the world. The city beautiful movement would soon wither, however, stigmatized 'as excessively concerned with monumentality, empty aesthetics, grand effects for the well-to-do, and general impracticality' (Wilson, 1989, p. 285), but the basis of a city planning tradition had been laid.

The importance of recognizing the very different origins of town planning in at least four countries (Britain, Germany, France and the United States) is to acknowledge the international character of the emergent movement. It followed that no country was entirely independent in the course of the movement's evolution, given the opportunities for cross-fertilization of ideas and practice. In the event, Britain, while not in all respects the quickest to advance its town planning reputation, actually gained the most. European countries had relatively little to learn from the United States; not much of French insight was exported; and the rivalry between Britain and Germany ended by Britain having the card of strongest appeal – the garden city. So in explaining the origins of British town planning, its emergence as the dominant player on the international stage comes to rank as being of great significance.

Exhibitions and conferences of all kinds increased in number during the second half of the nineteenth century; those with an urban focus proliferated around the turn of the century and up to 1914. The international peace movement encouraged the adoption of ideas which would appeal to all nations. The first international Garden City Congress was held in London in 1904; the garden city was seen as commonly applicable. International housing congresses reinforced the message. International road congresses were also held. Meanwhile conferences on public art proved useful for the furtherance of the British Arts and Crafts ideas of creative design. Meller (1995) observes that the period from 1890 to 1914 was unique:

> It was the only period when ideas on the future of life in large cities were discussed by international bodies unfettered, to a large extent, by the constraints of practical politics. For a brief moment, charity, self-interest and welfare had been brought into an international town planning movement aimed at securing the greatest good for the future. (p. 307)

In this context the first international conference on town planning, organized by the Royal Institute of British Architects in London in 1910, took place, attracting 1,250 people.

Institutionalized Town Planning

In certain respects both Germany and the United States had taken steps earlier than Britain to institutionalize their town planning arrangements in terms of governance, professionalization and education. In Germany urban planning was recognized as a municipal activity by the early 1900s. The term 'Stadtebau' had been used since around 1890. Town planners (*Stadtebauer*) had begun to regard themselves as a separate profession, training programmes were established and technical literature was available. *Der Stadtebau*, the first journal in the world to deal specifically with town planning, was launched in 1904. Town planning exhibitions devoted to city development were held, notably in 1910 to promote the planning of Greater Berlin. In the United States the first permanent city planning commission was set up in 1907 and others quickly followed. The first university course in city planning, at Harvard, enrolled students in 1909. An increasing number of zoning ordinances came to be adopted and many cities commissioned plans. The American City Planning Institute was founded in 1917.

Institutionalization in Britain came with a rush, between 1909 and 1914. Bodies found it convenient to acquire a town planning appellation: the Garden Cities and Town Planning Association and the National Housing and Town Planning Council were examples (in 1909). The early 1900s had seen all the formative influences established; a Town Planning Act served to bring them together.

From 1906 pressure was being exerted on the Local Government Board for housing and town planning legislation which would give powers to local authorities to take steps to order the physical arrangements of towns, or parts of towns, in order to promote their health and efficient functioning, and to impart an aesthetically pleasing environment. Health, convenience and beauty were the key concepts, achieved it was believed through low-density suburban development, integration of street networks, and the introduction of open space. Such legislation would be novel and potentially far-reaching in British affairs. The notion that public control might be exercised over the use of private land in towns, in order to secure an arguable end product, quite surpassed all previous considerations. On the other hand, as Ashworth (1954) argues:

> However great the novelty of statutory town planning, it was not concerned primarily with a problem that was either new itself or newly-recognized. It was an extension of the attempts . . . to remedy the unhealthy conditions of towns. (p. 167)

Nettlefold made an official visit to a number of German towns in the summer of 1905 (Cherry, 1982). He reported to Birmingham City Council later that year and submitted a fuller Report in 1906 in which he made a plea for a policy of municipal purchase of suburban land, encouraging others (individuals and Public Utility Building Societies) to build 'at the lowest possible rate healthy, cheerful houses for people with small incomes'. Money spent on judicious land purchase so as to create ground rents and direct the development of building land on sound lines had been successful in Germany, and a similar model should be pursued in Britain. However, to enforce town expansion plans and to carry out a vigorous policy of land purchase, fresh legislation was essential. The City Council supported Nettlefold's motion for a parliamentary bill. A year later a Conference of Local Authorities on Town Planning, held in Manchester, brought the matter before the Association of Municipal Corporations (AMC). Nettlefold was chairman of the Town Planning Committee of the AMC, and the Association proceeded to prepare a draft bill. A deputation from the AMC went to the Prime Minister and the President of the Local Government Board, when the Association was promised that sympathetic attention would be given to the matter. The National Housing Reform Council had also pressed the Prime Minister (in November 1906) for a programme of housing and town planning legislation, receiving a pledge that a bill would be introduced as soon as circumstances permitted. Meanwhile the Royal Institute of British Architects (RIBA) sent a deputation to John Burns urging the case of architects' advisory committees in town development.

In the event the Housing, Town Planning Bill had its First Reading in March 1908. The town planning provisions were confined to fourteen sections (54–67) at the end of what was essentially a housing bill which aimed to give further encouragement to house building. The objects were 'to secure, by means of schemes which may be prepared by local authorities or landowners, that in future, land in the vicinity of towns shall be developed in such a way as to secure proper sanitary conditions, amenity and convenience in connection with the laying out of the land itself and of any neighbouring land'. In other words projects for building development would be encouraged and co-ordinated through Planning Schemes, the provisions of which, once adopted, would become mandatory on developers. In practice local authorities rather than landowners became the agencies for the preparation of the schemes, their adoption, and their subsequent implementation. Thus the bedrock of twentieth-century statutory town planning was laid: public powers were granted to oversee the form of urban development – the arrangement of land uses in designated parcels of land, the disposition of house building, including layout and density, and the co-ordination of street patterns. The Bill included no powers to enable municipalities to buy land in their urban peripheries and failed to make town planning a mandatory activity for local authorities.

The bill made little progress during that parliamentary session; it was withdrawn and brought forward again in 1909. There were difficulties in the Lords both over compensation and the extension of bureaucracy implied in the arrangements which emphasized central control by the Local Government Board, but it finally passed – just a week before the government fell after the Lords refused to pass Lloyd George's Budget on 30 November 1909. It was a close-run thing: further delay would have modified the bill or even destroyed it altogether.

The act fell far short of the hopes of those who had pressed for much more over the previous three years. Yet the legislation met with successes which could scarcely have been imagined. Birmingham in particular used the new planning powers with enthusiasm. George Cadbury Jnr. (1915), a member of the City's Town Planning Committee, thought the Act 'a great instrument of progress' in that it gave the community for the first time 'an adequate control of the town's future development' (p. 139), though he went on to regret that the question of municipal land ownership had not been addressed.

Nettlefold, now highly critical of an over-cautious Local Government Board, left the City Council and was succeeded by his half cousin Neville Chamberlain. He became chairman of a newly-established Town Planning Committee (the first such local authority committee in the country) and the city found the 1909 Act to its liking. It was the first authority in the country to submit a request to the Local Government Board for authority to prepare a Planning Scheme. This was in respect of 2,320 acres in the west and south-west of the city covering the parish of Quinton and parts of the parishes of Harborne, Edgbaston and Northfield. With approval to proceed forthcoming in February 1911, the procedures took their course, and the scheme was finally approved in May 1913 – an indication of the cumbersome bureaucracy that was entailed. But by 1914 three other schemes in the city were in the pipeline, for East Birmingham, North Yardley and South Birmingham. Elsewhere in the country, take-up of the legislation was slender, and in any case the war had a severe impact, planning work being disrupted because of seriously depleted staff.

The situation was that in 1919 there were 172 schemes in England and Wales which had been authorized to be prepared, or had been adopted by local authorities; these covered little more than 300,000 acres. But in only 13 of these cases had schemes actually been submitted, and five of them were in Birmingham. In Scotland progress was even slower with not one scheme having yet been approved (Cherry, 1974). These achievements represented the slenderest base on which further progress could be built; the circumstances in which this first happened are sketched in chapter 4.

Although the legislative foundation to the institutionalization of town planning came relatively late and was half-hearted in its objects, the activity was practised on an ever-widening scale. The consequence was that the practitioners involved found it convenient to see their activity as distinctive within a number of professions which came to engage in this area – architecture, surveying, municipal engineering and the law. At first the call was for the professions to work harmoniously together, though each profession was loathe to admit that the new activity could be undertaken equally well by another. It seems that Thomas Adams played a leading part in discussions that went beyond mere co-operation. From 1910 onwards (by which time he had been appointed the first Town Planning Inspector at the Local Government Board) he was meeting regularly with a small group of practitioners in the field. The notion of town planning being an area of distinctive expertise within the ambit of cognate professional interests took root.

In July 1913 a provisional committee of the group was set up at a meeting in London. A membership list was drawn up, derived not only from the professions, but also 'amateurs' associated with none. An invitation was sent to them to join a Town Planning Institute and a first meeting was convened, chaired by Thomas Adams in November of that year. A Council was elected and met for the first time in December; Adams was elected president. An inaugural dinner in January 1914 marked the public launching of the institute and the articles of association were signed in September. The institute dates its founding from this time – 1914. The initial membership totalled 115 of all categories; 17 were qualified surveyors, 18 were engineers and 28 were architects. It was a neat balancing act: the honorary vice-presidents included the President of the Local Government Board (John Burns), a past president of the Surveyors Institution (Sir Alexander Stenning) and Sir Aston Webb of the Royal Institute of British Architects. A bevy of honorary members included the great and the good. From such beginnings grew the town planning profession, in due time liberating itself from the hold of the other professions, gaining its Charter, acquiring a Royal prefix, extending its activities world-wide and, being now the institutional home for 18,000 members.

These developments over the period 1910–14 were undoubtedly helped by initiatives in the field of town planning education at the same time. The origins lay with W. H. Lever, of Port Sunlight fame, and C. H. Reilly, the Professor of Architecture at Liverpool (Wright, 1982). In 1907 Lever won a successful libel action against a group of newspapers and was awarded £50,000 in damages, a sum later increased through subsidiary actions to £91,000, or £84,000 net of costs. Reilly wrote to Lever (they had met previously) asking for money for a Chair of Town Planning, a lectureship and the publication of a journal on the subject. Lever obliged. A Chair of Town Planning and Civic Design was endowed, a Department of Civic Design established in 1909, a research fellowship funded, and a journal, *The Town Planning Review*, was published, the first issue appearing in April 1910. The new professor was Stanley Adshead, an Architect in private practice in London; the research fellow and editor of *TPR* was Patrick Abercrombie, an assistant lecturer in the School of Architecture. Both Adshead and Abercrombie were founder members of the Town Planning Institute.

Demand for town planning 'knowledge' was growing, and other academic initiatives unfolded. With financial support from the Cadburys, the University of Birmingham appointed Raymond Unwin as a part-time lecturer in town planning; he gave two courses each year between 1912 and 1914 in the Department of Civil Engineering. Summer Schools of Planning were held under the auspices of the University of London around the same time and in 1914 a Department of Town Planning was established in the Bartlett School of Architecture at University College; Adshead moved from Liverpool to take the chair.

The Developing Agenda

Legislative, professional and educational developments quickly under-pinned the town planning movement which burst on the scene in the ten years before 1914. Within a remarkably short time they helped to transform a single-minded activity concerned with a new style of housing provision, in the resolution of a set of urban problems, into an altogether wider frame of reference – no less than the design, appearance and functioning of cities as a whole and the nature of community life within them.

The RIBA International Town Planning Conference, held in London in 1910, particularly the exhibition held at the Royal Academy, was an early indicator of the strides that were being made in Britain to catch up with continental and American work. The occasion appealed to architects and civic designers, but while it encouraged the notion that the end product of town planning was a derivative of architecture, none the less the totality of the process could not fall solely within the province of the architect, nor indeed within that of any profession. Town planning was not just a matter of co-ordination between the participant professions, with the architect or the surveyor as the lead player; it was also something 'above and beyond' with an agenda of its own.

This agenda responded to newly emergent issues. Road traffic is one example. By 1914 there were 132,000 private cars and vans licensed in Britain; there were also 51,000 public transport vehicles and 82,000 goods vehicles, to which should be added over 123,000 motor-cycles. In public transport horse-drawn buses had virtually given way to motor-buses. Well before this time the question of what new arrangements should be made to accommodate growing numbers of traffic on urban streets had come to the fore. The model of circular road schemes had already appeared in America, and a paper by G. L. Pepler at the RIBA 1910 Conference adapted this for a 'ringway' around London approximately 10 miles in radius (Cherry, 1981). The proper development of arterial roads was also part of the answer, and the Local Government Board convened an Arterial Roads Conference in July 1913 to address the traffic planning problem of Greater London. The linked question of road layouts and urban design was firmly established.

Other aspects of design found their way into town planning affairs. Landscape architecture became a specialism of T. H. Mawson in a career that graduated from the design of parks and gardens to a comprehensive design of whole urban areas (Cherry et al., 1993). Idealistic notions of ringing cities with green belts had already been advanced by Lord Meath who advocated a green girdle for London which would link existing parks in a continuous chain of verdure (Aalen, 1989). Pepler expanded his proposal for a 'ringway' around the city into the notion of a circular road scheme as a 'parkway' which linked outer open spaces, in emulation of schemes which had already appeared in the United States.

The growing town planning movement fed avidly on these broader matters, and was soon able to proclaim competence in the design and layout, not just of suburban estates, but of whole cities. In Birmingham Neville Chamberlain, as early as 1911, called for a 'skeleton' plan for the whole of the city of Birmingham, showing open spaces, roads and a land use division into residential, business and factory areas. The international competition in 1914 for plans for the future development of Dublin, sponsored by Lord Aberdeen, Lord Lieutenant of Ireland (won by Abercrombie in partnership with Sydney and Arthur Kelly), finally indicated that Britain was catching up with those other countries where city competitions had long been held.

A personal view of town planning was given by Unwin (1909) in *Town Planning in Practice*. The subtitle to the book, 'the art of designing cities and suburbs', confirmed a design bias to the activity. He began with the home and the importance of uplift of surroundings:

> We have forgotten that endless rows of brick boxes, looking out upon dreary streets and squalid backyards, are not really homes for people, and can never become such, however complete may be the drainage system, however pure the water supply, or however detailed the bye-laws under which they are built. Important as all these provisions for man's material needs and sanitary existence are, they do not suffice. There is needed the vivifying touch of art which would give completeness and increase their value tenfold; there is needed just that imaginative treatment which could transform the whole. (p. 4)

But he went on to apply design principles to conscious arrangements for towns as a whole:

> Hitherto our modern towns have been too much mere aggregations of people; but it must be our work to transform these same aggregations into consciously organized communities, finding in their towns and cities new homes in the true sense, enjoying the fuller life which comes from more intimate intercourse, and finding in the organization of their town scope and stimulus for the practice and development of the more noble aims which have contributed to bring them together. (p. 11)

This was flowery language perhaps, but it showed that a simple aesthetic objective was placed within a wider frame of reference. An intellectual polymath, Patrick Geddes, was particularly influential in addressing this broader setting (Meller, 1990). As a young man in the 1870s and 1880s he was open to all the ideas that were circulating at the time. With an early interest in biology and the natural sciences, he was attracted to theories in evolution and enrolled on Huxley's classes in London; while in Paris he discovered the work of Le Play and tried to marry evolution to the social sciences; and through an awareness of spatial form he introduced a regional perspective to cultural studies. A great synthesizer, never laying claim to any particular body of knowledge, he was a pioneer in bringing together threads of knowledge about the organization of society in relation to the environment; these and the theoretical constructs he drew up proved of great value to a town planning movement which lacked any single disciplinary home.

He secured his first permanent post in 1889 at the age of 35 when he was appointed to the Chair of Botany at Dundee College, then affiliated to the University of St Andrews. He remained there for the next 30 years, though for much of that time his career was more in the social sciences, while he engaged in educational, philanthropic and town planning activities. His Outlook Tower in Edinburgh was a centre for the synthesizing of knowledge; he developed the notion of 'civics' in applied sociology; and he achieved early prominence in being invited to advise the Carnegie Dunfermline Trust on the layout of Pittencrieff Park in that town. He was heavily involved in the RIBA 1910 Conference, where he was Director of the Cities and Town Planning Exhibition, which he subsequently took to other centres. In the years before 1914 he invested a lot of time in Dublin, and became an assessor to Lord Aberdeen's town planning competition for the city. In 1915 he published *Cities in Evolution*, one of the few books then available on the general development of cities; it was a passionate call for civic awakening and the flowering of a renewed urban civilization, realizable through town planning.

Geddes' great contribution in these early years was that he gave town planning the rudiments of a theoretical base which went beyond the disciplines of the built environment. Through applied sociology and geography, he provided it with a capacity to engage systematically in analysis and rational plan-making at spatial levels from local to regional and national.

3 The Notion of State Planning

The previous chapters have outlined developments in two important areas which have contributed to the emergence of twentieth-century planning. One of these areas saw the adoption of various measures to secure the regulation of an industrializing and urbanizing nation; progressive steps were taken to address the pressing problems of the late-Victorian city, particularly in matters regarding health and housing. The other area saw initiatives promoted to advance new forms of town building, especially in the layout and design of residential areas. An emergent professional expertise gave substance to a town planning movement which sought, first, the restoration of beauty and order to urban living and, subsequently, developed schemes for the comprehensive planning of town and country.

Coincidentally, a ground swell of political speculation favoured new forms of state organization and an increase in measures of social regulation. This chapter reviews these developments. By the end of the nineteenth century the idea of a much more active role for the state was gaining ground as arguments were advanced that an increasingly complex industrial society required forms of systematic organization which current arrangements did not provide. The portents were recognizable enough, as Greenleaf (1983) has shown. The German historical school stressed the role of corporate authority. Many economists were explicitly rejecting laissez-faire. The housing conditions of the working classes prompted calls for government to bear greater responsibility for the improvement (and increasingly the provision) of dwellings. Developments in the new field of social studies lent weight to this agitation.

During the half century from the 1880s to the 1930s collectivist forms of state organization were progressively adopted; it proved to be a period very different in character from the laissez-faire individualism of the mid-Victorian years which had preceded it. Hall and Schwarz (1985) argue that the sharp historical discontinuity which marked this period from its predecessor represented a crisis of liberalism, when it came to be recognized that the liberal state could no longer be reproduced by liberal policies. Major adjustments had to take place. Thus it was that in the quarter century up to the outbreak of the Great War in 1914, and in the two decades following cessation of hostilities in 1918, the state assumed a form which can be seen as characteristically 'modern'.

The main agencies for mass political representation also appeared at this time, with a new political party (Labour) in time usurping an old one (the Liberals). The twentieth-century socio-political world was born in which new collectivist aspirations unfolded. Imperialists sought to build up the strength, health and efficiency of the state. Fabians sought to destroy the perceived anarchy of the capitalist market; in so doing, it drifted to the Labour Party, elevating the expert, the administrator and the bureaucrat to new heights of power and influence. The New Liberals also sought greater state intervention, though aiming to preserve individual liberties in an agreed balance of rights and duties. The Conservatives were the most sceptical of the collectivist trends, but even here an important 'Middle Way' gained support.

The late-Victorian period saw the beginnings of a steady expansion of state interventionism as attitudes shifted over the years away from self-help and individualism and towards protection. However, the outreach of the state into the lives of the citizenry was slow to find popular favour. Exceptional politicians such as Joseph Chamberlain in Birmingham had advanced the cause of municipal socialism, his civic gospel proclaimed during his mayoralty 1873–6 commanding considerable local support. Municipal enterprise in taking over public utilities and transport from private companies was a widespread feature of the fourth quarter of the century, and local schemes in public health and housing improvement were commonplace. But we should remember that increases in public spending caused resentment and that, for the working-class, at least, occasions for state intervention could arouse no little antagonism. There had been persistent hostility by the working-class to the Poor Law system, for example. Compulsory education could also provoke; parents might resent the fact that their children were kept at school until the age of 12 when they could be earning wages. The practical effects of state intervention always seemed to impact adversely on the working classes; public housing policy may clear the slums but it exacerbated overcrowding. Equally, state expenditure appeared to benefit the better off because the tax burden fell disproportionately on poorer people.

So to begin with, working-class communities regarded state intervention in their lives with suspicion and hostility. But Pugh (1994) makes the point that by the Edwardian years this sentiment was plainly in transition. The introduction of old-age pensions in 1908 received warm support, for example; there was no cost to the beneficiaries and none of the indignity associated with seeking relief from the Poor Law guardians. Thereafter, the particular circumstances of the Great War saw the tentacles of the state extend in all directions, and although they withdrew briefly, the second half of the inter-war period suggested that a serious shift in political attitudes (though as yet without much practical effect) was taking place. The Second World War proved a major catalyst and by 1945 views of the form of the state in modern society had been completely transformed.

In the meantime the argument for change was being advanced amongst political movements: essentially the old parties, Conservative and Liberal; a new party, Labour; and a society, the Fabians. A new set of assumptions was paraded, a new political vocabulary heard, and ultimately a new message proclaimed – the virtues of planning. In due time the professionals in the town planning movement would be hypnotized by the siren song of state planning and for half a century their paths would be intertwined.

Political Movements

The Fabians

In the period between October 1883 and January 1884 a small number of 'young provincials adrift in the capital', as the Mackenzies (1977, p. 15) describe them, began meeting in London as a radical fellowship group. It became the Fabian Society. Edward Pease, from the well-connected Quaker family, was chairman; Frank Podmore, a young clerk in the Post Office, was secretary. At first the Society was little more than a congenial club, its members only casually linked. Two years after it was founded its membership was only 67, and no fixed views had been proclaimed.

The Society attracted broadly middle-class members; they ranged from the ascetic and high-minded, to the bohemian and those who scandalized society. The principal figures to dominate the Society in the early years included George Bernard Shaw who joined in 1884, still trying to scratch a living in journalism. He had heard Henry George lecturing in London on the taxation of land values, and he became a convert to land nationalization. On reading a French translation of *Das Kapital* he abandoned George's limited socialism in favour of the nationalization of all forms of capital. He was followed by his friend Sidney Webb, a civil service clerk, in 1885. Annie Bessant, divorcee from a clergyman husband and espouser of atheism, joined the same year; she went on to organize the matchmakers' strike in 1888 and subsequently form their union. Graham Wallas, who much later would become Professor of Political Science at the London School of Economics, joined in 1886.

The Society gathered momentum slowly, but by the close of the 1880s it had assumed a definitive direction. As political radicals the members distanced themselves from the socialists, revolutionaries, insurrectionists and militants. Rather, they were attracted to the significance of reforms in local government. They specialized in publishing pamphlets, an activity in which Webb was prominent. He had a particular gift for effective propaganda, his early tracts including *Facts for Socialists* (1887) and *Facts for Londoners* (1889). *Fabian Essays in Socialism* (1889) was edited and published by Shaw, who also contributed a paper, 'The Economic Basis of Socialism', and the text of his address, 'The Transition to Social Democracy', to the British Association. Webb also made a contribution to *Fabian Essays*.

In 1890 the Society's membership stood at 150; by the next year it had doubled to 300. Political activity was now being undertaken in the provinces, though it was within London that the Society's major significance lay. In 1892 Sidney Webb won Deptford for a seat on the London County Council, one of six Fabians on a Council of 118. From 1897 to 1903 Shaw also participated in municipal government – as a vestryman and later Borough Councillor of St Pancras, an experience which led him to publish *The Common Sense of Municipal Trading* (1904).

The Society continued to be dominated by personalities, and its direction by conflicts amongst them. The marriage of Sidney Webb to Beatrice Potter in 1892 provided the society with an indomitable partnership. The daughter of a wealthy railway and industrial magnate, Beatrice helped her cousin's husband, Charles Booth, in his survey, *Life and Labour of the People in London*. Sidney became chairman of a trust fund to manage a £10,000 inheritance for the Society; it was decided to use part of the money to found a school of economics in London – for teaching and research, not to endow socialism. Later, the Webbs founded the influential journal, *The New Statesman*. H. G. Wells joined the circle in 1903, but retained his membership for only five years, when he resigned. For some years he was openly critical of the Society; he advocated reform, though with no clear ideas as to the future, and his manner was disruptive. He stimulated the Fabians, but finally his petulance and unpredictability exasperated the Society.

Initially there was uncertainty as to whether the Fabians should be allied to Labour or the Liberals. For many years the Webbs dominated the Fabian line with the argument that socialism would be achieved gradually by the extension of state and municipal enterprise ('the inevitability of gradualism' as the doctrine had it). But an attraction to socialism strengthened after 1910 when the notion of society built around productive labour caught on. In due time G. D. H. Cole became one of the leaders of this group. He joined the Fabian (later Labour) Research Department in 1913; he was its honorary secretary from 1916 to 1924. Progressively, Reader in Economics and Professor of Social and Political Theory at Oxford, he was secretary and later chairman of the New Fabian Research Bureau in the 1930s and chairman of the Fabian Society from 1939 to 1946.

During the first half of the twentieth century the reputation and influence of the Fabians was ascendant. The Society had 2,000 members in 1907; interestingly, one-quarter were women. Beatrice Webb remained a pinnacle of intellectual authority. Sidney achieved Government office; elected MP for Seaham Harbour in 1922 (at the age of 63) he became President of the Board of Trade in the Labour Government in 1924. In the second Labour Government in 1929, as Baron Passfield, he became Secretary of State for the Colonies. Between the wars the Fabians became a brains trust for the Labour movement, issuing policy tracts and propaganda, conducting summer schools and producing advice notes for councillors.

Before the Second World War ended the Society had more than 10,000 members, with a network of local societies. Young intellectuals had turned to Fabian summer schools for their political inspiration. A new political generation of the Labour Party grew up as Fabians – Dalton, Morrison, Attlee and Laski as examples. In 1945 more than half the Labour MPs who won seats were Fabians; the Government included 45 of them and 10 were in the Cabinet. The socialist mainstream was informed from Fabian perspectives, strong on local government, quick to point to municipal enterprise. The notion of planning had fertile ground in which to grow. The Fabian influence had in fact been remarkable. At the time of their founding, the extent of state powers was very small and any increase observable was a result of pragmatism rather than ideology. But the society changed the political agenda, becoming the first British organization to promote a justification, coherently argued, for the extension of state power in pursuit of specific economic and social aims.

The Liberals

Towards the end of the nineteenth century Liberalism began to change its form and emphasis (Greenleaf, 1983; Eccleshall, 1986). A small network of friends and collaborators explored and propagated new Liberal doctrines which increasingly favoured positive action by the state in social and economic affairs. Over time the idea of the minimal state, which Liberalism had previously espoused, was progressively abandoned by the mainstream of the party.

The key players in the move towards an enlarged state included some eminent names. Alfred Marshall became Professor of Political Economy at Cambridge. Thomas Hill Green was Professor of Moral Philosophy at Oxford. Leonard Trelawney Hobhouse was Professor of Sociology at London. J. L. and Barbara Hammond were established authorities on economic and social history. John Atkinson Hobson, a journalist, was one of the founders of the *Progressive Review* in 1896. Under their influence progressive Liberalism took shape, rejecting the old Liberalism which had been marked by individualist perspectives. Fabianism was an influence even here, particularly on Hobhouse, but a creed hidebound by notions of class conflict proved unpalatable.

The Liberal Government of 1892–5 had already moved in the general direction of addressing social problems. But Liberal politicians were still divided at the end of the century between two camps: those faithful to the Gladstonian tradition, opponents of bureaucracy and any whiff of state socialism; and the others, largely newer and younger members, more open to the emergent philosophies which favoured positive action by the state. Campbell-Bannerman's government from December 1905 until his death two years later maintained a lukewarm stance to state intervention, though some social reform measures were promoted. But the real force of the new Liberalism came later, through the impact of David Lloyd George and Winston Churchill, supported by R. B. Haldane and H. H. Asquith (who succeeded Campbell-Bannerman as Prime Minister). C. F. G. Masterman and Herbert Louis Samuel were others of influence to expound the new political radicalism.

But no sooner had a new creed taken hold than splits weakened the party. Fragmentation had been seen early on with Joseph Chamberlain's organization of the Liberal Unionist faction in opposition to Gladstone's Home Rule Bill. But this split in the ruling bloc was followed by wounding disputes during the Great War when political sentiment turned critically on personality considerations, and the Liberal Party was divided between the followers of Asquith and Lloyd George. As a party of government, and indeed as a major political force, the Liberals did not survive the traumatic leadership split, on top of the issues arising from the coalition with the Conservatives in 1915 and the emotion surrounding the introduction of conscription.

But the new Liberal ideas survived and indeed took on a further lease of life. The first annual Liberal Summer School met in 1921. For one week each year throughout the 1920s the schools provided a forum in which ideas could be exchanged about the social reconstruction of the country. Businessmen, politicians and academics combined to formulate an alternative industrial policy to the Labour Party. The Summer School of 1926 established an inquiry, which reported in 1928: this was *Britain's Industrial Future*, the famous Yellow Book.

Its authorship was impressive, being the work of a committee whose members included Lloyd George, Hubert Henderson, J. M. Keynes, Ramsay Muir, B. S. Rowntree, Herbert Samuel and Sir John Simon. The publication represented the aims of the then Liberal intelligentsia in an extensive analysis of Britain's social and industrial problems. It recommended an increasing measure of control by government over private industry, particularly where monopoly conditions prevailed, and in connection with investment requirements. It urged a vigorous policy of national reconstruction so as to achieve planned development across a wide economic front of infrastructure (roads, housing and electricity), employment (docks and waterways, agriculture and mining) and education. The proposals represented a coherent alternative to the increasingly fashionable policies of nationalization and state protection as espoused by the Labour Party, and indeed in time some were taken over by both Labour and the Conservatives. Lloyd George continued the theme throughout the 1930s. Indeed, his 1935 election campaign offered a new deal for 'Peace and Reconstruction'; unemployment would be combated by a massive programme of government expenditure, and more effective machinery for economic planning would be introduced.

The Conservatives

It would be quite misleading to suppose that for much of the nineteenth century the Liberals advocated laissez-faire and that the Conservatives opposed it; equally, that in the twentieth century the positions were simply reversed. Letwin (1992) argues that the basic ingredients of opinion were the same in both parties. Hence movement across parties (such as by Gladstone, originally a High Church Tory, but forsaking that party allegiance over the repeal of the Corn Laws) was occasioned by attitudes to particular issues, personal loyalties or animosities, rather than by disagreement on fundamental principles.

In any case laissez-faire was a term introduced late into Britain, in the 1880s by French writers, the physiocrats, as a term of abuse; the term is not to be found in Adam Smith's *Wealth of Nations*. The meaning usually ascribed to the term is the principle that governments should not interfere with competition among individuals engaged in the making and exchange of goods and services. It is therefore synonymous with wholly unfettered competition. But Smith was arguing against a particular kind of restriction, namely that sought by the mercantilists who advocated the fixing of prices to keep out foreign goods which forced down the prices of English goods.

Throughout the nineteenth century there were numerous occasions when the Tories took measures to combat unfettered competition. Lord Shaftesbury attacked the system which led to the employment of children in factories and mines. Later, Disraeli promoted social and reformist measures. There was always a recognizable thread of sentiment, as in Tory Democracy, eager to secure the improvement of the working classes. Joseph Chamberlain was keen to urge the positive role of the state to achieve social reform.

But by the early twentieth century important currents of political thought left the Tories somewhat beached. State control in civil and military affairs was held to be a legitimate posture to adopt; but not in economic affairs. By contrast, as we have seen, political sentiments elsewhere were leaving the Tories rather isolated. The Fabians had a growing confidence in a benevolent state and the Liberals came to see the state as a humanitarian agency in social welfare. The socialists, to whom we turn next, would also soon define their statist stance.

It was not until the 1930s that a section of the Conservatives themselves began to argue for increasing state intervention in social and economic affairs, adopting postures and advocating measures already well articulated by their political rivals. Greenleaf (1983, vol. 2) observes that Neville Chamberlain in the 1930s conducted 'a not unenterprising programme of collectivist reconstruction even though there were others who would have pushed on faster and farther and more systematically' (p. 244). But it was Harold Macmillan's 'middle way' between the extremes of laissez-faire and state socialism which promised most for a Conservative Party. His book, *The Middle Way: a study of the problem of economic progress in a free and democratic society* (1938), urged wide strategic intervention by public authorities, almost akin to a national plan, whereby economic life might be revived and radical social reform undertaken, financed from the additional wealth created.

The Labour Party

The origins of the Labour Party are to be found in the last two decades of the nineteenth century. The Social Democratic Foundation emerged in 1884, the same year as the Fabian Society. The Independent Labour Party was born in 1893. By this time the essence of an alternative political order was being thrashed out, key propagators being Beatrice and Sidney Webb. In the meantime around the turn of the century the gospel of Labour was taking root in the mill towns of the Pennines and in the industrial areas of Scotland. It soon displaced Liberalism in the northern mining areas. Early in the twentieth century it swept into the South Wales valleys. In February 1900 the inaugural conference of the Labour Representation Committee was held in a Memorial Hall near Ludgate Circus, London; after 1906 the Committee became the Labour Party.

Under the new Party the essential shift was completed from guild socialism to state socialism. Doctrinal stress was given to public ownership, which, together with government control and planning, increasingly defined socialism. The public ownership of major industries, utilities and natural resources was seen as inseparable from the socialist idea (Morgan, 1987). Nationalization was regarded as vital if property relations were to be transformed. Miners became strongly committed to the nationalization of the coal-mines early in the century and it became a policy stance formally adopted by the Labour Party and the Trades Union Congress from 1906 onwards. The nationalization of railways was endorsed at Labour annual conferences before 1914.

But public ownership represented an aspiration rather than a programme. In large measure it was still a response to deteriorating labour relations, and could scarcely be regarded as a well-prepared model for either social change or technical modernization. A boost to public ownership came during the Great War, however, with steps taken by the war-time administrations to protect essential services and supplies. Moreover, during the latter stages of the conflict the aims of post-war reconstruction were widely discussed; in 1917 a Ministry of Reconstruction was set up, the activities of which encouraged political pressure for new social and economic arrangements. A Labour Party policy document of 1918, 'Labour and the New Social Order: a report on reconstruction', largely drafted by Sidney Webb, outlined a new order based on consciously planned cooperation, rather than on competitive struggle.

In 1918 Labour adopted a new constitution which included the famous clause (later renumbered as IV), committing the party 'to secure for the producers by hand or by brain the full fruits of their industry and the most equitable distribution thereof that may be possible, upon the basis of the common ownership of the means of production and the best system of popular administration and control of each industry and service.' (The words 'distribution and exchange' were added in 1929.)

The success of Labour in the 1922 general election signalled the debut of a strong third party into the mainstream of national political life, alongside the Conservatives and the Liberals. In 1924 they led a minority Labour Government for the first time, repeated on a second occasion from 1929 to 1931. But even then only coal nationalization was being proposed with any seriousness. (Perhaps this was due to the influence of R. H. Tawney, having served on the Sankey Coal Commission.) We have to turn to the 1930s to see the full flowering of the arguments for public ownership and planning.

One early line of approach was the aim of efficiency in public service. When Herbert Morrison was Minister of Transport in the second Labour Government his main legislative preoccupation was to acquire control of London Transport. His scheme would follow the precedents set by the British Broadcasting Corporation and the Central Electricity Generating Board – in other words the autonomous public corporation free from both parliamentary interference and internal dictation by workers. In 1933, when Morrison was chairman of the London County Council, the London Passenger Transport Board was established on this model. His book, *Socialisation and Transport* (1933), became highly influential.

But the main changes came from another direction, the immediate stimulus dictated by political events. The fall of the second Labour government signalled an early political casualty of the world depression, and the crisis of 1931 had the effect of triggering moves in party policy. Labour's reformism had finally proved too aimless. By the end of the 1920s there was already a substantial body of economic and political support for a radical unemployment policy based on a programme of substantial government investment. But the Labour Party did not have such a policy and in the election campaign of 1929 it attacked the Liberals for espousing expansionist aims. In office it followed the orthodox policies of the Conservatives, with only minor modifications. During this time the Liberals consistently advocated a bolder strategy. True, Labour did not have a parliamentary majority; but neither did it have the policies. Skidelsky (1967) explains this failure in terms of the party's commitment to a Utopian socialism which prevented it from coming to terms with economic reality. 'It was a parliamentary party with a Utopian ethic. It was not fit for the kind of power it was called upon to exercise' (p. xii). The National Government was formed in August 1931 and the Labour Party, humiliated at the polls, took revenge. The gradual evolutionary approach of MacDonald and his chancellor, Snowden, was rejected, and a new generation of leaders which replaced them embarked on a strategy of devising a practical programme for the introduction of socialism to Britain.

With hindsight, though it may not have appeared so at the time, conditions for this political change of direction were remarkably conducive to its ultimate success. First, intellectual underpinning to arguments for government intervention had been pressed for many years. Indeed it was embodied in the new Liberalism of the late-nineteenth century which held that it was the government's responsibility to intervene to ensure that social freedom might be translated into social justice.

Second, Britain's profound economic problems during the 1920s and into the 1930s raised fundamental questions about the appropriate role for government in the market system. Socialists held to the need to restructure the market, and, therefore, the role of government in the management of economic affairs was crucial to their alternative. Nationalization, the Labour Party's official policy for many years had not been implemented; now was the time to put in hand a practical programme.

Third, there was the on-going revolution amongst economists, in which J. M. Keynes emerged with a key which promised to restore economic health to market economies. His advice justified government intervention in order to bolster investment and increase expenditure, without the need to relinquish complete economic authority to the state. For democratic socialists his message reinforced their redistributive goals; it suggested the ways in which full employment could be maintained in the socialist state; and it provided a forceful argument for central planning. As Durbin (1985) summarizes: 'Thus both the intellectual ferment within the economics profession and the policy exigencies of the divided and defeated Labour Party opened up the way for socialist economists to examine the problems of economic management and its role in the socialist state' (p. 70).

Between 1931 and 1937 Labour evolved a clear, socialist programme, with nationalization central to it. A moderate performance in the 1935 General Election was a disappointment to the party, as the main lines of political and economic strategy had by then been worked out. The movement did not know that there would not be another chance for power until 1945 – under very different circumstances. In the meantime the party's sails were filled with moral rectitude under the guiding philosophy of R. H. Tawney and his contemporaries.

A new generation of Fabians helped to redefine and rearticulate the revisionist case for democratic socialism in Britain. The actors included Colin Clark, lecturer for University Tutorial Classes, London; Douglas Jay, staff writer for *The Times* and later *The Economist*; Robert Fraser, leader-writer for *The Daily Herald*; and G. D. H. Cole, Hugh Gaitskell, Hugh Dalton, and Evan Durbin. Durbin's daughter, Elizabeth Durbin (1985), describes them as optimists, believing that problems could be solved rationally, that the state could properly intervene to correct and improve economic performance, and that socialism represented the only ethical course to improve human society. Dalton's *Practical Socialism for Britain* (1935), followed by Jay's *The Socialist Case* (1937) and Durbin's *The Politics of Democratic Socialism* (1940) became influential texts expounding their cause.

The public ownership of major industries, utilities and natural resources had been inseparable from the socialist ideal since the early days of Keir Hardie's Independent Labour Party. What happened in the 1930s amongst the British Left was that a new school of university-trained democratic socialist economists not only appropriated public ownership as part of their rationale, but adopted 'planning' as a keyword of Labour policy. The imperatives of the world financial crisis in 1929 focused new attention on the relation between state and capital, and the intellectual foundations of the managed economy were laid. The notion of economic planning promised conscious and systematic control over resources, through which there would be an effective rationalization of industry, steered investment, technical development, and a prevention of unemployment. There may then have been no experience of central planning and control (that would come later with war-time administration), but at least the promise of a rational technocratic system was observable in the USSR.

Events moved quickly. In 1934 the Labour Party agreed on a detailed socialist programme in which socialist economic planning under central direction was promised. There would be a full scale extension of nationalization including the public ownership of land, a state medical service, and the raising of the school leaving age to 15. Durbin (1985) summarized the heady days as follows:

> By the outbreak of war the Labour Party had travelled light-years in the depth and sophistication of its knowledge of British financial institutions and economic policy options since the dark days of 1931. In a long process of research and debate, a practical programme of institutional reform had been officially adopted, which would ensure central control over the forces determining money supply, exchange rates and investment. The Party had also committed itself to a series of proposals to reduce general unemployment and to direct particular investment projects to distressed areas. A complementary programme to nationalize railways, coal and electricity had been thrashed out. (p. 261)

The dream, whether refreshingly positive, or dangerously simple-minded, was that social injustice could be removed through redistribution and that the capitalist market system could be transformed.

Little was yet said about the role of planning. The Party had no proposals to establish planning machinery, but faith was strong both in the power of enlightened government and political control established over economic institutions. Planning simply became an essential ingredient in the socialist economic alternative.

Meanwhile there was the experience of the USSR where British socialists noted the efficacy of planning to achieve the growth needed to ensure full employment. Communism was regarded by socialists as an alternative version of their own goals; inapplicable to England, it was yet a distinctive experiment in collective living and working and in the effort to advance scientific research, public health, education and social welfare. Left-wing travellers to the Soviet Union (Leventhal, 1987) reflected a general fascination with Stalin's work. An account of a tour by Sidney and Beatrice Webb (now the Passfields) of Russia in 1935 appeared in *Soviet Communism, a New Civilisation?* In its second edition in 1937 the question mark was omitted.

The Communist Party

Prior to 1917 the two principal Marxist organizations were the British Socialist Party (BSP) and the Socialist Labour Party (SLP). The BSP, a direct descendant of the Social Democratic Foundation (SDF) dating from 1883, was formed in 1911. By contrast, the SLP had split from the SDF at the turn of the century. Both were isolated from the British working class, and though Marxism had influence in central Scotland, South Wales, the north-east, and parts of Lancashire and Yorkshire (typically Manchester and Sheffield), the labour movement was captured by the Labour Party.

The Communist Party was founded in July 1920. For some years British Marxism had been militant, seeking an active role in the trade unions and fomenting unrest in key industries. It had also been anti-war, thriving in the heightened class tension seen throughout Europe between 1917 and 1921. Revolutionary strategies were encouraged by the Russian revolution. But the Communist Party proved unable to compete with the Labour Party and remained alien to the mainstream of the labour movement (Macintyre, 1980). Membership remained small, with distinct geographical foci: South Wales, Central Scotland and south and east London. Its strategy remained that of providing a militant lead in trade union affairs. It derided the reformism of the Labour Party, preferring to emphasize the incompatibility of class interests.

It was in retreat after the failure of the General Strike in 1926. Theorists among its working-class members proved unable to provide leadership; and with the input during the 1930s of a few university-trained intellectuals conversant with Soviet Marxism, alienation with the working class was further heightened. Moreover, after 1926 the leaders of the Labour Party and the Trades Union Congress opened up a drive to outlaw the Communists and isolate the rest of the labour movement (Branson, 1985). The TUC in effect said 'never again' and the Labour Party set its face against any kind of direct action. The Communists were left with the struggle to abolish capitalism on their terms, with ideas based on Lenin's views (expressed in *State and Revolution* written just before the 1917 October Revolution) that the state machine, including Parliament, was an organ of class rule – of oppression of one class (the working class) by another (the capitalist class). The working class could not use the state machine and wield it for its own purpose, rather it must replace it with a system of direct democracy for the workers. The far left isolated itself from the wider inter-war debates about planning and forms of economic management.

Keynesian Economics

As the 1920s unfolded, the argument that government spending could be an instrument of public policy was increasingly advanced in economic and political circles. The 1930s saw the flowering of Keynesian economics, which provided a rationale for public expenditure and the basis for programmes of state intervention designed to rescue Britain and the West from the breakdown of laissez-faire capitalism. For the Labour Party, as we have seen, the Keynesian doctrine was seized upon to bolster its own theoretical propositions about state enterprise and planning.

John Maynard Keynes was born into an intellectually gifted and successful family. A Cambridge economist, he had a short spell in the India Office before returning to his college. During the Great War he worked in the Treasury, though he grew to despise the government, regarding their aims as criminal. (He was a conscientious objector, but was exempted by the Treasury from enlistment under the Military Services Act, 1916.) He carried this private fury with him to the Paris Peace Conference, where he represented the Treasury. He had a mistrust of Lloyd George, contempt for the Americans, an anger that politics had ousted reason, and a genuine fear of a general impoverishment to follow. As Skidelsky (1983) remarks, 'Keynes carried to the conference a burden not just of collective guilt but of personal guilt for his part in the war' (p. 353).

His rage burst out in his book, *The Economic Consequences of the Peace* (1919), in which he condemned the harsh reparations policy of the Treaty of Versailles. He argued for the retention of Germany as the central support for the European economic system. Affirming the virtues of the capitalist system, he stressed the need for the accumulation of capital in a balanced equilibrium between the old world and the new. Keynes resigned from the Treasury in 1919 and returned to Cambridge. But the war had marked the start of his career as a radical economist, and his book would make him world-famous. A best seller world-wide, it gave him a position of intellectual leadership on which he would build later in moulding the economic perceptions of a generation and more. Additionally, his anti-war stance made him a hero of the Left (to which he never belonged), of significance in the 1930s when the Labour Party embraced his interventionary doctrine.

Back in Cambridge, aged 37 in 1920, Keynes had so far given no hint of greatness in the sphere in which he would now excel – economics. Indeed, but for the war he may not even have stuck to economics. But he now set out to save a capitalist system, where persistent mass unemployment after 1921 suggested that the self-regulating market had broken down. Stability and progress in a world cut adrift from its nineteenth-century moorings had to be restored. We should recall his Victorian and Edwardian background – a period when prices and interest rates were relatively stable. In 1914 prices were 11 per cent below the level of 50 years earlier and during the same half-century the range of fluctuation of long-term interest rates had been between 2.5 and 3.4 per cent. Moreover, the age was one when the government of Britain was in the hands of an intellectual elite, membership of which, for him, was unquestioned (Moggridge, 1976).

Keynes' ultimate genius was that he developed an analysis of economic disorder which justified forms of state intervention compatible with traditional liberal values. He was the last of the great English liberals (Skidelsky, 1992). Throughout the 1920s Keynes and others in a circle, which included Walter Layton, Hubert Henderson, Philip Kerr and Seebohm Rowntree (Greenleaf, 1983), worked on the theoretical foundations for a fundamental reform of capitalism. Layton was editor of *The Economist*, Henderson was a Cambridge economist who became editor of *Nation and Athenaeum*, Kerr was private secretary to Lloyd George from 1916 to 1921, and Rowntree, while chairman of his company, was prominent in the field of scientific management and industrial welfare. It was typical that from 1921–2 Keynes opposed the deflationary policy adopted by the Treasury and the Bank of England, and that in 1925 he attacked the return to the gold standard. A rapprochement with Lloyd George saw him serving on the Liberal Industrial Enquiry between 1926 and 1929 in an effort to provide an economic programme for the revival of Liberal fortunes.

Two books by Keynes, *A Treatise on Money* (1930) and (particularly)

The General Theory of Employment, Interest and Money (1936), finally laid the foundations for Keynesian economics. Keynes started with the theme that the specific virtues associated with economic self-regulation depend on the stability of the price level. Post-1918 economic disorder was manifest in the collapse of that most stable indicator – money – as seen in inflation and deflation in western economies. From analysis to prescription: for Keynes money became not so much the cause of the uncertainty of the post-1918 world, but a means whereby that uncertainty might be tackled.

The Depression of 1931 and its aftermath allowed Keynes to establish practical policies to supplement theory. Laissez-faire capitalism may have a self-adjusting mechanism, but recovery happens neither automatically nor necessarily quickly. Revival has to be encouraged by state policies to revitalize industry: these may include reduction of interest rates, cutting taxes, or increasing government spending to aid recovery in trade and manufacture. Society's self-governing mechanisms had broken down, and it needed more governing from the centre; public expenditure was needed to restore idle resources to work. External intervention was required to restore an economy to new vigour, so that it might once again produce wealth (a message seized upon by the Left in its concern for redistribution).

Keynes argued that government levels of spending, investment and taxation should be set in accordance with an appropriate level of aggregate demand. If demand was too low (in which case additional unemployment would result) then government should budget for a deficit and encourage both public and private spending through a combination of tax cuts and reduced interest rates. On the other hand, if demand was too high (in which case inflation would be higher) then government should budget for a surplus by reductions in its own spending and a blend of increased taxes and higher interest rates. An active government role was thereby justified: state spending should not be regarded in negative terms, but could itself generate income and spending power, so promising to control, if not eliminate unemployment.

The stimulation of fresh consumption and the creation of pump-priming investment found early adherents in all political parties: David Lloyd George and the Liberals; Oswald Mosley in the Labour Party, following his departure from the Conservatives in 1924; and Harold Macmillan and Robert Boothby amongst the Conservatives. Furthermore, there was a general openness to new interventionary initiatives outside political circles. For example, the problem of mass unemployment encouraged speculation as to new measures to overcome it; the Pilgrim Trust, founded in 1930 by an American millionaire, conducted studies in this area. Political and Economic Planning (PEP), an influential group of civil servants, business men and academics, was launched in 1931 as an independent, non-party group. In the United States Franklin Roosevelt's election as President in 1933 signalled an immediate leap forward in interventionary politics with acts concerned with unemployment relief, housing, industry and regional regeneration (in the Tennessee Valley).

The Keynesian revolution during the 1930s appeared to supply answers to the problem of economic management. It seemed possible to establish measures to confront the perceived collapse of capitalism; there was an answer to the mass unemployment experienced in the early 1930s. Democratic socialists recognized that Keynesian analysis could be used in the maintenance of employment and investment levels, as part of their own overall employment strategy. The Keynesian message also reinforced their redistributive goals.

But full employment per se was not socialism. *The General Theory* had little to say about the institutional reforms that were needed to control the banking system, for example, and the Labour Party for long housed suspicions of Keynes' Liberal connections. Theories which sought to make the capitalist system more workable, did not go far enough for the far left, and an explicit commitment to Keynesian policies for full employment did not come until 1944–5. However, for socialists the revolution in economic thinking confirmed their concerns to maintain full employment, enlarge the public sector and redistribute incomes. Planning became the keystone in the Labour Party's economic policy. It was an alternative to capitalism because it would provide political control over economic institutions, and promised administrative efficiency in place of the unregulated market.

There was of course another side. Economic liberals (and there were not many left in Britain between the wars) were nourished by the Austrian School of Economics, represented in particular by Ludwig von Mises and Friedrich von Hayek. They argued that socialism would decrease productivity and create widespread poverty, and were equally dismissive of the 'mixed economy'. (Some British politicians, it will be recalled, would be attracted to a 'middle way' between the extremes of central planning as seen in the USSR and the unbridled capitalism in Britain in past years.) At the low point of intellectual interest in economic liberalism, the political battlelines were drawn: on the one hand the belief that capitalist non-planning created and maintained social injustice, and on the other the argument that socialist planning would destroy political freedom. Robbins, Professor of Economics at the London School of Economics, was a standard-bearer for this view; his book, *Economic Planning and International Order* (1937), asserted the superiority of economic liberalism over socialism. But neither he nor his fellow Professor, Friedrich Hayek (recently arrived from Vienna) could stem the tide of theoretical advances in economic thinking. Hayek, distrustful of government interference of any kind, made his most effective contribution later in a new offensive against the political foundations of socialism in *The Road to Serfdom* (1944).

The Steps to State Planning

The Liberal governments of 1892–5 had already taken steps to tackle a range of social problems. There was legislation to give local authorities power to acquire land to provide allotments, to repair or close unhealthy houses and build new ones, to establish libraries and public baths, and to extend factory regulations. However, it was the period after 1907 when another Liberal Government gave the state a significantly enhanced role in social and economic affairs: old-age pensions, measures to deal with unemployment, the acceptance of public responsibility for feeding schoolchildren, and arrangements for national insurance. In 1909 came the first town planning legislation as an appendage of a Housing Act. The setting up of labour exchanges and the introduction of a national scheme of unemployment insurance, in particular, signalled the arrival of state welfare policies. It all happened relatively quickly: the term 'unemployment' only came into widespread use after 1895, yet by 1911, based on the theoretical work of Booth and Beveridge, major legislation had been embarked upon (Langan, 1985). Meanwhile, government intervention in economic matters was helped by improved knowledge (Schwarz, 1985). The Labour Department of the Board of Trade was set up in 1893 and the *Labour Gazette* introduced. The Census of Production Office was established in 1906 and the first ever Census of Production in the UK was conducted in 1907.

War decisively augmented the role of government between 1914 and 1918. Housing rents were controlled. Manpower was mobilized. There was control over the production, price and distribution of food supplies. Railways passed into the hands of a Railway Executive Committee presided over by the President of the Board of Trade; shipping was also controlled. Coal supplies were protected. In the last year of the war plans for post-war reconstruction were predicated on the assumption of an enhanced state role in national affairs, not least in housing and town planning, as we will see in chapter 4. On the basis of what had been done to meet the war emergency, an enhanced public sector role no longer seemed so distasteful.

These various instances of state intervention fell far short of any conscious programme of central planning. A distinct planning ideology was not formulated with any coherence until the 1930s, but the various steps taken constituted a vital prelude to later developments. In the event, the immediate period after 1918 offered more disappointment than encouragement. An ambitious housing programme was terminated, agricultural subsidies were abolished, and in 1921, Sir Eric Geddes' attempt to construct a state-organized transport system, dependent on the nationalization of the railways, was defeated. Amalgamation was imposed on the railway companies but the Railways Act, 1921, was a compromise between public ownership and private control; it proved well-nigh fatal to railway progress. Yet the 1920s did see some modest steps towards further state involvement in social and economic affairs. Attempts were made to promote a reorganization of the coal industry; and in 1926 the Central Electricity Generating Board was set up, making possible the development of the National Grid. Unemployment insurance was extended to many more workers, Joint Industrial Councils were set up for the negotiation of wage rates and the like. Housing Acts continued subsidized housing programmes. Unemployment relief programmes for public works were established, and areas of low unemployment were encouraged under an Industrial Transference Scheme to absorb work-seeking transferees.

Meanwhile, as we have seen, a struggle was being waged between economic radicals and economic conservatives, that cut across party lines. In the general election of 1929 it was the Liberal Party that propounded economic radicalism; and was attacked by Labour for its detailed programme of public investment. In office during the period 1929–31, Labour pursued the orthodox policies of its Conservative predecessors, with only slight modifications. The crisis of 1931 exposed limitations in Britain's system of government as it struggled to balance the budget when the increase in unemployment was carrying mounting deficits in the Unemployment Insurance Fund. Subsequently, the national government supervised a slow recovery, following policies which were increasingly interventionist.

The main feature of the background context was provided by the economic conditions of the period between the world wars. A short-lived boom in 1919 was followed by a sharp downturn in 1920, which was itself the prelude to a severe recession in 1921 when unemployment rose to 2.4 million in May (equivalent to 22 per cent of the insured labour force). There was labour unrest in the coalfields, in the cotton mills and on the railways. Economic recovery followed, but there were still a million out of work in June 1924. Severe labour problems featured in the middle of the decade, with the General Strike in 1926 and a prolonged stoppage in the coal industry. Recovery continued, but was then quite overtaken by the depression of 1929–32 – not quite so severe as 1921, but more prolonged. The US stock-market crash in October 1929 was followed by the international financial crisis in the summer of 1931, and unemployment in Britain peaked at 3 million in 1932. Particular regions in Britain suffered badly, particularly those economies which depended on coal, iron and steel, heavy engineering, textiles and shipbuilding. Another slow recovery set in, but the total out of work still numbered 1.4 million in the third quarter of 1937. Structural change was underway; while Scotland, the north and Wales did badly, parts of the Midlands and particularly outer London and the Home Counties did relatively well, with an expanding range of new industries (Law, 1980). The inter-war period, highly charged politically, proved conducive to new interventionary initiatives as the state took a heightened interest in social and economic affairs.

Nonetheless, the working out of coherent policies was a tortured business, conditioned by expediency, no little caution and an incrementalism which smacked of 'trial and error' experimentation. Government drifted into interventionary roles, and the most that can be said is that by 1939 important experience had been gained to stand the country in good stead for what followed. It was not engaged in planning by any stretch of the imagination; ad hoc policies were often seen as temporary solutions, programmes for long-term action scarcely existed, and in any case there was no available machinery of government to put them into effect. But nonetheless useful steps had been taken along the road. This becomes clear if we look in a little more detail at various interventionary measures in labour and industrial matters which, as we will see, came to have a close relevance to town planning.

With regard to agriculture, the 1920s saw little relief extended to the farming community. Subsidies returned, but only for a new crop, sugar beet. British agriculture was in depression, but it took a drastic fall in wheat and barley prices at the beginning of the 1930s, in the height of the depression, to sharpen the political arguments about state subsidies and guaranteed prices. Imperial preferences helped and so too did agricultural de-rating. The Wheat Act, 1932, prompted some recovery of the area, and Marketing Boards were set up (17 of them by 1939, of which the best known was that for Milk, established in 1933). In another area, the Forestry Commission, set up in 1919, was in effect creating a new rural state industry, planned afforestation designed to overcome the timber shortages of the Great War.

Much more far-reaching government involvement came with regional unemployment and the conditions of particular industries; certain measures were embarked upon which would ultimately flower into early speculation about forms of regional economic planning. It began with the objective of facilitating labour mobility by encouraging movement from areas where jobs were in short supply to areas where they were more plentiful. The Industrial Transference Board was set up in 1928, its purpose to retrain labour locked in declining industries and to provide grants and loans so that employment might be found in industries elsewhere. This policy continued throughout the 1930s, though the number of persons transferred peaked by 1936. In the 10 years from 1929 to 1938 over 200,000 adults, 70,000 juveniles and more than 30,000 families were transferred from Depressed Areas – by definition wider than the Special Areas themselves (McCrone, 1969).

This labour policy was effectively replaced by regional policy, initiated through the Special Areas (Development and Improvement) Act, 1934. Following studies of some of the worst-hit areas, where the average unemployment figure was around 40 per cent of the labour force, four Special Areas were designated: South Wales, North East England, West Cumberland and Clydeside – North Lanarkshire. Two Commissioners were appointed, one for England and Wales, and one for Scotland and £2 million was made available to them to promote the economic recovery of the areas. It was envisaged that the legislation should be temporary to meet an unusual emergency; the Commissioners' powers were regarded as exceptional. There were the usual problems associated with designation (important centres were excluded, though they were still part of the regional problem), and in fact the powers of the Commissioners proved to be extremely limited. Wider powers were contained in the Special Areas Amendment Act, 1937, and encouragement was given to the setting up of Trading Estates – which followed at Team Valley on Tyneside, Treforest in South Wales and Hillingden, Scotland. Meanwhile there were ad hoc measures of considerable local significance; for example loans were made to the Cunard Shipping Line for the building of the liners Queen Mary and Queen Elizabeth.

During the second half of the 1930s the focus on Special Areas changed when attention was also directed to the explosive growth and continued economic buoyancy of metropolitan London. The Third Report of the Commissioners (1936) referred to the question of the economic and social problems of the Special Areas to the possibility of diverting growth away from London to places elsewhere. The argument was advanced that the time had come for London's growth to be controlled in the national interest; the magnitude of the capital's territorial spread made it vulnerable to air attack; and new industrial production not dependent on location in London should be restrained from seeking premises in the area. A dispersal strategy sought official recognition, and in 1937 the government appointed a Royal Commission under the chairmanship of Sir Montague Barlow to examine the whole question. As we also observe in chapter 4, at this point developments in town planning converged with advances made in economic and regional planning. The publication of the Barlow Report in 1940 confirmed the new stage which had been reached in this common ground, but it required a totally different national context for the recommendations to be taken up – the exigency of total war and the blossoming of central planning.

4   Town Planning's Foothold, 1919–39

Town planning as a local government activity fell away during the First World War, with work on scheme preparation abandoned in most areas. Thomas Adams left Britain in the autumn of 1914 to start a new career in Canada as Town Planning Adviser to the Commission of Conservation. He was replaced by the able and effective George Pepler, but an important thread of continuity was nevertheless broken. Building activity was soon curtailed and consultancy practice largely ceased apart from some government-sponsored projects. But the propagandist element of town planning lost none of its enthusiasm and key figures in the Garden Cities and Town Planning Association remained active. Charles Purdom, who served with the British Expeditionary Force from 1915 to 1918, drafted a pamphlet entitled *New Towns After the War*; he, Howard, W. A. Taylor (a Letchworth publisher) and F. J. Osborn, who avoided active service, formed a group called the 'New Townsmen', and established the Association as the centre of a national campaign to build a hundred new towns. The booklet was published in 1918 under their pseudonym.

Nonetheless in 1919 it was a case of making a new start. Important developments had taken place before 1914; they could not be dismissed and they were there to be built upon. They included work in the local authorities as councils implemented the 1909 legislation, innovations in house building by co-partnership and other arrangements in garden-suburb style, and professional outreach of various kinds to secure a widening remit for town planning. But much had happened since 1914 and a new agenda was reformulated. The need to rebuild war-damaged cities in Belgium and France gave a higher profile to town planning, and in Britain post-war housing requirements called for bold action which, it was argued, demanded an enhanced state role. The rising tide of the involvement by government in national affairs had risen sharply during the war, but its incidence was as yet haphazard and failed to suggest any coherent strategy. It remained to be seen what fortunes would attend town planning in the years of reconstruction.

We turn first to developments in statutory planning; there was new legislation and a renewed take up by local authorities. We then consider housing, of equal importance in our story because for some years the closeness of housing to town planning matters suggested little difference between local authority housing projects and town planning schemes. Countryside issues unfolded (scenic protection, green belts, and national parks) and because of their land-use implications, there was a consequential affinity with town planning. Transport questions gained in importance as road traffic increased and again, because of their relevance to the processes of urban development, the core of town planning activity was ultimately strengthened. Finally, we draw the threads together by suggesting the underlying sentiments of town planning as they had come to be defined by 1939.

Statutory Planning

A Coalition Government was formed in January 1919 with Lloyd George as Prime Minister. Dr Christopher Addison, President of the Local Government Board, became minister in a new Ministry of Health (in which town planning matters resided), combining the duties of the Board and the Health Insurance Commissioners. He introduced a Housing, Town Planning etc. bill in March. It contained little apart from measures to streamline administrative procedures in order to stimulate the submission of town planning schemes (Cherry, 1974). The system was to be simplified; local authorities were to be allowed to prepare schemes without authorization of the Local Government Board, and later the minister. There was not much here, and indeed the weight of the bill was on housing matters. But there was pressure for the bill to go further than it did, particularly in regard to making town planning compulsory, rather than retaining the permissive nature of the 1909 Act. This pressure was continued in Standing Committee, notably by the persistent lobby of the National Housing and Town Planning Council. The bill was amended to include a new clause which made town planning compulsory on local authorities above 20,000 population. Addison stood firm against those who argued that for the state to wield compulsory powers on local authorities would be to weaken local government, and the clause stood. Schemes had to be prepared within three years of 1 January 1923. The bill was passed and a Scottish Act followed shortly afterwards. Town Planning Regulations were later drawn up setting out the required procedure in the preparation of schemes.

The housing provisions of the 1919 Act proved much the more important (see p. 74). Indeed housing questions quite overshadowed town planning and it is doubtful if Addison was bothered all that much by the extra-parliamentary lobby which pressed for compulsory powers. Perhaps it was not going to make all that much difference anyway in view of the fact that only a handful of local authorities possessed any obvious ability to proceed energetically with the new simplified powers. Indeed, deadlines by which schemes had to be submitted were progressively extended.

By April 1933 (when the next legislation came into force) just 94 schemes had been approved in England and Wales, from 50 local councils; in Scotland there were five schemes approved, from three councils. But that would be to disguise the fact that rather more activity was in fact underway. There were schemes in the pipeline which were not yet approved; others had been prepared and adopted by local authorities but not yet submitted; and a large number of councils had made resolutions to prepare schemes or gone further to draw up preliminary statements. The rudiments of a statutory town planning system were being taken up: more than nine million acres in England and Wales were covered by town planning schemes (albeit most of them at the resolution stage). It is highly likely that without the 1919 Act's adoption of compulsion, permissive powers alone would not have had this effect. The Chief Planning Adviser, George Pepler, showed great skill in inducing local authorities to adopt town planning powers, and guiding them in putting them into practice. He made it his job to know personally all town and district clerks in the country; it is said that he claimed to have played golf with most of them (Cherry, 1981). The adoption of town planning in these early days owed much to personal lobbying of this kind.

The measures of the 1919 Act were consolidated in the Town Planning Act, 1925 – the first planning legislation not to be an appendage of housing. There were two other significant legislative developments in the 1920s. Locked away in the Housing etc. Act, 1923, was a power which enabled the minister to authorize the preparation of a town planning scheme with the object of preserving the existing character and features of a locality with special architectural, historic or artistic interests. Soon taken up by Oxford and other historic cities, the provision was the forerunner to a century-long interest in urban conservation. Perhaps of more immediate importance was the Local Government Act, 1929, which extended to county councils the right to share in the preparation and administration of any joint town planning scheme, although it stopped short of giving them any direct power of initiating schemes themselves. It encouraged the operation of town planning on a wider territorial scale than a single local authority, and was a fillip to regional planning.

The provisions of the 1919 and 1925 Acts were superseded by the Town and Country Planning Act, 1932 – the term 'country' introduced for the first time. The act began its life in 1929 when Sir Edward Hilton-Young, a Conservative Private Member, adopting a line from the recently founded Council for the Preservation of Rural England, introduced his Rural Amenities Bill, designed to extend planning powers to rural land. The bill fell with the election of a new government (Labour). The minister, Arthur Greenwood, introduced a Town and Country Planning Bill in 1931, superseding Hilton-Young's earlier proposals. It was proposed to extend planning powers to built-up areas and was thus a significant step beyond the 1909 and 1919 Acts which had confined the preparation of schemes to land in the course of development or about to be developed. Of immediate impact was the intention that local authorities would be able to collect 100 per cent of the betterment generated by their planning schemes. The bill was surprisingly well received by the opposition parties, though at standing committee the betterment charge was reduced to 75 per cent.

However, political turmoil arrested further proceedings. In August 1931 a National Government was formed and the subsequent General Election in October returned an overwhelmingly Conservative Parliament. Financial rectitude was the order of the day in political sentiment, and further extensions of the state's role in national and local affairs were not looked upon with favour. So when Hilton-Young (now himself Minister of Health) reintroduced Greenwood's bill it was fiercely attacked. A powerful private property lobby secured the emasculation of the bill. Betterment (still nominally 75 per cent) was made virtually impossible to collect because of restrictive clauses, while provisions for compensation were rendered unsatisfactory. Town planning reverted to the 1909 situation, permissive once more, and while the powers applied to all land, developed or underdeveloped, it was expected that schemes would not be prepared for certain 'static' areas which would be exempt.

There is no doubting that the clock had been put back with a vengeance. Conservative supporters of town planning were conspicuous by their silence. The professional and propagandist pressure groups were routed and the Town and Country Planning Act, 1932, emerged as a substantially weaker measure than the original bill. The traditional Tory voice, considerably strengthened in the 1931 General Election, won the day in a manner which reflected the coming divide between 'middle way' Conservatism and the alternative, older view. Greenwood was left to protest: 'this Bill has been butchered to make a holiday for the diehard Tories. Their hostility is to the whole principle of town planning' (House of Commons 'Debates', 7 June 1932, quoted in Ward (1974)).

Town planning faced a period of uncertainty. Statutory town planning had recently attained its majority, 21 years on from 1909. It had some notable achievements to record: as a movement, encouraged by propaganda; as a profession discharging its work both in private consultancy and in statutory obligations for local councils; and in education. The actual practice of town planning was securing a more technical base as the principle of 'zoning' was taken up, whereby areas in which certain types of development would be allowed were delineated as land use parcels in scheme layouts. Chamberlain's hope for 'skeleton' plans, expressed in 1911 (see p. 40), was gradually being realized. But for the moment there would be little more encouragement from government by way of legislation, and further advances in town planning would largely come from initiatives in local government.

One such development was the widespread inauguration of joint town planning advisory committees and the encouragement they gave to regional planning. A notable early example (1920) was the arrangement for Manchester and District, stemming from a conference of 76 local authorities convened by Manchester City Council, covering an area of 15 miles radius from the city centre. The Midlands Joint Town Planning Council, set up in 1923, became the largest regional planning unit in the country, built up around six centres – Birmingham, Coventry, Kidderminster, Walsall, Warwick and Wolverhampton. By 1938 there were 138 joint committees and increasingly they had become executive rather than advisory in function. Both the opportunity for county councils to engage in town planning, provided by the Local Government Act, 1929, and the passing of the Town and Country Planning Act, 1932, helped to promote this wider geographical frame of reference.

By the close of the inter-war years an explicit regional perspective and the wholesale commissioning of regional plans placed town planning practice on a far more secure footing than the legislation of the time would have suggested (Wannop and Cherry, 1994). Some 60 joint committee-sponsored regional plans were published between 1922 and 1937, of exceptional significance in advancing the cause of town planning during its emergent years. They were important propaganda documents for the authorities themselves, rallying the interests of elected members to the cause; while their contents secured a working agenda for professional work around the common themes of the day. They were strong on the 'physical' aspects of town planning – the allocation of land uses, road networks, scenic protection and reservation of open and green land. Analysis was slender; presumption was everything. The social science input remained weak: there was a good deal about where houses should be built, but little as to who might live in them.

The most significant regional exercise was that for Greater London, for which area a Regional Planning Committee was constituted in November 1927 at the invitation of the then Minister of Health, Neville Chamberlain. Raymond Unwin was appointed Technical Adviser. His Reports (see p. 77) published between 1929 and 1933 may now be seen as an essential step in the history of the planning of Greater London. In the town planning retrenchment of that time the work of the Committee was wound down. On the other hand, town planning within the area of the London County Council received a great boost with the capture of the LCC in 1934 by Herbert Morrison for Labour.

There was one additional piece of legislation and even that came from local authority initiatives. County councils in the Greater London area were anxious to curb ribbon development – the practice by the building industry of extending frontage development along highways to the exclusion of developing in depth behind – and so limit the tentacular spread of the urban periphery. In 1925 Middlesex promoted a local bill which included provisions for the acquisition by the council of land up to 200 yards on either side of an arterial road. Surrey and Essex followed suit in 1931 and 1933 respectively and other counties were prepared to take similar action (Sheail, 1979). The Ministry of Health took up the cause: the Restriction of Ribbon Development Act was passed in 1935. Its provisions were that any highway authority could adopt a 'standard width' for any road in their area and that consent was required for access or development within 220 feet of the middle of a classified road. The legislation proved not terribly significant. It was belated, responding to a situation where the problem had already peaked, and those responsible for highway and planning interests often had different objectives in pursuing a particular policy.

Housing

A feature of the late-Victorian and Edwardian housing crisis was the burden of local taxation carried by ratepayers as local expenditure by municipal authorities rose sharply from the 1880s onwards. The rent increases that followed exacerbated an already worsening situation caused by a rising demand for working class housing while supply was virtually static. Tenant radicalism resulted (Englander, 1983) with rent strikes in English boroughs between 1911 and 1913; on Clydeside, where tenant eviction had worsened appreciably, a rent strike in 1915 could not have come at a worse time, with Britain at war. A particular problem stemming from war-time conditions was the additional demand for housing occasioned by the expansion of the munitions industry in key centres of the country. The government was prodded into action: the Rent and Mortgage Interest (War Restrictions) Act, 1915, froze rents of houses below a certain rateable value (£35 in London, £30 in Scotland and £26 elsewhere) at the figure paid on 3 August 1914. The act was to apply for the duration of the war and six months thereafter (though when the time came the period was considerably extended).

Rent control was not the only way government was sucked in to war-time housing issues. The provision of state housing for munitions workers was another. Intriguingly it reintroduced Raymond Unwin to the housing limelight. It was necessary to provide housing for the influx of workers required for the plants selected for major expansion of munitions production. The Well Hall Estate built in 1915 at Eltham, south-east London, contained over 1,200 houses and flats, designed under the direction of Frank Baines in the Office of Works. But there were other areas of housing pressure and Unwin was recruited from the Planning Inspectorate to act as Chief Housing Architect to the Explosives Department of the Ministry of Munitions. The immediate task was to service the vast explosives plant being built in Dumfriesshire on the Solway Firth. Townships were built at Gretna and Eastriggs, layouts prepared under Unwin's direction, though Courtenay Crickmer from Letchworth was resident site architect. Mancot Royal, Queensferry, west of Chester, provided the site for another, smaller, settlement.

These war-time model communities attracted American attention and US Federal projects for war-time housing in the years 1917–18 'bore traces of their transatlantic precedents' (Miller, 1992, p. 159).

However, Unwin's great wartime contribution was yet to be made; it had perhaps the biggest of all influences on the post-war housing policy. An informal group of heads of departments working with the prime minister was already active in March 1916 on the question of post-war reconstruction. There was much to be done if housing unfitness was to be addressed. The Royal Commission on the Housing of the Industrial Population of Scotland reported in 1917; it gave a stark reminder of the backlog of bad conditions in the burghs, especially Glasgow, and called for better housing for those who had been called upon to defend their country. In 1917 Lloyd George's reconstruction committee flowered into a Ministry of Reconstruction, led by Christopher Addison. Unwin was not a member of this Committee, but Seebohm Rowntree (who was) was closely assisted by him. Fabian influence, coming through Beatrice Webb, held that private enterprise could not be relied upon to meet the task of rehousing, and favoured local authorities in preference to public utility societies and co-partnership schemes. The Committee pressed for a study of post-war housing; a special committee was set up and in July 1917 Sir John Tudor Walters (a Liberal MP, Chairman of the London Housing Board and a Director of Hampstead Garden Suburb Trust) was appointed chairman. Membership included three architects – Unwin, Frank Baines and Sir Aston Webb.

The Tudor Walters Committee had to balance two very divergent views. Faced with estimates that the housing deficit in England and Wales at the end of 1918 might be of the order of 600,000 dwellings, Addison advocated bold solutions and leaned towards a radical state-aided housing initiative. On the other hand, Hayes Fisher, President of the Local Government Board (and therefore responsible for housing), thought that the housing demand figures had been much inflated; his attitude was altogether more sceptical and he was less inclined to follow the ambitious housing programme being suggested. The report was ready by the spring of 1918, but publication was delayed – a reflection of the rift between Fisher and Addison. Unwin's own position was delicate: he steered the committee towards ambitious solutions, yet his permanent post was with the Board (which, via Fisher, was cautious on these matters).

The report was published in October 1918. Its contents were far-reaching. The housing need was established at 500,000. The private sector was not expected to meet working-class needs until building costs were stable. A powerful Central Housing Authority and Regional Commissioners were required. Towns were urged to acquire suburban land and proceed with their schemes, leasing sites to housing societies and others for development. Densities of 12 dwellings per acre in urban areas and 8 per acre in rural areas were endorsed. Cottage designs and accommodation standards were laid down; they represented huge advances in working-class housing. Site planning advice was given. Every housing scheme should be based on architect-prepared designs. The state provision of working-class housing was underscored. There was Unwin's hand in every aspect.

The Tudor Walters Report met the political needs of the day; its timeliness ensured adoption. Lloyd George called a snap election soon after the Armistice of 11 November; later that month his campaign pledge to the voters of Wolverhampton that returning soldiers should have 'homes fit for heroes' indicated that bold reconstruction was in the air. Legislation followed in 1919. The Housing and Town Planning Act passed in July made it obligatory for local authorities to prepare surveys of their housing needs, to draw up plans to deal with them, and to carry out their schemes. Any loss incurred by the local authorities would fall as a charge on the Exchequer. But it was soon argued that houses would not be built in sufficient quantity, or speedily enough, without direct subsidy, and Addison rushed through a further Housing (Additional Powers) Bill in December to meet this omission. Meanwhile the Local Government Board's (1919) Manual on Housing Schemes adopted the Tudor Walters recommendations. Voluntary action by philanthropists, co-partnership arrangements and the unaided work of local authorities, let alone the private building industry, were overtaken: government assumed the obligation of providing good quality housing for the working class. It ushered in a 60-year period in which the state left an indelible stamp in this area of social and urban affairs.

It proved no smooth transformation from an old order of private landlords to a new pattern dominated by owner occupation and council tenants. Within little more than a year the costs of the housing programme were such as to lead to its abandonment. Only 29,000 houses were completed in 1920 and the cost of a house nearly quadrupled over the 1914 figure. Addison fell in April 1921, accused of waste and lavish public expenditure. But contracts which had been let were honoured and in 1923 houses were still being completed under the Addison scheme, so that in the end nearly 214,000 dwellings resulted from this programme.

The period 1918–23 was clearly a crucial one in the development of housing (and by association, planning) policy. It has been fashionable to argue, as with Orbach (1977), that the housing programme, including the obligatory building of council houses, was motivated essentially by a fear of industrial unrest. The measures promised industrial and social peace. Orbach argues that, 'Few in Government considered that they were building *for* the workers. They were building *for* themselves, and taking an insurance policy *against* revolution' (p. 116). Quite where this thesis places the housing reform movement which had infiltrated government circles for many years is rather uncertain, but we can agree that the history of housing legislation, particularly in this period, 'is the story of the permanent adoption of solutions to what was conceived as a temporary problem' (p. 46).

Another subsidy scheme was introduced in 1923 by the Conservatives. Neville Chamberlain's new scheme lowered the standards for grant eligibility, and smaller houses were built at lower rents. Moreover, local authorities could only use subsidies if they could convince the ministry that they could build houses better than private enterprise. In 1924 the Labour Government initially gave higher subsidies, though they were reduced somewhat subsequently; but John Wheatley's Housing Act of that year remained in operation until 1933. This new round of subsidies aimed specifically to encourage local authorities to build houses with controlled rents; they were further subsidized out of the rates. Between 1919 and 1934 nearly one-third of the dwellings built in England and Wales were by local authorities, and the proportion was higher in Scotland. It was an astonishing take-up, not least because it often represented a sharp reversal of attitudes and local authority practices. Birmingham, for example, after a slow start, proceeded to be an enthusiastic council house builder, with 40,000 to its credit by 1933.

In social welfare terms the subsidized council house was a major development, and was probably as effective as any state welfare initiative in targeting need. Tenurial arrangements were also transformed, with profound social and political consequences. From a town planning point of view, 20 years of garden suburb pressure and the thrust of an Unwin-inspired revolution in domestic architecture and estate layout came to fruition, though in a sadly debased and caricatured form. Council estates adopted standardized forms, incorporating geometric road layouts which were wasteful of space, and the massing of housing units (semi-detached or groups of four predominating) which lacked design intimacy. Low density prevailed, around 12 houses to the acre. Some very large estates appeared in the larger cities: when completed, Kingstanding in north Birmingham contained 4,800 houses and Becontree in south Essex, developed for the LCC, was the largest local authority estate in the world. They had problems in developing social cohesion particularly when the provision of community facilities lagged behind estate building.

The dwellings themselves represented a marked improvement on most other privately rented property. The houses were well-appointed and for many working-class families the new accommodation was a revelation: (typically) a hall, large living room, scullery, larder, bathroom, toilet, three bedrooms and gardens back and front. But the rents were still too high for lower-paid workers and council houses were not within the reach of the mass of poorer workers (Burnett, 1978). Typically the council tenant was in a 'sheltered' manual job; he earned slightly more than the average wage and had a family of two children. Those who could not afford council rents (and the other costs of journey to work, furnishing a new house and higher suburban food costs) continued to live in old, rent-restricted property.

The state took responsibility for working-class accommodation in an arrangement whereby houses were built by local councils and the critical subsidies were provided by government. The state went further, determining in what conditions and where the working class should live. House design and estate layout principles were established and slavishly adopted by the local authorities. Up until now the housing question had been dominated by the threat as well as the disgrace of insanitary, unfit dwellings, and their replacement by accommodation which met the objectives of health, amenity and convenience. To these ends the solution of dispersed housing had come into favour. The 1920s saw the beginning of suburban working-class house building by local authorities, responding to favourable subsidy provisions, in a way which in 1914 would have been unthinkable.

A decentralist perspective on urban affairs remained the prevailing influence and it showed no sign of weakening. On the contrary: within the circle of the Garden Cities and Town Planning Association the 'New Townsmen' seized power during 1918; in January 1919 Purdom replaced Ewart Culpin as Secretary, and with Osborn now out of hiding, the long campaign for new towns was engaged. In 1920 Ebenezer Howard (now aged 70), acting on his own initiative, bought an estate which had just come on to the market at Welwyn for a second garden city, and proceeded to set up a Second Garden City Company.

The outreach of the association persisted in government circles where Neville Chamberlain, on more than one occasion, showed a planner's awareness of the issues surrounding housing problems. In his very first year in Parliament, Addison appointed him chairman of a newly-established Unhealthy Areas Committee, set up to review the principles to be adopted in the clearance of slum areas. The actual remit was very broad and it allowed the committee to range far and wide, particularly about the problems of London. Of two reports submitted the Interim Report (1920) was the more important. It made some far-reaching town planning recommendations which implied a considerable extension of state powers: garden cities around London and the relocation of industries to them, the preparation of a general plan for the reconstruction of London, and the creation of a new authority covering an area larger than the LCC. No action was taken to implement the recommendations, but Chamberlain's work deserves recognition as the first official report to advocate urban reconstruction and decentralization on such a wide scale (Cherry, 1980).

The setting up of the Greater London Regional Planning Committee in 1927 followed the same perspective. Chamberlain, now in his second term of office as Minister of Health, constituted the committee covering the area of the LCC, the City of London and six surrounding counties – a region of 1,800 square miles. He had not abandoned his hope that a strategy of decentralization might be realized. Unwin was appointed Technical Adviser charged with preparing an outline plan. In four reports published between 1929 and 1933 he drew up a frame of reference, establishing the key strategic principles which should govern future development. The notion of concentric rings of development, with the periphery that of a green girdle, would survive in town planning thought and practice for many years.

Manchester's ambitious scheme (stemming from the City Council's Housing Committee) to build its own garden city at Wythenshawe also exemplified the prevailing ideology of dispersal. Barry Parker was appointed architect. Wythenshawe, built on the Tatton Estate which had been bought by the city, fell uncomfortably between a garden suburb and a garden city, but it showed what a large municipality could do in pursuance of a decentralist policy.

Wythenshawe helped to keep the idea of new settlements alive, but practical achievements came to an end. Idealism was not in short supply, however. A Hundred New Towns Association was formed in 1934 following an ex-serviceman's Armistice Day march through the slums of London the previous year; quite independent of the GCTPA, it succeeded in enlisting the support of the architect A. Trystan Edwards. The Association pressed for 100 new towns to relieve pressure on the metropolis: 5 million people would be rehoused in 40 new settlements built south of a line from the Wash to the Severn, a further 36 to the rest of England, 15 to Scotland and 9 to Wales. This was quite impracticable and when a Departmental Committee on Garden Cities and Satellite Towns, which had been set up in 1931 chaired by Lord Marley, finally reported in 1935, advocating the fullest adoption of garden city development, it was not surprising that there was silence on any official action.

In practical terms the housing question was entering a new phase. Governments had been fully exposed to dispersed housing solutions throughout this period, but by the early 1930s the arrangements for building new houses seemed less important than those for clearing away the old. E. D. (Sir Ernest) Simon (1929), former chairman of Manchester's Housing Committee, Lord Mayor, industrialist and Liberal politician (Parliamentary Secretary to the Minister of Health), observed in 1929 that 'the position of the slums is little or no better than it was at the time of the Armistice. The slum dwellers are not filtering into better homes, with the result that the overcrowding in the slums is not being relieved' (p. 66). His solution was to reinvigorate the house building programme with a supply of cheaper houses. But government policy in the 1930s followed a rather different tack, giving powers to local authorities to engage in huge clearance projects.

Arthur Greenwood's Housing Act, 1930, signalled the move away from council building for general need to encouragement of rebuilding on cleared sites. Local authorities were given extra subsidies related to the numbers of people displaced and the higher price of central area land. But while the general subsidies for suburban houses remained in force, local authorities showed a preference for using them, and the council estate building machine maintained its momentum. Subsidies were cancelled in 1933 and further developments had to await the Housing Act, 1935. In the event there was a far from direct, radical attack on unfit housing and much depended on local authority vigour and enterprise. The act simply encouraged slum clearance by extending new forms of subsidy directed to the rehousing of overcrowded families. Local authorities were obliged to carry out overcrowding surveys and to implement their own schemes for suitable alternative accommodation. The act used the term 'Redevelopment Areas' for the first time (Yelling,

1992): they were districts which contained more than 50 working-class houses, of which one-third were unfit for human habitation, and where land-use arrangements made comprehensive redevelopment expedient.

It was a curious piece of 'half-way' legislation, but it did produce some spectacular local developments, in which flats were represented largely for the first time (outside London, that is). Special subsidies for flats had been included in Greenwood's Act; the architectural ideals of the Modern Movement, well-represented in workers' housing projects in certain continental cities, found their way to Britain; and the new building method of prefabrication promised speed and economy. The time was ripe for experiment and, in the first serious departure from garden suburb orthodoxy, Leeds built nearly 1,000 flats by 1939, Liverpool over 5,000 and Manchester 9,000; even Birmingham's long-standing reluctance to build flats was overcome and some major schemes were on the drawing board at the outbreak of war. The initiative fell on local councils where key actors played a significant role. In Leeds it was the Rev. Charles Jenkinson, Labour's reformer on the Housing Committee, in harness with R. A. H. Livett, Director of Housing, who pioneered the celebrated Quarry Hill flats (Ravetz, 1974).

Meanwhile revised calculations for the number of slum dwellings nationally suggested a higher figure than previously estimated. In 1939 the officially accepted total for England and Wales stood at 472,000, by which time nearly half had been demolished or closed. Powers extracted from government on the back of moral indignation about the condition of old housing and the lobby over health and overcrowding had raised slum clearance and redevelopment to new levels. The state's involvement in urban reconstruction was pushed forward by some powerful municipalities and the professional confidence of their chief officers.

Scenic Protection and the Countryside

The origins of town planning were essentially urban in character, but once established, town planning displayed a relevance to a variety of functions and at various spatial scales, and a capacity to address problems which were far from housing-oriented. Thus it was that between the wars town planning was called in aid of various non-urban questions and, from 1932, was given the statutory title of 'town and country planning'.

The inauguration of Town Planning Schemes introduced the notion of amenity, though it was never defined. In regional plans, particularly, local councils were called upon to be the guardians of the visual appearance of their territory, urban and rural, and at a time when anxiety about the despoliation of the coast and countryside was being expressed, this proved to be an increasingly important matter (Cherry and Rogers, 1996). Pressure for development produced some objectionable eyesores: Hardy and Ward (1984) have described the way in which the old plotlands came to house huts, caravans, old railway carriages, bus bodies, temporary bungalows and shacks. Over many stretches of the countryside there was disfigurement from garish, ill-sited advertisements, electricity pylons, cafes, filling stations and camping sites. Then, in the south-east particularly, large-scale coastal development offended popular taste: at Peacehaven on the cliff-tops between Brighton and Newhaven, at Shoreham a straggle of railway carriages and timber bungalows, and at Jaywick Sands to the undying opposition of Clacton.

The destruction of the countryside was a theme adopted by town (and country) planning. The architect Clough Williams-Ellis (1928) provided a rallying call when he likened the urban spread from London and the big cities to the tentacles of an octopus. The planner Thomas Sharp (1932) called for the rejection of low density, semi-detached suburban sprawl. The beauties of an unchanging countryside were popularized and the founding of a new body in 1926 proved highly significant – the Council for the Preservation of Rural England (CPRE), the CPR Wales following shortly afterwards. Local authorities took what initiatives they could to exercise control over rural development. A number of counties promoted local bills, and hopes reposed widely in the contents of regional plans which by the 1930s almost uniformly expressed the objectives of countryside preservation.

Beyond these general matters, there were three particular rural issues to which town planning was drawn: national parks, green belts and moorland rambling.

In 1929 the Prime Minister, Ramsay MacDonald, appointed a Committee of Inquiry 'to consider if it is desirable and feasible to establish one or more National Parks in Great Britain with a view to the preservation of natural characteristics including flora and fauna, and to the improvement of recreational facilities for the people' (Cherry, 1975). The Chairman was Christopher Addison. The Committee, reporting in 1931, found favour in a system of 'National Reserves' and 'Nature Sanctuaries'; a small annual budget was recommended, also two authorities, either executive or advisory depending on the budget, for England and Wales, and Scotland. No government action followed, but an influential lobby was encouraged. In 1936, the CPRE and CPRW set up a Standing Committee on National Parks under the chairmanship of the lawyer, Sir Norman Birkett; its membership included representatives of many amenity organizations. It proceeded to proselytize vigorously for national parks, and demanded state action to establish them. National parks figured prominently in town planning and national reconstruction debates which would be engaged in just a few years' time (see chapter 5).

The problem of unrestricted suburban spread and the loss of vulnerable countryside around the periphery of London had already attracted prescriptive solutions from around the turn of the century (see chapter 2), culminating in Raymond Unwin's proposal for a narrow green girdle surrounding Greater London. During the late 1920s and into the 1930s county councils and other local authorities were acquiring land and properties, before they fell into the hands of speculators, beyond the girdle delineated in the Greater London regional planning exercise. In this way they built up a discontinuous ring of green belt estates around the metropolitan fringe, preserved as open spaces and farmland. The London County Council launched its own green belt scheme in 1935, making available £2 million to fund half the cost of acquisition. Subsequently it was necessary to legitimize the grant offered to authorities outside its jurisdiction, in the Green Belt (London and the Home Counties) Act, 1938. Birmingham, Sheffield and Oxford also promoted small green belt schemes before the war. As with national parks, the opening shots in a long town planning story had been fired.

During the 1920s the leisure pursuit of walking and rambling, having already been taken up by professional and generally middle-class people, spread to the working class. It became increasingly popular in the northern industrial towns where rambling clubs were loosely organized in federations. Their destination for weekend mass rambling was typically the Pennines. The philosopher and rambler himself, C. E. M. Joad (1946), would later write that hiking 'replaced beer as the shortest cut out of Manchester' (p. 17). Unfortunately this brought them into immediate conflict with landowners and sporting tenants because the heather-clad moors constituted an area of prime grouse shooting. As rambling peaked in enthusiasm in the early 1930s militant trespass marked the clash of interest. Access to the Peak District was a particular problem: only twelve footpaths exceeded two miles in length and there was no footpath at all to the Kinderscout Plateau. The story of the organized trespass there on Easter Day 1932, the arrest of the ringleaders and their subsequent imprisonment, has entered into the folklore of national rambling (Stephenson, 1988). The Ramblers' Association was formed in 1935. Attention turned to government for help; in fact it was a case of returning to Parliament because on seventeen previous occasions Private Members' Bills had been introduced with the objective of gaining unlimited access, as of right, to British mountains. The eighteenth occasion was successful: an Access to Mountains Bill passed through all its stages and was enacted in 1939, but no access agreements were ever made under its provisions. By the outbreak of war the government had been dragged into countryside affairs; the relationship between rambling and town planning as then understood was marginal, but within a short period of time countryside leisure and recreation was firmly established on the agenda of reconstruction.

Roads

The setting up of the Roads Department of the Ministry of Transport in 1919, born out of the disappointment of the Roads Board (established in 1910), effectively separated the issues of road traffic and town planning for the whole of the inter-war period. Indeed, although there was a brief coming together of two professional disciplines in the 1940s, it was not until the 1960s when some sort of common ground for mutual action was established, albeit reluctantly and with suspicion. The irony is that the design and layout of roads are integral parts of the process of town building, but government made no attempt to take initiatives in an area where professionals feared to tread.

The new ministry got off to an uncertain start. Its energies were concentrated on battles with the Treasury about taxation and the Road Fund set up in 1909. When the first minister, Sir Eric Geddes, resigned in 1921, the First Commissioner for works doubled up in that appointment; the separate post of minister was only recreated by the Conservatives in 1924. For many years the insistent questions before government were how to tax the motor vehicle and how to pay for roads, but by the 1930s the major problem was that of road accidents, and because these were matters for the police, it involved the Home Office (Plowden, 1973). These were the years when the 'politics' of roads were dominated by the self-protective lobbying of the motorists' organizations, the AA and the RAC, Treasury pleas to limit government expenditure on highways, and the fearful statistics of road accidents.

Thus it was that governments were sucked in to enforcing programmes of road safety measures including the 30 m.p.h. speed limit in built-up areas, the inauguration of driving tests and the installation of pedestrian crossings marked by the Belisha beacon, named after Sir Leslie Hore-Belisha, the then Home Secretary. Meanwhile technical innovations by road engineers saw the introduction of traffic lights, centre road markings, the dual carriageway, roundabouts, staggered road junctions, and building set backs and sight lines for improved visibility. These were elements in the built environment, and road layouts remained essential components of statutory planning schemes.

It was well into the 1930s before wider issues came to the fore. London's traffic problems had led to early attempts to regulate passenger traffic in the London area (Dyos and Aldcroft, 1969). It was 1933 before the London Passenger Transport Act introduced an effective scheme of control, by putting an end to competition and setting up the London Passenger Transport Board. In 1934 a comprehensive survey of highway developments required in the London traffic area for the next 30 years was inaugurated by the Minister of Transport. An Origin and Destination census was conducted in June 1936 in respect of London Docks. A Highway Development Survey was prepared in 1937 by Sir Charles Bressey, a former Chief Engineer at the Ministry of Transport, assisted by Sir Edwin Lutyens to impart (a very limited) architectural gloss. In the meantime the Trunk Roads Act, 1936, prescribed a rationale of the country's roads into four categories: Trunk, Class I, Class II, and Unclassified. The Ministry of Transport became directly responsible for 4,505 miles of Trunk roads. There was no question of embarking on motorway building, though projects in Germany and Italy had already begun. Moreover there was no emulation of US innovation in segregating pedestrians from motor traffic in residential development; the revolutionary layout by S. Stein and H. Wright of Radburn, New York, although unfinished, showed that the traditional forms of estate road and house frontage could be dispensed with and the motor vehicle accommodated in a quite different way. In the future the very name 'Radburn' would signal new approaches to British residential and traffic planning, but the 1930s proved too cautious a decade.

The Road Fund lost its independence in 1937, after protracted political debate. With the petrol duty finally seen as revenue duty and not as a contribution to road costs, in some ways this was among the most significant developments of the inter-war period. Otherwise it was a case of government, only just recently faced by an altogether unknown phenomenon, maintaining a balance between competing pressures of police, private organizations, local authorities and the general electorate. But inexorably, a process was begun whereby one by one individual aspects of the car would be brought under government control, and the road building established as a major function of the state.

The Sentiment of Town Planning

By 1939 statutory town planning had been undertaken in Britain for 30 years. It was well understood and reasonably in evidence, particularly in those parts of the country where building development was taking place. The activity of town planning was prescribed by statute as the preparation of schemes and the control of development in accordance with them, but in practice the scope was widening to embrace other factors, notably the question of countryside amenity. A professional cadre had been built up, competent in technical expertise, as demonstrated in a host of regional plans.

This was progress, yet the failure to achieve more during the post-1919 period was all too evident. The town planning movement, both amongst the profession and its amateur supporters had been introspective, wedded to the shibboleths of its own ideals for better housing and future cities of beauty and harmony. Its vision still rested on notions of civic design, the future seen in terms of art form. Consequently it was largely excluded from the intellectual thrusts which in the 1930s proclaimed planning as a social and economic activity of the state. Town planning had no obvious place in regional economic questions and the initiatives of the Special Areas. The canvas of a planned distribution of industry and population was understood, yet the immediate threads on offer were no more than garden cities and satellite towns. The economic costs of traffic congestion and long journeys to work were also recognized, but an ad hoc list of improvements was all that was to be seen – bypasses, an impressive bridge (over the Tyne), a tunnel (under the Mersey), improvements to London radials and the London North Circular.

The achievements of the inter-war years did not amount to all that much. Development within the area of a planning scheme did not seem all that different from that outside it; the supply of garden cities had dried up; and the private building industry proved capable of creating semi-detached dream-worlds of its own. As far as the great changes in inter-war population geography were concerned, town planning had simply been a spectator. London increased its population by two million between the wars, 1.25 million by inward migration, but town planning, while professing an ability to discharge a co-ordinating regional role, was denied any such administrative involvement.

There may have been relatively little by way of practical achievements to record, but its practitioners still proclaimed an ideological supremacy: they rested their case on the common sense of rejecting the haphazard in urban development in favour of conscious organization. They argued that it was a mark of human progress when a comprehensive plan could be worked to in an orderly manner, with the objective of securing the most efficient and effective use of land. The contrast of course was with the inconveniences and evils of nineteenth-century development. Unwin (1921) writing on London, put it this way:

> the conditions of town life are of man's own making . . . All he needs to do is to regard the city as a great human activity, needing to be guided like any other. The fact is, the growth of towns has become a scramble, and reminds one of a crowd at the ticket office that has not learnt to form a queue. Citizens must learn the queue habit . . . (p. 178)

Patrick Abercrombie (1933) in a widely-read text expressed the philosophy in very much the same terms. He considered the 'natural' (i.e. unplanned) growth of cities 'synonymous with complete muddle' (p. 10) and was typical of a large part of nineteenth-century Britain. The promise of planning was that it was 'a conscious exercise of the powers of combination and design' (p. 12). Following some curious analogy with bees and spiders, he continued: 'such insects share with mankind a passion for creating symmetry, regularity and neatness in protest against inanimate nature's dishevelled prodigality' (p. 18). He concluded:

> Town and Country planning seeks to proffer a guiding hand to the trend of natural evolution, as a result of careful study of the place itself and its external relationships. The result is to be more than a piece of skilful engineering, or satisfactory hygiene or successful economics: it should be a social organism and a work of art. (p. 27)

Unwin and the younger Abercrombie were the key town planning spokesmen of the 1919–39 period. They communicated the shared sentiments of their time, based unerringly on idealistic certainty and a faith in the reforming power of technical expertise harnessed to managerial skill. They had a rationalistic belief that optimal solutions could be found to problems; sceptical about the competence and preference of the average citizen, distrustful both of big business and politicians, they held that professional objectivity was the most trusted way forward. Town planning possessed understanding and imagination, and could be relied upon to address the problems of an industrial society in ways that would create futures of vision. It did not matter that in advancing claims for urban utopias, all demands posed by the market, financial and otherwise, could be side-stepped. Town planning was visionary, revolutionary and grounded in social realism. The professional myth was born.

The preferred British model remained the decentralist tradition based on Howard's garden city and Unwin's style of cottage architecture, though both, by the 1930s, had been modified and adapted almost out of recognition. But there were other models, as Fishman (1977) has described, though Britain remained strangely aloof from them. Frank Lloyd Wright's Broadacre City was not for Britain anyway, but le Corbusier's Radiant City had more insistent claims. The new architecture of the Modern Movement, seen in new blocks of workers' flats in Frankfurt and other European cities, could not have been more different from the recommendations of the Tudor Walters Report. As we have seen, replacement housing in slum clearance schemes flirted with the new model, but by and large Britain stuck doggedly to low density, suburban style development. Britain's isolation from town planning speculation, rife elsewhere, was also seen in the fact that the call for 'functional town planning', laid down by the International Congresses of Modern Architecture (CIAM), an organization set up in 1928, went largely unheeded in this country.

Britain's instinctive town planning preferences were sympathetic to the legacy of housing reform, its vernacular traditions in house design and spatial composition, and to its institutional structures in local government. It went on to share a belief in the scenic virtues of a farmed countryside and the importance of separating town from country. By 1939 these views were well entrenched, and while the objectives espoused fell far short of realization, nonetheless an important foothold had been gained. Above all, town planning had developed a capacity to appeal to 'higher instincts', offering rationality and objectivity – features which would soon stand it in good stead.

5 Planning and the Corporate State, 1939–45

In the quarter century between the outbreak of one world war (1914) and the onset of another (1939) discernible strides were made in the furtherance of state interventionary policies in economic and social affairs. 'Planning' had entered into the vocabulary of political parties; town planning as a statutory activity was well represented in local government affairs. The advances made were intermittent, and reversals could and did occur, but nonetheless a progression was clear. Greenleaf (1983) sees it thus:

> something of the collectivist wrack left by the tide of the Great War did remain; though not so much as many wished. Then there was the impact of the inter-war depression and the continuing growth of social services. So that when the second even greater conflict broke out, only two decades after the end of the first, it began at a higher level altogether and proceeded much farther. (p. 61)

The advent of war augmented the role of government in the country's affairs. Extensive state intervention seemed justified as national organization and centralized control proved more effective than either high prices or laissez-faire in stimulating supply for the war effort.

Within a remarkably short time the elements of the corporate state were established. We look first in this chapter at the remarkable system of central planning that was devised. Then we turn to the way in which the ethos of planning suffused national conduct and was implanted into hopes for post-war recovery. Third, we consider the enormous elevation of town planning in professional prestige during these years. Finally, we assess the performance of Churchill's Coalition Government and consider the consequences for the century-long story of the planning ideal.

The Establishment of the Corporate State

The first impact of war was dislocation and disruption: evacuation of school children, air-raid precautions, troop movements and mobilization affected many lives within a very short period of time. The impact on the government was just as profound. In July 1939 Chamberlain set up the Ministry of Supply and within weeks of the outbreak of war further new ministries were added – Economic Warfare, Food, Home Security, Information, Labour and Shipping. The Ministry of Aircraft Production followed in 1940, and in 1941 the Ministry of Labour added National Service to its responsibilities. In 1942 the Ministry of Production was set up. The size of the Civil Service almost doubled in little more than four years, from 388,000 in April 1939 to 719,000 in July 1943. Furthermore, the number of Cabinet Committees proliferated, to include the Lord President's Committee for Home Affairs, the Food Policy Committee, the Manpower Requirements Committee and the Production Executive. A central planning system was put in place; the duties of existing Departments were extended and, with the new departments added, a network of co-ordinating machinery was established.

The real spur to action came with the fall of Chamberlain and the formation of the Coalition Government under Churchill on 10 May 1940. Later that month (the 22nd) the Emergency Powers (Defence) Bill passed through both Houses and was enacted in the one day. The powers were remarkable: they enabled the government to assume control of all persons and property in the country. Britain proceeded to mobilize resources for total war. Within 18 months, say by the close of 1941, a command economy had been established, the basis being state control of industry, though without state ownership. The economy of war-time Britain was subjected to a greater degree of state supervision than even that of Nazi Germany. At the conclusion of hostilities it would be unlikely for the situation to revert quickly, or even at all, to the economic and political situation obtaining before the war. A return to the *status quo ante bellum* was improbable, and this recognition affected all other considerations as the war years unfolded.

For example, the war gave a great boost to the notion of public ownership (Morgan, 1987). Control was effected over industries such as coal and shipping; and nationalization was introduced into the production of munitions. This war-time extension of state regulation of economic activity gave encouragement to advocates of public ownership that the practical effects of their policies were indeed preferable to unfettered market operations. Moreover, with some planned redistribution of industry successfully carried out, an extension of state supervision of economic activity after the war seemed all the more likely. Attitudes in general were profoundly affected. It came to be argued that if weapons of war could be produced in such profusion, seemingly regardless of expense, then community facilities in the subsequent peace could not be denied; tanks, aircraft and ships would give way to houses, schools and hospitals, just as much by the effort of the state. By 1945 it could safely be assumed that government would continue to play a major role in directing the economy.

The corporate state was established as a consequence of major developments in three fields. First, a tripartite structure of relations was successfully established between Whitehall, the employers and the trade unions. Lloyd George had attempted this in the Great War, but had failed. A modest flourish of corporatism during the 1930s now fully bloomed in the exceptional conditions of the Second World War. There was no break with the past, rather an acceleration of past trends. The keys to success rested with the Ministry of Labour, which controlled manpower, and the three Supply Departments (Supply, Admiralty and Aircraft Production) which implemented the manpower and production programmes.

Secondly, there was a transformation of the civil service. An influx of temporary civil servants invigorated the establishment; scientists were attracted to the service ministries, captains of industry to Supply and Aircraft Production; and town planning benefited from the work of such experts as John Dower, William Holford and Thomas Sharp. The most illustrious recruits were Beveridge to the Ministry of Labour and J. M. Keynes to the Treasury. Many of the new recruits, particularly liberal or socialist academics, were reformist by inclination, and an institutional momentum was given to the promotion of radical policies and planning after the war. Permanent officials were swept along to work on new legislation; in the town planning field this is well described by Cullingworth (1975).

Thirdly, the Treasury finally capitulated to the Keynesian ideas of demand management. These were ultimately acknowledged in the

White Paper on employment policy (1944): in its opening words the Government accepted 'as one of the primary aims and responsibilities the maintenance of a high and stable level of employment after the War'. This included only a modest statement of Keynes' approach, however. Keynes, recruited to the Treasury again, worked mostly on matters of external finance and the reconstruction of the international economy, and the full impact of his more general ideas took time to penetrate the thinking of the Coalition Government. The 1941 Budget reflected his approach to the potential inflationary consequences of the war, but it required the efforts of three groups of academic economists working in Whitehall to secure acceptance of the new orthodoxy (Addison, 1987). These were Evan Durbin, Douglas Jay and Hugh Gaitskell working under the patronage of Hugh Dalton; the Prime Minister's Statistical Section; and Lionel Robbins, then Director of the Economic Section of the War Cabinet.

So the five years of the Coalition Government saw huge advances made in the structures of a collectivist state. New power relationships were forged in which the expert and the administrator came to the fore and a new apparatus of departmental administration was set up. What also happened in this period was that Labour became an effective governing party for the first time. The devolution of power to Labour in the Coalition implied that the Party would be able to join in the creation of post-war Britain. Labour's ideals from the mid-1930s would find expression after all. In Churchill's inner circle Clement Attlee grew in authority; Ernest Bevin reigned supreme on labour matters; Tom Johnston (a former red Clydesider) became Secretary of State for Scotland; Herbert Morrison was Home Secretary and Minister for Home Security; and Hugh Dalton, first Minister of Economic Warfare, later became President of the Board of Trade.

In this context, it is not surprising that the Coalition Government became a radical reforming Administration. An early keynote was the Beveridge Report, *Social Insurance and Allied Services* (1942), a publication which attained huge readership figures (635,000 copies were sold within a few weeks), and which propelled a little known academic into becoming a household name. It was the most popular blueprint for social reform ever published in Britain, benefiting from a unique timeliness. The welfare state had been on the British political agenda for at least 30 years, and even before 1914 the state was providing benefits for some people in old age, ill health and unemployment. But by 1939 it was still the case that only half the population was covered by national health insurance. The promise of radical reform was almost bound to be well received.

The genesis of the report was almost an accident (Addison, 1987). In 1941, Bevin, wanting to remove Beveridge from the Ministry of Labour, persuaded Arthur Greenwood, Minister without Portfolio in charge of reconstruction, to appoint him chairman of a committee to enquire into social insurance. The committee was initially conceived simply in terms of rationalizing and co-ordinating existing schemes of social insurance, but this modest beginning was enlarged into a comprehensive scheme for the abolition of poverty. In effect it became a political manifesto, published over the signature of one man; the stakes were raised when five other matters were highlighted, which government must tackle in measures of post-war reconstruction – Ignorance, Want, Squalor, Idleness and Disease. As Beveridge himself wrote, 'a revolutionary moment in the world's history is a time for revolutions, not for patching' (pp. 6–7). The Government was obliged to respond to this aspect of post-war social policy, but no immediate political consensus was apparent when in 1943 the House of Commons debated a motion calling for an immediate commitment to the implementation of the Beveridge Report not one Conservative MP voted in favour (Hennessy, 1992).

The publication of the Beveridge Report, and the popular reception accorded to it, marked an important point in both the wartime attitudes and the life of the Coalition. Liberalism was experiencing a startling eclipse; society must be co-operative, not competitive. The Report revealed basic ideological divisions; in the words of Cockett (1994), it was 'a searing experience for politicians of all sides' (p. 62). Everyone seemed to be swept along by Beveridge and there was remarkable little opposition in public to the proposals. The obvious counter-argument was muted: that the country's post-war priority should be to restore industrial and trading strengths rather than embark on a costly and open-ended scheme of comprehensive social provision.

Beveridge proceeded to argue in his second privately financed report, *Full Employment in a Free Society* (1944), that the avoidance of mass unemployment could be achieved in peacetime. Through the application of Keynesian policies of demand management he thought that a margin of unemployment of not more than 3 per cent was possible. Another target for post-war Britain was set.

The reforming nature of the Coalition Government was already clear. By 1943 schemes for social security for all, family allowances, and a universal and free health service had all been introduced. The next year would see educational changes proposed, a commitment to full employment and comprehensive arrangements for town and country planning.

The Planning Ethos

The impact of war on government accelerated the implementation of new arrangements for the governance of a collectivist state. It also had a profound effect on the national psyche; it fostered a determination for change and for meeting the future with a resolve to sweep away the past. This meant making plans, and prospects for planning received a huge fillip in national life.

. One important thread in the development of social attitudes was the German bombing campaign on British cities, which reached its height between September 1940 and May 1941. Night attacks continued in 1942, day attacks were started in 1943, and from June 1944 flying bomb attacks caused particularly indiscriminate damage. In England and Wales a total of 475,000 dwellings were destroyed or made permanently uninhabitable. London (especially the riverside areas around East and West Ham) took the full force of the destruction, but the effect bore on the whole country: estuarial complexes such as Merseyside and Clydeside; individual ports including Portsmouth, Hull, Southampton, Plymouth, Bristol and Belfast; inland industrial towns exemplified by Greater Manchester, Birmingham, Coventry and Sheffield; and inland cathedral towns such as Norwich and Exeter. War damage on this scale, and with a country-wide distribution, provided practical opportunities for the professionals to rebuild. Just as importantly, however, it encouraged a social psychology of deep purpose and determination to aspire to a new future. Rebuilding meant planning. This gave weight to the political ideology which already embraced the notion of planning, while the professionals and experts who would engage in the rebuilding process stood to gain immeasurably from an elevation to new importance.

But physical reconstruction would not be enough. Moral and spiritual recovery was also entailed, and this needed to be woven into a new social order. The cynics may have a field day as we reflect on the conscious manipulation of social attitudes that undoubtedly took place. Government was aware early on of the need to counter Nazi propaganda about Hitler's New Order in Europe. The War Cabinet set up a committee under Neville Chamberlain in August 1940 to look ahead to a post-war European and world system, and to consider the means whereby the new-found national unity might be perpetuated through social and economic arrangements to secure quality of opportunity and service amongst all classes of the community (Addison, 1992). Chamberlain was soon to resign through illness (he died in the December), but the remit of the committee spoke volumes about the expanding role of government in relation to future social arrangements.

A socialist Archbishop of Canterbury, William Temple, appointed in 1942, urged a Christian programme of social reform. In *Christianity and the Social Order* (1942), he called for an end to inherited wealth and priority for wages over dividends; his long list of reform measures clearly entailed more government intervention than ever before.

Government propaganda may have been contrived, and a single prelate did not speak for the whole of his Church, but it is undeniable that national sentiment strongly endorsed a vision of a just and fairer society. After a people's war there would be a people's peace. The working classes would be rewarded for their participation in the war effort. In the midst of war, a community beset by privations saw social justice in the post-war world as the light at the end of the tunnel. Unlike the Great War there was no doubt about the aggressor and the absolute need to overcome a tyrant and his regime. Britain was right in its mission. The determination to reconstruct and reward the victors was assiduously promoted, and Government would both show the way and provide the means. The war radicalized the civilian population and made possible a popular reception to collectivist proposals that would have seemed unthinkable just a few years earlier. Planning has rarely had a more conducive set of circumstances in which to flourish.

There was an early dispute between those who said that Britain should have 'War Aims' (in other words the sort of Britain people were fighting for) and those who advocated concentrating on the war and thinking later about the future. Churchill is said to have preferred the latter, but the argument that discussion about the future would be disruptive proved fallacious – rather it served to heighten purpose and direction. As an example, the issue of *Picture Post* for 4 January 1941 was devoted to 'A Plan for Britain'. It was stirring stuff, about the need for planning, imagination and 'being prepared'; unlike at the end of the last war, the next peace would be different. But it was the language of expectation that was so arresting. The Editor, Tom Hopkinson wrote:

> We believe that, after this war, certain things will be common ground among all political parties. It will be common ground, for example that every Briton – man, woman or child – shall be assured of enough food of the right kinds to maintain him in full bodily health and fitness. It will be common ground that we must reform our system of education – so that every child is assured of the fullest education he can profit by. It will be common ground that our state medical service must be reorganized and developed so as to foster health, not merely battle with disease. It will be common ground that the agricultural land of Britain must not again be given up to thistles and bracken; and that the beauty of our country and our buildings is the nation's heritage, not to be pawned away in plots to speculative builders.

Common ground, the sweeping aside of party or private interests, interdependence on one another, a vision not of the unlikely, but a determination to secure the attainable: these were the matters which turned Britain into a nation of planners. Post-war reconstruction became an integral part of the war effort.

Labour captured this war-time mood at the same time as the Conservatives began to be blamed for the circumstances of the past. It was as though the retreat from Dunkirk, the capitulation of France and the onset of the Blitz marked a turning point in British political sentiment. Pre-war foreign policy was now repudiated as weak. The social conditions of the 1930s were held up as shameful. Conservativism as a political creed lost its respectability. The socialists denigrated the anarchistic principles of laissez-faire and attached it to their opponents. New life was breathed into planning with the belief that it was a necessary ally in the saving of democracy. The town planner Thomas Sharp (1940), in a 6d Pelican Book which sold a quarter of a million copies, asserted that:

> It is no overstatement to say that the simple choice between planning and non-planning, between order and disorder, is a test-choice for English democracy. In the long run even the worst democratic muddle is preferable to a dictator's dream bought at the price of liberty and decency. But the English muddle is nevertheless a matter for shame. We shall never get rid of its shamefulness unless we plan our activities.

And plan we must – not for the sake of our physical environment only, but to save and fulfil democracy itself. (p. 143)

There was a leftward shift in politics; even communism took on a greater appeal, inspired no doubt by the Russian war effort. Collectivist state programmes in all spheres of life were looked for; *The Times* and *The Economist* were consistent advocates of bold approaches. Labour politicians attacked the domestic record of the National Government. Labour was increasingly identified with programmes for economic and social reform. There were tell-tale signs as the Conservative share of the votes at by-elections tended to fall, and between 1943 and 1945 four Conservatives loyal to the government were defeated by Commonwealth or Independent Socialist candidates.

Developments in Town Planning

During the war, town planning made considerable strides. Its practitioners were called upon to prepare ambitious plans for reconstruction and to outline new propositions for the post-war era. Official reports fuelled expectations that new policies would be taken up to address both the deep-seated problems of the past and the immediate hardships of the present. Pressure groups, notably the Town and Country Planning Association (adopting its new name in 1941), advanced the planning cause. New machinery of government was established for town and country planning; and new legislation was enacted. In a remarkably short time town planning became elevated in the public mind to heights far beyond anything reached previously. As an enthusiasm was generated for planning in national economic and social affairs, so the principles and practice of town planning became part of war-time expectations. War-time circumstances provided the crucible in which the full flowering of contemporary town planning took place.

Plans and propositions

War damage was the immediate trigger which prompted the commissioning of a number of plans for the reconstruction of bombed cities. They provided the opportunity for consultants to demonstrate their professional skills to a lay public already conditioned to a sympathy with proposals which would sweep away the past and inject 'modern' notions of design into the very appearance and structure of towns and cities. They became the vehicles whereby town planning principles, which had been well aired in professional circles for at least a decade, assumed conventional wisdom in the public mind: the need to decongest our cities and provide conditions for spacious and airy living, with all the trappings which anticipated the future rather than reconstructed the past.

Plans for London ushered in a remarkable period of endeavour, generating five advisory plans during the war years (Marmaras and Sutcliffe, 1994). Two of these were official plans; three were independent in origin. The former became the main centre of interest, but the latter were important forerunners. It is interesting that the authors of all five were architects and planners of London and its region, which reflects a built-in bias in British town planning at this time; planning solutions for one of the world's biggest cities became the model for Britain's urban areas as a whole.

The Plan of the Modern Architectural Research (MARS) Group was published in the form of an exhibition in 1942. The MARS Group had been founded in 1933 by architects keen to promote Modern Movement architecture in Britain. Its Town Planning Committee, chaired by Arthur Korn, set up in 1937, displayed its early ideas, including a linear layout structure for London as early as 1938. The MARS master plan concentrated heavily on matters of communication and was a theoretical model expressing movement and distribution. There was an east-west axis which grouped transit, heavy industry and metropolitan services along which, to north and south, were hung in herring-bone fashion, 16 linear strip-cities, each two miles wide and eight miles long, housing 600,000 people. The drawings in the exhibition were accompanied by a long essay, authored by Korn and Felix J. Samuely (chair of the MARS Committee on transport and economics) in the June 1942 issue of *The Architectural Review.*

Later that year in October the Royal Academy Plan, prepared by the RA Planning Committee, was presented at an exhibition at Burlington House; a text and a selection of the drawings were published by *Country Life.* This plan was in effect an extension of the work on London's roads undertaken by Sir Thomas Bressey and published in 1938. The architectural implications were taken forward with treatments worked up for major junctions and attention given to vistas. A dominant feature of the plan emerged as a ring road round London's central area, with most of the main line railway termini moved to meet it. The Royal Academy Plan could scarcely have been more different from the MARS plan: it was Beaux Arts street architecture on a grand scale compared with the

Corbusian statement on Modern Movement lines, though there was a common denominator – roads and communications.

Interestingly, the same thread was also well represented in the plan of the London Regional Reconstruction Committee of the RIBA (Royal Institute of British Architects) exhibited in the National Gallery in May 1943, and published by the Institute later in the year as *Greater London: Towards a Master Plan*. The chairman was Arthur Kenyon. In addition to communications, the plan considered the reconstruction of the main urban areas, the location of the industrial areas and the preservation of historical features. The proposals of the plan were more realistic than the MARS and Royal Academy Plans, but consideration of its merits was curtailed by knowledge that the first of the official plans had already captured the stage.

In 1941 Lord Reith, in his capacity as Minister of Works and Buildings, asked the LCC for a reconstruction plan for the County of London. This was undertaken by the Council's architect, J. H. Forshaw, in conjunction with Patrick Abercrombie (who had also been involved with both the Royal Academy and RIBA Plans), Professor of Town Planning at University College, London. Their *County of London Plan* was published in July 1943.

The authors declined to wipe the slate clean and posit some ideological utopian scheme, as the MARS Plan had done; furthermore they made no architectural statement to compare with that of the Royal Academy. Theirs was more a matter of fact, down to earth, land-use planning oriented plan which took the existing structure of London and offered proposals for making it work better. To this end, Forshaw and Abercrombie focused on four major problems: traffic congestion, poor housing, inadequacy and maldistribution of open space, and land use intermixture.

To resolve traffic problems the *County of London Plan* once more built on the Bressey Plan of 1937. To ease the congestion afflicting through traffic from west London via the centre to the Docks, the plan proposed to add to the two already partly-built outer ring roads (the North and South Orbital and the North and South Circular) by the construction of two corresponding inner rings: 'the fast traffic ring road and (innermost) the sub arterial station ring'. The concentric ring of London's roads articulated the 'spoke and wheel' model that sufficed for London for over 30 years, and even now has not been totally abandoned.

With regard to reconstruction, the plan envisaged giving spatial shape to community territories known as neighbourhoods, of between 6 and 10,000 persons based on the catchment area of the elementary school concerned. This concept, which built on American sociological theory, helped to give structural definition to the perceived amorphous anonymity of London's spread; the plan's drawings showed a constellation of residential areas appearing as eggs in a basket, against a backcloth of open space.

The authors acknowledged the centrifugal sprawl characteristic of outer London. But this was a plan for the area of the LCC, basically the built-up area which contained London at the end of the nineteenth century. From the outset therefore it was limited to earlier geographical confines long outdated by subsequent territorial spread. This implicit drawback was addressed even before the *County of London Plan* was completed. While it was still in preparation arrangements were afoot for work on a far wider remit – Greater London.

As we have seen in chapter 2, the Greater London Planning Committee was set up in 1927. It was served by Raymond Unwin until it was stood down in 1931, to be replaced in 1937 by a Standing Conference on London Regional Planning. Beyond the compact amalgamation of the City of London and the London County Council with its constituent metropolitan boroughs, lay a further 143 local authorities, urban and rural districts in the surrounding shire counties, extending over almost 2,600 square miles, all tributary to the LCC heartland. Nearly every one of these administrative units had planning schemes prepared independently of its adjoining authority. Furthermore, there was a large number of statutory authorities, all with independent investment and development strategies, including such bodies as the Port of London Authority, Drainage Boards, public utilities, railway and canal companies. At a time when the notion of co-ordinated planning promised so much, the challenge as well as the opportunity could not have been greater.

In 1942 Lord Reith asked the Standing Conference to agree to the preparation of a Plan for Greater London and to the appointment of Abercrombie to work in collaboration with the Technical Committee. Hence, before the *County of London Plan* was completed, Abercrombie had embarked on his wider study. In the event, the *Greater London Plan 1944* (actually published in 1945) proved the seminal document of all five London plans.

Abercrombie's plan captured the dominant town planning themes of the day and wove them into a coherent strategy. It gave a structural framework to Greater London which spoke the language of rational order in land use terms. It offered a transport model which would afford ease of communications and a solution to congestion. It bowed to the pressure of the decentralists by incorporating proposals for new housing beyond the periphery of London's present suburbs. It emphasized the need for an enhanced provision of open space, including an extensive green belt. It promised modernity: reconstruction of the blitzed and the outworn and the lowering of high densities in inner London.

In spatial terms the overall design for Greater London followed the form of concentric rings. The core represented the older areas of the capital, congested and high density, from where up to over one million people would be decanted to more congenial living conditions elsewhere. The surrounding ring was in effect inter-war suburban London, up to 12 miles from Charing Cross. Beyond that would be the Green Belt, up to 15 miles wide in parts, built up from the Green Belt Estates acquired in the 1930s, but added to with other open land. Finally, at the very perimeter would be the 'outer country ring' which would receive the dispersed population from inner London, in the form of additions to existing towns, immediate housing programmes for the LCC and Croydon, and eight new towns. The concentric functional rings were overlain by a similarly annular network of strategic roads: ten radials and rings of 'express arterial roads'. When added to the proposals for industrial relocation and other measures, it is clear that it far surpassed any previous strategic plan for London and its region.

The words of Abercrombie's personal foreword to the plan spoke volumes in the context of the time:

> There is now a chance – and a similar one may not occur again – of getting the main features of this programme of redistributed population and work carried through rapidly and effectively, thereby reducing overcrowding and locating industry in conjunction. The difficulties in normal times of moving people and industry are rightly stressed; but people and industry will go where accommodation is made available. Moreover the war has made migration a familiar habit. Give a man and his wife a first-rate house, a community, and occupation of various kinds reasonably near at hand, within a regional framework which enables them to move freely and safely about, to see their friends and enjoy the advantages of London; add to these a wide freedom of choice, and they will not grumble in the years immediately following the war. The industrialist, if he is asked whether he is prepared to submit to the guidance of a Government official, will probably protest. But if he is offered a choice of sites, with every modern facility (including labour) provided, and in addition a license to build and access to building materials and labour, he will jump at the chance to get started as quickly as possible. (pp. v–vi)

Abercrombie concluded: 'Courage is needed to seize the moment when it arrives and to make a resolute start.'

Local authorities up and down the country also 'seized the moment' and in the mid-1940s there was a veritable spate of plans for towns and cities. Abercrombie himself was heavily involved in a number of consultancy schemes: plans for Plymouth (1943), Kingston upon Hull (1945), and the Clyde Valley (1946). The City Engineers of Manchester (1945) and Sheffield (1945) produced reconstruction plans. Thomas Sharp was consultant to Durham (1945) and Exeter (1946) for their historic city plans. There were other plans for Chester (1945), Merseyside (1945), Middlesbrough (1946) and Worcester (1946), to quote just a selection.

While spatial strategies and design-oriented plans attracted most attention, other contributions to the technical aspects of town planning were being made elsewhere. One example of this was with regard to roads planning where the source of the new input was a police administrator, Alker Tripp. (This provenance should not surprise us too much as road traffic had long been a matter for the police because of the concern over road traffic accidents.) In *Town Planning and Road Traffic* (1942), Tripp outlined the importance of designing and planning complete road systems as one comprehensive exercise. This would provide a solution to both road safety (previously seen in terms of the design of junctions and implementation of local improvement schemes) and road communication generally (so far confined to the provision of new roads such as bypasses). Tripp acknowledged a hierarchy of roads: arterial, sub-arterial and local, each serving a different function and designed according to the type of traffic it would carry, such as local or heavy, inter-urban traffic. This allowed him to think in terms of precincts of local roads from which through-traffic would be deflected. A combination of the hierarchy and the structural composition emanating from a concept of road systems had the effect of confirming that an ideal town plan was a gigantic cart-wheel of spokes and rims, or, equally figuratively, a spider's web or a dartboard – precisely the same arrangement of radials and ring roads that Abercrombie favoured for London. Just for a brief moment there was the promise of road planning and town planning being seen as one integrated activity – an eventuality to be dashed repeatedly over the next 50 years.

Reports

By the end of the war the preparation of commissioned plans for the reconstruction and development of towns and cities was in full swing, informed from the pioneering work of a group of architect/planner consultants, among whom Abercrombie's reputation was outstanding. They borrowed heavily from prevailing notions in geography as to ideal forms of city structure, from sociology regarding communities and neighbourhoods, and from road engineering concerning highway hierarchies and communication patterns. Meanwhile, throughout the war years, but particularly after 1942, there was a steady stream of officially-sponsored reports in respect of various aspects of national planning.

Taken overall they established important positions concerning distribution of the industrial population, land compensation, rural areas, housing and national parks. By 1945 the essential directions of national planning had been established.

The work of the Royal Commission on the Distribution of the Industrial Population, set up in 1937, has been described in chapter 3. A strongly decentralist line was pressed on the Commission; the need for planned regional dispersal away from London and the south-east and the reduction of overcrowding and congestion in the central parts of cities were common themes. The Commission's Report (the Barlow Report) was ready in 1939 but was not published until 1940. In the event it was a report which advanced the cause of planning very substantially.

Barlow recommended a set of objectives for national action:

(a) Continued and further redevelopment of congested urban areas, where necessary.

(b) Decentralization or dispersal, both of industries and industrial population, from such areas.

(c) Encouragement of a reasonable balance of industrial development, so far as possible, throughout the various divisions or regions of Great Britain, coupled with appropriate diversification of industry in each division or region throughout the country. (para 428)

These parameters for town planning and economic planning seen within a national framework went far beyond any previous official report. Moreover, Barlow recommended a new national authority, 'the National Industrial Board', comprising a chairman and three other members to oversee the work that would be necessary to implement the objectives. The Board would provide information relating to the location of industry; it would undertake research; and advise Government, local authorities and industrialists.

The majority report was accompanied by three supplementary notes. One was a 'Note of Reservations' signed by three Commissioners; this pressed for an extension of the executive powers proposed for the new National Industrial Board. Another was a longer 'Report' signed by a further three Commissioners, including Patrick Abercrombie; this recommended the setting up of a new government department to undertake the tasks which were necessary. A further one was a 'Dissentient Memorandum on Planning in Relation to the Location of Industry' submitted by Abercrombie himself. He argued that if industrial control were to be exercised on a national basis, then it must be integrated into regional and local planning in all their aspects.

The stakes were raised, and later in this chapter we shall see how Barlow's four-man National Industrial Board was comprehensively overtaken by events. But however tentative Barlow's proposed Board appeared, and however premature a new government department must have seemed, a positive thrust to central planning had been firmly established. Bomb damage and other consequences of the war soon confirmed the need for national planning.

Attention turned to precisely how the new arrangements would be carried into effect. One immediate problem was that in any national planning system the allocation of land for various purposes would have to proceed on the basis of selecting the most suitable land for particular purposes irrespective of the existing values which may attach to that land. The operation of the land market would have to be overridden. But this was practically impossible under existing planning legislation because local planning authorities were obliged to compensate landowners for loss of development value. The great obstacle to the sort of effective planning that was now advocated had to be removed. The problems of compensation and betterment in respect of public control of the use of land had bedevilled statutory town planning since its outset in 1909; now was the chance to crack the nut once and for all.

Lord Reith set up an Expert Committee chaired by Mr Justice Uthwatt in January 1941 to examine this question and to advise on the steps to be taken so that reconstruction work would not be prejudiced. An Interim Report presented in July 1941 contained three far-reaching recommendations: that compensation in respect of the public acquisition of land be 'pegged' to values obtaining at 31 March 1939; that building and development control be extended throughout the whole country; and that special redevelopment areas be defined to widen the scope of reconstruction projects. The Final Report followed in September

1942. A lengthy, complex and technical document, its proposals powerfully underpinned the extension of central planning powers then being considered by Government. It suggested the immediate vesting in the state of the rights of development in all land outside built-up areas on payment of fair compensation, and a periodic levy on increases in annual site value. For developed land it recommended the compulsory purchase of war-damaged or other reconstruction areas, as well as land elsewhere to provide accommodation for persons displaced.

Outside the formal recommendations Uthwatt offered an observation on the nature of the central planning authority which had emerged in the Barlow Report. Uthwatt thought it would be wrong to create a government department concerned with National Development which would rank with existing government departments. 'What is wanted is thought at the centre, an informed vision, unified control of land use and co-ordination between the existing Departments' (para 362). The concept of a Minister for National Development, with no departmental cares, was one which the War Cabinet would wrestle with, as we indicate later in this chapter.

Lord Reith was also responsible for launching an enquiry into Land Utilisation in Rural Areas; a committee was established in October 1941, chaired by Lord Justice Scott. Reith's original intention was for an investigation into rural industries, especially those suitable for location in the countryside. But much broader terms of reference were established which enabled the committee to make sweeping recommendations on a wide range of rural planning matters. The tone of the report (1942) was set very much by the vice-chairman, the geographer Dudley Stamp, and the two secretaries, the planner Thomas Sharp and Basil Engholm, who would later be head of a new Land Use Division in the Ministry of Agriculture. This is not the place to dwell on the essential thrust of the report, namely that farming was an inevitable and benign mainstay of landscape protection and nature conservation (an uncritical chicken that would come home to roost 30–40 years later), rather to emphasize the sheer breadth of the recommendations which underlined the likely extent of the planning outreach in post-war Britain. Going far beyond the inter-war agenda, expectations were raised about improved rural services and amenities, national parks, green belts and the development of a national footpaths system.

It was inevitable that housing would figure significantly in plans for the post-war era. In chapter 4 we saw that housing expectations were raised towards the close of the Great War, the Tudor Walters Report (1918) then recommending higher design standards for public sector housing. In fact these endured for a quarter of a century until the Dudley Report (1944) performed much the same function on the second occasion.

The outbreak of war saw the immediate contraction of house building, and also brought a halt to slum clearance. New cottages for agricultural workers were permitted in 1943, but basically the later war years were devoted to a reassessment of housing policy for the post-war period (Taylor, 1995). Early in 1942 two committees were set up by the Central Housing Advisory committee to report to the Minister of Health (the minister responsible for housing) on matters relating to post-war housing rebuilding. One (the Burt Committee) considered prefabrication and other forms of non-traditional construction. The other (chaired by Lord Dudley) established the forms, and space and equipment standards, for post-war housing; in conjunction with a team from the Ministry of Town and Country Planning, they advised on matters of housing layout and densities. Their Report (the Dudley Report) was published as *The Design of Dwellings* (1944).

The Dudley Committee saw the need for a much wider range of accommodation than had so far been provided; part of this emphasis was no doubt the desire to establish forms of home design to foster the virtues of family life, so important in the psychology of war-time resistance as Bullock has suggested (1987). The committee was drawn into the debate about preferences for flats and houses. In recommending a range of densities (30 persons per acre for town centres, rising to a maximum of 120 for the largest cities), it was inescapable that flats would be necessary to accommodate the highest densities. Between 25 and 30 per cent of the population in the biggest cities, at 120 persons per acre, would have to live in flats – an issue that would remain at the forefront of planning policy for the next 30 years. It was evident that the form of post-war housing would be different from that which had characterized the inter-war period. The individualism of low-density suburbia was under threat from communitarianism. A good example was the plan prepared by Sir Charles Reilly, Professor of Architecture at Liverpool, for Birkenhead where he had been appointed planning consultant in 1944. He prepared an estate layout which showed houses arranged round greens, and 'the greens themselves arranged like the petals of a flower round a community building, the modern equivalent of the village inn' (Wolfe, 1945, p. 10). The so-called Reilly Plan attracted political comment, hailed by the Labour and Communist parties as a forerunner of planned neighbourly co-operation..

It was abundantly clear that post-war housing in Britain would have a substantial measure of central direction. When the Central Housing Advisory Committee met in 1942, the Ministry of Health suggested that the pattern of pre-war housing provision would be followed after the war, with local authorities building between one-third and one-quarter of the total. But quite quickly government moved to a position of regarding local authorities as essential rather than secondary in meeting housing needs. It was assumed that most houses would be built by the state, to centrally-established design criteria, in forms which would be dictated by density considerations, in turn guided by planning policy relating to the need to decant over-congested populations to other areas. The nation's house building would accord to a set of centrally-devised criteria.

Neither was rural housing neglected. A third sub-committee of the Central Housing Advisory Committee, chaired by Sir Arthur Hobhouse, concerned rural housing. Their report (1944) acknowledged that there were particular problems to address, such as the shortage of houses for agricultural workers and the disrepair and deterioration of existing property. Extra financial assistance and improvements in administration were seen as crucial for an 'expansive policy' for rural housing after the war.

Another official report at this time, which indicated the breadth of assumptions relating to the scope of central direction over national affairs, concerned the country's scenic heritage. In chapter 4 we noted the increasing pressure exerted by the various amenity associations for national parks; a national body was formed – the Standing Committee on National Parks – its drafting secretary, John Dower (Sheail, 1995). Dower enlisted as soon as the war began but was invalided out of the army. Lord Reith's successor, Lord Portal, appointed him in August 1942 as a temporary civil servant charged with preparing a factual report on various park areas. This work was undertaken over the next two years, though interrupted by bouts of ill health. His report *National Parks in England and Wales* (1945) considered that 8,000 square miles in England and Wales constituted potential national park areas: 3,600 square miles in ten national parks, and the rest in a further twelve reserves. A third list of 34 tracts specified other amenity areas. Dower made it clear that these were *national* areas; hence their cost should fall on national funds and their administration should be the concern of an appropriate national body. Fully sympathetic to the outreach of the collectivist state, he argued that if national parks were to be provided *for* the nation they should be provided *by* the nation.

Meanwhile a committee chaired by Sir Douglas Ramsay had surveyed potential Scottish national parks; their report was published in 1945. Five areas were recommended as suitable for national parks and a further three were placed on a reserve list for future consideration.

Pressure for planning

Plans and official reports had their place; they clearly signalled considerable developments in the acceptance of town planning during the war years. But an unofficial planning campaign was also waged, the cudgels being seized by the Garden Cities and Town Planning Association (GCTPA). Founded in 1899 as the Garden City Association, to pursue the ideals and objectives of Ebenezer Howard, it had changed its name to the GCTPA in 1909, but remained a body very largely reflecting a garden city and satellite town movement (Hardy, 1991a). After 1936 the leadership and style changed with a direction towards national planning for achieving the Association's goals. It became the Town and Country Planning Association in 1941 and under Frederic Osborn, its secretary, it achieved considerable success in its proselytizing zeal, with annual conferences and a prolific output of pamphlets. Espousing policies of dispersal, green belts and new towns the Association's aims became almost official policy.

With less flamboyance, and regional rather than local appeal, yet with no little significance, the Bournville Village Trust was already promoting a wider town planning view in the West Midlands. In 1935 it had set up a programme of housing research in Birmingham, collecting data from 7,000 respondents and mapping an area of 1,100 square miles. *When We Build Again* (Bournville Village Trust, 1941) set out a list of far-reaching planning objectives for the city.

But the trust was simply one of a large number of organizations to advance the aspirations of town planning at this time. These included the professions – the Town Planning Institute and the RIBA; housing bodies such as the Co-operative Building Society and the Housing Centre; and the 1940 Council set up to promote aspects of social planning.

Machinery of government

In this chapter we have argued that between 1939 and 1945 town planning made enormous strides and was propelled into a public sector arena. The results were seen in Whitehall and in legislation.

Before the war, town planning resided in the Ministry of Health, but a rather different departmental structure was soon called for. In September 1940 the old Office of Works, enlivened as a consequence of the commencement of the rearmament programme, became the Ministry of Works and Buildings. Perhaps even more importantly, Sir John Reith became the first minister, exercising considerable influence on subsequent developments relating to planning, particularly reconstruction. Before Reith was replaced by Lord Portal, all town and country planning functions had been transferred to a new Ministry of Works and Planning. The full logic came into effect with the setting up of the Ministry of Town and Country Planning in 1943, with responsibilities for England and Wales (north of the border central responsibility remained with the Department of Health for Scotland). The arguments for a 'central authority' stemming from Barlow were finally repulsed: the Board of Trade was responsible for industrial location and the Ministry of Health for housing.

Legislation in 1943 extended planning control to all land in the country not already covered by a scheme, or a resolution to prepare one. The slow process of extending planning control during the 1930s was suddenly completed. But it was the Town and Country Planning Act 1944 which demonstrated the hugely increased planning powers granted by the state. In its gestation, however, it also exemplified the sharp political divide inherent in land-use planning – the profit element in the development of land, and to whom it should accrue. Ministers and officials were still wrestling with the recommendations of the Uthwatt Report. Legislation was required to help local authorities tackle the reconstruction of their blitzed areas, but the problem was as yet unresolved as to the level of compensation to be paid for land and property, and the procedures to be followed. The official historian of the period, Cullingworth (1975), quotes from a memorandum by the Minister for Economic Warfare, the Earl of Selbourne, who put his finger on the point of contention:

> It must necessarily sometimes be difficult for Conservatives, Liberals and Socialists to agree about post-war legislation. In Town and Country Planning the Socialist and the Liberal will wish to extend State interference with private trade and property much further than most the Conservatives will think necessary or desirable. Many Conservatives hold that State planning can easily be carried to a point where it will impede development and impair freedom, without improving anything.

> For the sake of avoiding controversy that might delay measures of
> reconstruction desired by everyone, I would make many concessions to
> my socialist colleagues, and do not contest the unprecedented powers
> of land acquisition embodied in the Bill. No compromise, however,
> appears to be legitimate on the question of fair compensation to persons
> dispossessed of their property. (p. 128)

The principle was established that compensation would be based on
1939 prices. This allowed the Conservatives to object that landowners
would get no more; and Labour to object that the LCC and other blitzed
local authorities would not be able to pay less. Property owners regarded
the principle as a concession to nationalization. The bill had a difficult
passage in Parliament and although Labour abstained on the second
reading, it required work by a committee under Attlee's chairmanship
to devise an acceptable compromise. The 1939 ceiling was adhered to,
but all owner-occupiers were given the right to a supplementary payment
(up to a 30 per cent addition) according to the circumstances of each
particular case.

The act provided sweeping powers to local authorities to engage in
reconstruction and redevelopment. They were enabled to buy land,
simply and expeditiously to deal with areas of extensive war damage
and areas of 'bad layout and obsolete development' – blitzed and blighted
land. This was the first occasion when a General Act permitted planned
redevelopment on an extensive, central area scale. The legislation enacted
that after a compulsory purchase order had been authorized, a new,
expedited procedure for transfer of ownership could be exercised,
whereby the vesting of land *preceded* the assessment and payment of
compensation instead of following it. A local authority could give notice
of its intention to enter on land and take possession after 14 days. It
was argued that these remarkable measures were required because of the
exceptional circumstances of the time. One city, Birmingham, became
a slum landlord virtually overnight, when in taking advantage of the
legislation it acquired redevelopment areas in its inner ring containing
30,000 houses accommodating over 100,000 people, some 2,650 shops
and 2,300 commercial and industrial premises (Cherry, 1994).

This strengthening of local authority power was accompanied by
statements clarifying government policy for the future. A White Paper,
The Control of Land Use (Ministry of Town and Country Planning,
1944), laid out intentions with regard to compensation and betterment
and proposed 'a single reconstruction programme' in which the various
claims on land should be harmonized – housing, reconstruction, schools,

distribution of industry, agriculture, national parks and forests, roads and airfields. Never before had such a prospect been advanced whereby the right use of land would be planned so comprehensively.

Regional planning received an impetus when ten Regional Planning Officers were appointed by the Minister. Joint Planning Committees proliferated: a new Committee for Merseyside was formed, and in Scotland three Regional Committees were set up (for the Clyde Valley, Central and South East Scotland, and East Central Scotland).

Regional economic planning was the province of the Board of Trade. The President, Hugh Dalton, was given to settling location decisions in a piecemeal way: ad hoc agreements entered into with industry gave rise to a new strip mill at Margam, petrochemicals and car manufacture at Linwood and Grangemouth, synthetic fibres at Pontypool and petrochemicals at Wilton, Teeside. He devoted his last few months in office to getting a Distribution of Industry Bill on to the statute book. Against the opposition of some Cabinet colleagues, but supported by Bevin, the bill was published in February 1945, with the Second Reading on 21 March. He told the House: 'It is the first instalment of a debt of honour which we owe to some of the best and bravest of our fighting men, from Scotland, from Tyneside, from County Durham and from elsewhere' (Pimlott, 1985, p. 406). Clause 9 of the bill aroused controversy. It enabled the board to declare any area a Restricted Area, within which permission would be needed to build or extend an industrial building. Dalton in the last days of the Caretaker Government offered a concession on this, and the bill received the Royal Assent on 15 June 1945, the day Parliament was dissolved. We may reasonably claim Dalton as the architect of post-war Development Area policy. His act renamed the pre-war Special Areas 'Development Areas' and aided factory building and the provision of infrastructure.

The End of Coalition

With the war in Europe at an end, though with hostilities unabated in the Far East, Churchill announced the termination of the Coalition on 23 May 1945; it had governed for five years since the resignation of Chamberlain. A Conservative Caretaker Government was formed which would carry on throughout a General Election campaign of three weeks, beginning on 15 June. Election day was 6 July. Time had to be allowed for the counting of service votes, so the Election results would not be known until 26 July.

During the final period of the war economic liberals had a late shout against the collectivism shown by the Coalition. It fell to Friedrich von Hayek to catch the tide of debate over planning and post-war policy. Born in Vienna in 1899, he had been appointed Professor of Economic Science and Statistics at the London School of Economics in 1931; advocate of the free market, he was an arch-critic of Keynesian state intervention and demand management. Hayek retained a conviction that it was quite impracticable to substitute a central authority for the decentralized decision making of the market, regarding planned economics as not only inefficient, but morally corrupting. He consistently argued against state intervention into social and economic activity in order to produce a certain outcome – a vain desire which he was to call 'the fatal conceit', the title of his last book (1988).

He remains best known for his one popular book, *The Road to Serfdom* (1944), in which he warned against the potential for the creeping totalitarianism which he perceived in the burgeoning welfare-'ism' of the Labour Party, post-Beveridge. Prosperity, he argued, would come not from central planning but from a market system that released the energies of free people. The book was dedicated 'to the Socialists of all Parties', suggesting that all parties were now suffering from the same delusions, namely that collectivism would decrease freedom and was inherently undemocratic.

When it came to the election, the Conservative Party manifesto was entitled simply, 'Mr Churchill's Declaration of Policy to the Electors'. The party relied heavily on Churchill's success and popularity during the war, but the manifesto reiterated pledges on full employment, national insurance and a national health service, all made earlier.

The Labour Party was in a very different position. It had been out of power since 1931, but had made enormous strides during the 1930s in putting together a coherent package of socialist policies, and in the Coalition Government its leaders had proved effective and competent. There was undeniably a leftward shift in political opinion and at the 1944 Labour Conference in December 1944 Ian Mikardo successfully moved the adoption of a more radical programme than had been proposed by the National Executive Committee. The NEC's programme had included no measure of nationalization other than the Bank of England. The adoption of the revised programme now meant that the public ownership of land, large-scale building, heavy industry and all forms of banking, transport and fuel and power were included (Eatwell, 1979).

Labour's manifesto in 1945 was entitled 'Let us Face the Future', It made the same commitments as the Conservatives to insurance, health, housing and education, but added specific promises on nationalization. Aggressively, it nailed its colours to the mast, declaring that, 'The Labour Party is a Socialist Party, and proud of it. Its ultimate purpose at home is the establishment of the Socialist Commonwealth of Great Britain – free, democratic, efficient, progressive, public-spirited, its material resources organized in the service of the British people'. The manifesto commitments, like those of the Conservatives, were built on an administrative platform, already partly erected by the Coalition. Labour proposed to complete the superstructure, carry through the revolution of reform and extend it in directions recognizably socialist.

Among the Conservatives, the Tory Reform Committee formed in 1943 shared in the concern for social justice, but overall the party was not successful in refuting the long-standing charges of privileged sectional interests laid at its door. It was Labour that benefited from the war-time shift in public opinion. The party was considered very much in harmony with the wartime ethos of 'fair shares' imposed by rationing, controls and the sacrifice of war. It was also uniquely identified with the new social agenda, and successfully exploited the vogue for planning and egalitarianism.

The Coalition had been a remarkably successful government. Its war record is not for analysis here, but on the home front it was one of the most reformist administrations since before 1914. In three heady years between 1942 and 1945 it published a series of White Papers which promised major initiatives in the fields of education, health, housing, industry, employment, social security and land-use planning. Its welfare record was particularly good. It helped with supplementary pensions, supply of milk to mothers and babies and school milk and meals for all school children. Free schooling was provided under the Butler Education Act 1944 for all up to the age of 15. It set up a new apparatus of administration, with new departments and an invigorated civil service.

Barnett (1986), on the other hand, has seen more failings. The war-time movement for social reform is interpreted as the creation of an intelligentsia, successful in the manipulation of popular opinion, but ultimately creating unrealistic expectations of what could be achieved in the post-war world. Further, there is an alleged failure by government to reconstruct and reorganize British industry, an omission which would later impact severely on a sluggish economy and a fragile balance of payments. Such dissent from the widely accepted favourable view, namely that an overblown future was unattainable and that the long-term needs of British industry were ignored, has its point, but it is difficult to see what more the Coalition could have done at the time either to keep British public opinion under control or to attend to the macro-investment needs of the economy.

In the terms of town planning, the creation of a separate ministry in 1943, the bringing under effective planning control of all the land in Britain, and the 1944 Town and Country Planning Act attending to 'blitz and blight' were major steps forward. The war-time reports (Barlow, Uthwatt, Scott, Dudley and Dower) proved seminal. Greater London received a notable plan, some of the major provisions of which can be seen today. Regional planning made advances. The bedrock of a national planning system was being worked upon and was almost ready to be put into place. Town planning was actively proselytized and found favour with the community at large.

The Coalition had done its job. The Caretaker Government's short span came to an end. On 26 July 1945 the votes were counted. A Labour landslide victory was the result. More than 2 million middle-class voters had voted for Labour, many for the first time. 'At 7 p.m. Churchill set off for Buckingham Palace in a chauffeur-driven Rolls, to tender his resignation and at 7.30 Attlee arrived at the Palace in a Standard Ten driven by his wife' (Addison, 1992, p. 385). A new government took office – Labour, for the first time with a majority.

6 The Attlee Years, 1945–51

Labour was swept to power in July 1945. It survived a General Election in February 1950, with an overall majority reduced to five (though with a clear lead of nearly one million votes over the Conservatives). It returned to the opposition benches in October 1951 when Conservatives gained 321 seats to Labour's 295. Attlee had presided over six eventful years. During this time the machinery of government, inherited from the Coalition, proved effective in the discharge of a socialist programme of state intervention in economic, social and related affairs including that of town and country planning.

Yet the two Labour governments were not as doctrinaire as might have been anticipated. They were constrained from pursuing more radical and expensive policies by a succession of economic difficulties and financial sanctions. However, 30 years on, they could be regarded as the 'most reforming Administrations of the century' (Seldon, 1981, p. 5), renowned for their nationalization programme and welfare state measures.

They were governments which established the language and the battle-ground of post-war British politics for a period lasting three decades. The basis was a moderate political and intellectual consensus which rested on the success of a mixed economy, full employment and the trappings of the welfare state. Some observers, including Peter Jenkins (1987), have sought to play down the post-war consensus, but all three main parties fought the 1945 election on the same commitment to use the state for economic reconstruction and social redistribution. Moreover, until the late 1970s this was the common agenda for all the principal political parties. None seemed to be excluded: the Liberals could claim the contributions of Beveridge and Keynes, the Conservatives from Butler to Heath regarded many of Attlee's achievements with favour, while

Labour's flagship was founded on their measures of public ownership and the welfare state. The consensus originated in part of course in the fact that previous governments, particularly the War Coalition of 1940–5, had provided the ground for Attlee's legislation.

We have already seen that the colleagues whom Attlee had led on the Home Front during the war were trusted and loyal, had become used to power, and were skilled in the art of government and departmental administration. In an atmosphere conducive to the furtherance of centrally directed programmes of national reform, Attlee could scarcely have wished for a better team – a cabinet of veterans whose instincts were rooted in the early history of their Party: Bevan, the youngest of the new Cabinet ministers was born in 1897, otherwise they were mainly in their sixties – Bevin born in 1881, Attlee in 1883, Dalton in 1887, Morrison in 1888 and Cripps in 1889. They were pragmatic politicians and relatively non-disputatious, at least in the early years. The government's general stability was helped by a number of powerful permanent secretaries, a general acceptance of continuity from the past and, especially, support from the trade unions. Labour's victory in 1945 was also a victory for the unions. Before 1939 they had not been regarded as an estate of the realm, but once propelled into necessary prominence, they retained it until the late 1980s.

Reformist and consensual, the government retained a large measure of popular support and loyal party political backing during its period of office. One past dragon was soon slain: national unemployment rates fell to less than 2 per cent of the insured labour force; in north-east England in 1949 it was only 3 per cent, Scotland 4.5 per cent and in South Wales 5.5 per cent. New factories started up in the Development Areas and in Scotland. A popular legislative programme giving nationalized industries and welfare measures maintained an impetus of change. There was a generally supportive post-war mood: as in the war years the people would all pull through together.

Yet for the country at large the period after 1945 was one of austerity. As late as November 1948 the Minister of Food, John Strachey, told the Cabinet that for the first time since 1944 it would be impossible to increase the meat ration in Christmas week (Eatwell, 1979). Rationing in fact continued for longer than expected: potato rationing did not end until the spring of 1948, bread until July and jam until December that year. There was a concerted attack on rationing and controls only as the General Election of 1950 approached, with (in March 1949) the Board of Trade announcing the removal of nearly one million licences, which led to the abolition of all clothes and textile rationing. But the British people were in a highly disciplined condition. A population long accustomed to a seige economy at home, or military service abroad, was inured to a continuation of strict regulation and the perceived follies of civil servants. (An oily tasteless fish called snoek, bought in large quantities from South Africa proved unpopular; and a plan to grow ground-nuts in East Africa taken up by the Ministry of Food proved a fiasco.)

It was against this background that the flowering of the planning ideal was fully demonstrated. With great self-confidence, Britain would be reconstructed as the war effort had demanded.

The Outreach of the State

Labour came to office with a clear commitment to planning and the restructuring of the whole economy. The commanding ethos was that collective endeavour would be channelled by central government, through powerful and revitalized local authorities and a variety of public bodies. As Morgan (1984) puts it, 'The planners were in the ascendant, the new conquerors of mankind' (p. 297).

As we have seen in chapter 5, Labour, for the first and only time in its history, went before the electorate in July 1945 with the nationalization of major industries and utilities as its prime objective (Morgan 1987). Its manifesto had a bravado which associated nationalization with the patriotism and social unity which had won the people's war. Nationalization was indeed to be one of the centre-pieces of the government's programme. By the autumn of 1946 four nationalization statutes were in place, covering the Bank of England, civil aviation, cable and wireless, and coal. Railways, long-distance transport and electricity followed in 1947; gas in 1948; and iron and steel in 1949. In all cases the administrative model followed was that of Morrison's London Passenger Transport Board, set up in 1934. The structure enabled Whitehall departments to sponsor public corporations, and ministers to appoint experts to boards which would then run the industries at arm's length from political involvement.

We observed in chapter 3 that nationalization was not new, in that public ownership in varying degrees had been established for many years: between the wars the Central Electricity Generating Board, the British Broadcasting Corporation (in addition to Morrison's London Passenger Transport Board) were set up and during the war the North of Scotland Hydro Electricity Board was created. It is also true that in some industries (gas, electricity and civil aviation, for example) there was already a high degree of public intervention, and that in the case of the Bank of England only a modest reform was effected. Yet the nationalization measures indicated a substantial advance in the state direction of economic affairs.

But public ownership in Britain had not yet run its full course. The fuel crisis in the harsh winter of 1947 called the consequences of nationalization into question when coal shortages provoked criticisms about failures in the planning of adequate supplies. Strong political opposition to the nationalization of iron and steel was mounted and as 1950 approached, the government's attitude to further measures weakened. Labour went to the country that year with a shopping list of proposals to nationalize an assortment of industries including cement, water supply, meat wholesaling, sugar refining, industrial assurance, shipbuilding and chemicals. No action was taken. When it came to the 1951 election the party manifesto contained no such list, merely a vaguely worded pledge to take over (unnamed) industries which were 'failing the nation'.

During the last 18 months of Attlee's government there was clearly a retreat from the early enthusiasm for nationalization. It had moved away from the command economy of wartime to the managed economy of Keynes. As Addison (1987a) observes: 'In 1945 the initiative in politics lay with socialists and planners. By the end of the 1940s the initiative lay with Keynesians and businessmen' (p. 253). This feature would remain over the next decade and beyond with governments of very different hues.

Inevitably the economic problems encountered by the government were not generally those it had expected. A course of action marked out in a manifesto programme soon takes on a different reality in the light of changing circumstances. The marvel in many ways is that a radical programme with a consistent theme was maintained for so long. Within a month of taking office Attlee was faced with President Truman's abrupt termination of US Lease Lend; Keynes negotiated a new loan which was indispensable if the government's welfare measures were to be implemented. The year 1947 was a difficult one, beginning with the coal crisis and ending with the devaluation of sterling against the US dollar.

Then 1951 proved even more contentious with the consequence of the Korean War soon felt with a soaring defence expenditure requirement, the fateful dispute between Gaitskell and Bevan over NHS charges on dentures and spectacles, ministerial resignations (Bevan, Harold Wilson and John Freeman), and the party divisions opened up by the rise of the Bevanite group. Later that year a disastrous collapse in the overseas balance of payments produced further austerity measures. No wonder public sentiment felt that Attlee's administration was running out of energy and ideas, though had Attlee delayed going to the country until the spring of the next year, and had not the Liberal Party severely curtailed the number of its candidates (thereby allowing the Conservatives to benefit), he may well have won a later election. However, a chill had been cast on socialist thought, though the practice of economic planning was not to be dismantled yet.

There was little political will to change the broad parameters of the economic measures set in place for the post-war years. The Conservatives entered their period in opposition in a state of some intellectual disarray (Greenleaf, 1983). The Coalition may have formulated an extensive programme of economic and social reform, but the degree of state intervention caused unease on the right wing of the party where the irony was not lost that Britain had fought a war to preserve freedom only to lose liberties at home. In the event, the Conservatives did not resist nationalization measures to any great extent until opposition was mounted to the 1947 Transport Act – mainly over road haulage.

At the first post-war party conference (Blackpool in October 1946) Churchill acceded to demands for policy reformulation. He appointed a committee of the Shadow Cabinet (the Industrial Policy Committee) chaired by R. A. Butler to draw up a statement on economic and industrial affairs. The result was the Industrial Charter, published in May 1947; it accepted nationalization of the mines, railways and the Bank of England; pledged the party to the maintenance of full employment; and, confirming a strategic role for the state in the economy, acknowledged the need for appropriate machinery for economic planning and the fixing of wages. In the next year (May 1948) an Agricultural Charter broadly accepted the interventionism of the 1947 Agriculture Act, with its guaranteed price support for farmers.

It may not have been apparent at the time (Schneer, 1987) but a broad consensus had been established. Politically the parties subscribed to Keynesian economic policies. The administrative elite in governance and business saw merit in the virtues of planning. The country at large were happy at the prospect of improved economic conditions.

The main building blocks of post-war policy had been set in place and there was little incentive to change them. Nationalization lost its immediate appeal, and in 1950 was no longer a major electoral issue, but the broad thrust of economic management by the state remained.

Meanwhile another important element in the consensus was established by two Welsh Ministers, Aneurin Bevan (at Health) and James Griffiths (at National Insurance). The Family Allowances Act 1945, promoted by the Coalition, was already law; it was followed by the National Health Act in 1946 and the National Insurance Act in 1946, also the Industrial Injuries Act and the National Assistance Act in 1948 (the latter dealing the final blow to the nineteenth-century Poor Law). The National Health Service came into being in July 1948. Beveridge's earlier work and government guarantees of improved social conditions had come to pass, to widespread popular approval. The new arrangements had a long pedigree. For centuries the state had accepted a minimal obligation to the destitute who fell within the scope of the Poor Laws. Before the Great War there had been Lloyd George's National Insurance Act and Winston Churchill's Unemployment Insurance Act. National Insurance was now given a striking feature – universality. Although there was provision for a few exceptions, there was no contracting out, and those who wished to make separate arrangements could do so as an addition, but not as an alternative to the national scheme. The new provisions for pensions similarly built on earlier schemes. Before 1908 state pensions had been restricted to those who served the crown in military or civil capacities. From 1908 old-age pensions were paid to certain people over 70 who were deemed worthy in terms of evidence of having saved money. The contributory principle was introduced in legislation of 1925 which provided for pensions to poorish people at the age of 65. The 1946 Act chose 65 for a man's retiring age and 60 for a woman's.

Bevan clearly was a key figure in the welfare programme, yet his housing record was poor. In the second Attlee administration he was Minister of Labour and National Service, but if we consider the six years between August 1945 and December 1951 Labour's performance was consistently disappointing, with only 1,016,000 dwellings built during that time. Over the last four years, when it might have been expected that the shortage of materials would have been overcome and that the organization of the building industry made effective, annual totals for

England, Wales and Scotland showed little variation and certainly no growth: 227,000 (1948), 197,000 (1949), 198,000 (1950) and 194,000 (1951). The bulk of these completions was in the public sector, private house building having scarcely got under way. Bevan emphasized that the national housing programme would focus on building houses to let, and that local authorities would be the main instruments for that objective. The post-war council house came into its own, built to high standard, and costly on the public purse. The annual totals may have disappointed, but they were still far in excess of the local authority completions pre-war.

But stagnating building rates were of little popular comfort for the many in housing need, the seriousness of which was evidenced by the highly visible squatter problem in London. The claim that state control and regulation meant efficiency in production sounded increasingly hollow; and the Conservatives (as indicated in their 1950 election manifesto) promised to restore to the citizenry personal freedom and a power of initiative in property and house ownership. The slogan 'setting the people free' suggested that the ethic of the war years was giving way to the imperative of individualism. But as we shall see, the political rhetoric did not seriously chip away at the framework of the economic and social post-war settlement for many years to come.

This is not to say, of course, that fires were not being stoked which would rage in future years. The argument about the extent of state involvement burned slowly, but while the flash points of popular irritation at bureaucratic control could be damped down, the deeper heat of intellectual concern glowed from time to time. A socialist George Orwell used novels to reach a general public: in *Animal Farm* (1945) he attacked excessive centralism and suppression of free thought, and in *Nineteen Eighty Four* (1949) he denounced the threats from centralization, state planning and conformity.

From an economist, John Jewkes (1948), a war-time head of the Economic Secretariat of the Cabinet, came a vivid denunciation of central state planning:

> (it) ultimately turns every individual into a cipher and every economic decision into blind fumbling, destroys the incentives through which economic progress arises, renders the economic system as unstable as the whims of the few who ultimately control it and creates a system of wire-pulling and privileges in which economic justice ceases to have any meaning. (p. 9)

Jewkes argued that the case for planning rested on misrepresentation and pure ignorance of the nature of the economic system. In a vigorous defence of the market system, he pointed to the moral sickness of a planned society, derided planners as a species and revealed the flaws of planning as a scientific method. In an onslaught on planning in action, he concluded that 'No pen could fully describe and no mind could wholly grasp the vast mesh of controls in Great Britain that now circumscribe everyday action' (p. 217). In a catalogue of cases he described how the dispatch of a small shipment of lubricating oil necessitated the completion of no less than 46 forms; the instance of a provincial corn merchant who operated under 14 licenses and with 160 fixed prices; and the case of a company fined for selling 60,000 frying pans on the home market because of delays in the supply of an export license by the Board of Trade.

Jewkes attended the first meeting of Hayek's Society of liberal academics which held its first conference at the Hotel du Park on the slopes of Mont Pelerin overlooking Lac Leman in April 1947. It became known as the Mont Pelerin Society and proceeded to meet every one or two years thereafter. Economic liberalism was still alive – but only just, in Britain. A Keynesian perspective prevailed and a fashion for planning captured political sentiment for the vast majority. Hayek, Jewkes and Robbins were swept aside. Barbara Wootton, responding to Hayek in *Freedom under Planning* (1945), argued that socialism creates conditions in which 'the wise and the public spirited' would rise to power; as with Plato's 'Philosopher–Kings', they could be trusted to work wholly for the public good to administer the New Jerusalem. For the time being the pendulum of opinion stayed there, though in the same year Karl Popper, then living in New Zealand, published *The Open Society and its Enemies* (1945). Within a year Hayek and Popper had laid the intellectual foundations for a sustained attack on Socialist Society, but it was some years before much support was attracted.

Developments in Town and Country Planning

There was scarcely any break in continuity in matters regarding town and country planning between the Coalition and the Attlee government. The same issues were on the political agenda; for some time the officials were the same; and apart from the finance provisions of the Town and Country Planning Act, 1947, no particular policy was contentious. The difference between pre- and post-1945 lay simply in the political context: a socialist administration, buoyed by its nationalization and welfare state programmes and committed to a general interventionary role, would naturally see land planning and related matters of regional development, agriculture, housing and transport as central to its broad policy objectives. We shall never know how far a Conservative administration would have taken the matters inherited from the Coalition, but Labour did not shrink from the tasks it inherited.

Three matters were before Lewis Silkin, Attlee's Minister of Town and Country Planning when he was appointed in August 1945: control of land use, satellite towns and national parks. The Labour Party manifesto had contained an undertaking 'to bring forward proposals for improving the law with regard to compensation and betterment so as to secure for the future the best use of land in the public interest, including proper reservation of open spaces and the best location of industry and housing'. Nothing was said about new towns, yet in the event a New Towns Bill took precedence over the measure on compensation and betterment, which had exercised the Coalition Government from 1942.

New towns

The Abercrombie *Greater London Plan* proposed eight or ten 'new satellite towns' beyond the green belt, to accommodate 383,000 people in a massive redistribution of population. Their broad locations were: White Waltham (Berkshire); Chipping Ongar, Harlow and Margaretting (Essex); Stevenage, Redbourn and Stapleford (Herts); Meopham (Kent); and Crowhurst and Holmwood (Surrey). The whole question of the desirable machinery for satellite development was under consideration by officials from the beginning of 1944 (Cullingworth,1979). By March 1945 Stevenage was being recommended as a first new town experiment; and was before ministers to the very end of the Caretaker Government.

Silkin, though under pressure from the Town and Country Planning Association to act speedily, acknowledged that the incoming government had other priorities before it. He opted for delay and in October appointed a departmental committee, chaired by Lord Reith, to give further advice. The committee worked quickly. A first interim report, published in March 1946 (Cmd 6759), emphasized that the building of new towns would be a public sector venture requiring a government-sponsored corporation to plan and develop them. A second interim report, published in April (Cmd 6794), was largely concerned with the powers the agency should have for the acquisition of land. The final report, published in July (Cmd 6876), gave attention to the various planning principles which would govern the building of a new town, such as its size (a population of between 30,000 and 50,000 was thought desirable). As a child of its time, the final report struck a clear egalitarian note with regard to the social composition of the new urban settlements:

> if the community is to be truly balanced, so long as social classes exist, all must be represented in it. A contribution is needed from every type and class of person; the community will be poorer if all are not there, able and willing to make it. (para 22)

It was convenient for Silkin to proceed with legislation because the issue of compensation and betterment had still not been resolved and a bill would be delayed until 1947. A Satellite Towns Bill (as it was first known) could come first, in 1946, particularly as it was not expected to be controversial. Estimates of likely costs were hastily prepared and a provisional national programme drawn up with Westwood, Secretary of State for Scotland; a total of 26 new towns was envisaged – 13 for London, seven for the rest of England and six for Scotland. Meanwhile a decision had already been taken for Stevenage to be developed as a new town and land was being purchased.

The New Towns Bill was introduced in the House of Commons in April 1946, shortly after the publication of Reith's second interim report. It received an unopposed second reading; the previous minister, W. S. Morrison, gave it general support, though Lord Hinchingbrooke thought it 'frankly totalitarian in form'. At an unopposed third reading it was again denounced by Hinchingbrooke as 'a State experiment in the life and happiness of our people and in my opinion like all State experiments, it will work havoc, bitterness and grave social damage' (Cullingworth, 1979, p. 25). Royal Assent was given to the bill in August. The New Towns Act, 1946, provided for the designation of sites for new towns; the planning and building agency would be a development corporation and it was granted a range of powers for its use.

This particular story exemplifies particularly well the bi-partisan nature of much of town and country planning at this time. The state's primary role in determining where people would live, in what social mix, and in what sort of houses (rented from public authorities) was not seriously questioned. The building of a new town was simply not a fit subject for private enterprise; on this the major political parties were all agreed. Not even local authorities would be granted a role. New towns fitted very well into a centralist framework for town planning. Wasteful sprawl had characterized the unco-ordinated activities of the building industry pre-war; it was more rational and socially effective for the state to determine the distribution of its population and it was more efficient for the state to organize the huge scale of building development that would be necessary. The new towns themselves would be gracious experiments in community living, well in tune with the psychology of post-war reconstruction, while they would make an additional contribution to relieving the overcrowded conditions of London and other large cities elsewhere.

A programme of new town building was quickly begun. It started with the designation of Stevenage, though the consultation process was marked by acrimony and dispute. The designation order (made in November 1946) was challenged by the residents' protection society and the High Court found in their favour; the minister had made up his mind before the public inquiry and had therefore not considered the objections fairly. On appeal, the Court of Appeal reversed the earlier judgement and the reversal was upheld by the House of Lords.

Thereafter the actual designations were untroubled but this was not to say that the new towns programme ran at all smoothly. Policy was made on the hoof. A shopping list of possible sites in England and Wales provided a constantly changing menu of opportunity, though in Scotland the options were rather clearer due to the earlier work of the Clyde Valley Regional Planning Committee. But there were other dimensions to the policy: conformity with industrial location proposals, requirements for highway expenditure, and overall costs generally. Nonetheless by the summer of 1947 Silkin managed to get approval from Cabinet Committee for a clutch of new towns before the economic crisis of the autumn of that year obliged him to delay any further commitments for expenditure until the spring of 1948. The programme slowed down, but by 1950 fourteen new towns had been designated: eight for London, two for Scotland, two for the north-east, one for Wales and one in Northamptonshire to assist with the development of Stewart and Lloyds steelworks at Corby. With this total the programme came to an end for a number of years.

Silkin left the government after the General Election in 1950; he was replaced by Dalton, who had never been as enthusiastic about new towns as his predecessor, but in any case there were further rumbling anxieties about the scale of committed expenditure and priorities generally.

But after five years there was no disguising the extent of Silkin's achievements. In order of designation the new towns were:

Stevenage 1946	Welwyn 1948
Harlow 1947	Hatfield 1948
Hemel Hempstead 1947	Peterlee 1948
Crawley 1947	Basildon 1949
East Kilbride 1947	Bracknell 1949
Aycliffe 1947	Cwmbran 1949
Glenrothes 1948	Corby 1950

Abercrombie's new town objectives in the *Greater London Plan* had been realized, the congestion problem for Glasgow and its region had been addressed, coalfield regions in Scotland, Durham and South Wales had received an injection of new development, and arrangements were in hand for a small local authority (Corby) to cope with a massive employment expansion in its area. The actual amount of new house-building was as yet small, but a state-directed enterprise had so far attracted much praise from the professionals.

Controlling land use

Labour's 1945 election manifesto read:

> Labour believes in land nationalization and will work towards it, but as a first step the State and local authorities must have wider and speedier powers to acquire land for public purposes wherever the public interest so requires.. In this regard and for the purposes of controlling land use under town and country planning, we will provide for fair compensation; but we will also provide for a revenue for public funds from betterment.

Silkin was faced with the fact that planning powers, though extensive, were inoperable while ever local authorities shouldered the burdens of compensation and purchase and so long as the amount of compensation and the collection of betterment remained undetermined (Cullingworth, 1975). In chapter 4 we referred to the Uthwatt Report (1942) on compensation and betterment; from 1943 onwards officials had been giving further attention to it. Silkin inherited a highly technical issue from which there was no escape; a scheme had to be devised whereby the state would benefit from the development rights in land.

The technical details of a compensation and betterment scheme, which inevitably involved the wider arrangements for the control of land use, were handed over to a committee of officials chaired by Sir

Geoffrey Whiskard of the Ministry of Town and Country Planning. The committee prepared three reports and it was early 1947 before the Town and Country Planning Bill began its passage through Parliament. It had begun as a bill to deal primarily with the recommendations of Uthwatt, but it ended as a comprehensive measure which provided the machinery for national land use planning.

Enacted in August 1947 it came into operation on 1 July 1948. Its financial provisions ensured that when land was developed, the increase in its value resulting from the granting of planning permission was secured for the community by the imposition of a development charge, which would be assessed and collected by a Central Land Board. This recoupment of betterment was in effect the nationalization of appreciating land values, released when development was approved by a local council. The corollary was that any refusal of permission to develop did not give any entitlement to compensation, because the development value had been vested in the state. When compensation was paid (to owners whose land was depreciated by restrictions imposed by the act) payments would be made from a sum of £300 million which was set aside for the purpose.

The act introduced a new development plan system in succession to that based pre-war planning schemes. The development plan, the preparation of which was obligatory and no longer permissive as had been the case under the former legislation, was intended to outline a basic framework of future land use against which development proposals would be considered. It was expected that development plans would cover the whole country within a few years. The act also ensured that, with certain technical exceptions, and with the exclusion of agriculture and forestry operations, all development was made subject to the permission of the local planning authority. The number of authorities with planning powers was substantially reduced: from 1,441 to 145, they were simply the counties and the county boroughs. The former situation whereby *all* local authorities (including urban and rural districts) exercised planning powers was removed.

There was cross-party support for further planning legislation, but there was disagreement on the form it should take. Opposition focused on the financial provisions. As in 1944, the threat to private property and the nationalization of land values established a political divide. As we shall see in chapter 7, the compensation and betterment scheme was modified by the Conservatives after they were returned to power and was ultimately abolished, but a later variation was twice reintroduced under Labour. Consensus on this matter proved quite impossible. But the other essentials of the1947 Act have largely been unchallenged and have provided the basis for the post-war system of land planning control. The principle that land ownership alone confers no right to develop has remained: development can only take place if planning permission has been granted – by a local council popularly elected by the people, or by the minister (or today, the Secretary of State) on appeal. The system remains an obligatory one, local planning authorities bound by law as a statutory duty to prepare their development plans. On these points the post-war system has registered a marked continuity.

National parks

We noted in chapter 5 that in May 1945 the Minister of Town and Country Planning failed in his attempt to use the report by John Dower to set up a Preparatory Commission on National Parks. Dower's work became instead a personal report to the minister which led to the setting up of a committee to give further advice. This put the situation for England and Wales on a similar basis to that for Scotland where a further committee followed the work of the Scottish National Parks Survey Committee. For England and Wales the minister appointed Sir Arthur Hobhouse to chair an appropriate committee; in Scotland the Secretary of State asked Sir Douglas Ramsay to continue as chair of a second advisory committee (Cherry, 1975).

The Attlee government saw no need to change direction. Silkin regarded national parks as priority, but they had to follow after legislation on new towns and town and country planning. Hobhouse reported in 1947 (Cmd 7121), recommending 12 national parks and an additional 52 'conservation areas' of high landscape quality; a National Parks Commission was proposed with Park Committees at the local level. Of Dower's list of ten, Hobhouse omitted one and added three. For Scotland, Ramsay proposed five national parks, a Commission and Park Committees (Cmd 7235).

Having just established the new land-use control system, operated through a much smaller number of local planning authorities, it was now arguable whether a separate commission was really necessary to look after areas of scenic beauty. It was feared that an independent commission might compete with the ministry in matters of country planning. Meanwhile the Treasury was anxious about the financial implications of the commission's work, and there were unresolved conflicts over the degrees of central as opposed to local control. But Silkin proceeded, introducing his bill in March. At the second reading he described it as 'a people's charter for the open air, for the hikers and the ramblers, for everyone who likes to get out into the open air and enjoy the countryside' (Cherry, 1975, p. 105). There was no serious opposition, indeed much cross-party support and the National Parks and Access to Countryside Act 1949 received the Royal Assent in December.

It was always assumed that a Scottish bill would follow at once. In fact Woodburn, the Secretary of State, showed less enthusiasm than Silkin, and the Scottish Office in 1950 decided to prepare no bill at that time. In 1951 there was a change of government and the matter lapsed.

Meanwhile there were related matters of importance. From July 1946 Sir Arthur Hobhouse was also chairing a Special Committee on Footpaths and Access; his recommendation (Cmd 7207) for a complete survey of all rights of way was incorporated into the 1949 Act. More importantly Sir Julian Huxley was chairing the Wildlife Conservation Special Committee, an offshoot of the main Hobhouse Committee. From this source stemmed the setting up of the Nature Conservancy (Sheail, 1976). National parks and nature conservation went their separate ways, the former remaining the responsibility of the Minister of Town and Country Planning, the latter the province of the Lord President of the Council who represented scientific concerns in the Cabinet. The subsequent tortured history of the Conservancy is described in Cherry and Rogers (1996).

Planning-related Initiatives

The Minister of Town and Country Planning had responsibility for new towns, the control of land use and national parks, and his department gave the new planning authorities a kit of technical tools for the professional job in hand (plot ratios, daylight indicators, parking standards etc.), as published in *The Redevelopment of Central Areas* (Ministry of Town and Country Planning, 1947). But other issues which affected the development of land were in the remit of other ministers: the President of the Board of Trade and the Ministers of Agriculture, Health (for housing) and Transport.

Industrial location

The Attlee government used the Distribution of Industry Act, 1945, piloted by Dalton in the final months of the Coalition, and made it the foundation of British regional policy post-war (McCrone, 1969). The pre-war Special Areas were redefined and renamed Development Areas; they were more extensive and included a greater population – 6.5 million, compared with 4 million pre-war. These were the areas which had experienced the most severe economic hardships between the wars, and the act targeted them for special help. The Board of Trade was empowered to build factories, give grants or loans, provide infrastructure for development and reclaim derelict land. An important additional power was introduced in the Town and Country Planning Act, 1947 – the Industrial Development Certificate, which replaced the building license system introduced during the war. Before development could proceed, the certificate (IDC) was necessary for industrial development of more than 5,000 sq. ft. In pursuance of regional policy to aid the disadvantaged regions 'carrot and stick' measures were employed – inducements to develop in those regions which would benefit from economic regeneration, and refusal of permission (i.e. the non issue of the IDC) to develop in areas already economically buoyant. In the interests of a nationally balanced distribution of industrial development, the state sought to override the operation of regional labour markets in an attempt to redress the balance between favoured and unfavoured parts of the country.

To begin with, the development areas were South Wales, the north-east, West Cumberland and West-Central Scotland with an outlier in Dundee. The act permitted flexibility in its geographical coverage and in 1946 Wrexham and Wigan-St Helens were added to the list. In 1948 north-east Lancashire, Merseyside and Scottish blackspots (Dingwall and Inverness for the Highlands) were also added. This list was not changed until 1958 – a testimony to continuity. Northern Ireland received its own inducements administered by the Provincial Government.

Between 1945 and 1947 circumstances were conducive to a successful regional policy. Unemployment had fallen to very low levels during the war and rates remained low; the traditional industries in the Special Areas had worked flat out and trade remained reasonably buoyant; former munitions factories were being converted; and there was an unusual opportunity for securing some redistribution of economic activity. But in the financial crisis of 1947 the building of 'advance' factories stopped and over time pressure was relaxed on industrialists to locate in development areas. This was due not so much to political opposition to regional policy in principle, nor to any hint of failure in application, rather a realization that regional unemployment was no longer the problem it once had been.

Agriculture

We saw in chapter 3 that the government's promise to the farming community after the Great War was broken (in 1921). By contrast, the promise after 1945 was kept (Cherry and Rogers, 1996). War-time encouragements to increased production found their way into post-war legislation, and policies were pursued which guaranteed prices at levels negotiated annually between government and leaders of the farming industry.

The Hill Farming Act, 1946, introduced a system of grants to improve farming in upland areas and to provide infrastructure in the form of electricity and roads. Farming efficiency country-wide was encouraged through Advisory Services. But it was the Agriculture Act, 1947, which was the critical measure for the post-war period, creating a mechanism for guaranteeing prices for major agricultural products. The Agricultural Holdings Act, 1948, allowed tenant farmers to have a lifelong tenancy; this was designed to give tenants the confidence to invest capital in new farming practices.

The 1947 Act gave stability and self-sufficiency to the farming industry; better incomes and living conditions for the labour force; and low food prices (from subsidies stemming from the taxpayer) for the nation. There would be clear continuity of all these features, together with enhanced efficiency in production based on the application of science and technology, over the next quarter of a century. The state underpinned a veritable revolution; the conditions obtaining between the wars were banished, and apart from occasional rumblings about 'feather-bedded' farmers there was no political mood to change the new arrangements.

Quite apart from the assistance given to the farming industry, the 1947 Act addressed the issues examined in the Scott Report (1942). It provided the conditions whereby the proper maintenance of the countryside would be secured by reason of a prosperous economy, and local communities rescued from their previous poor living standards. This at least was Scott's argument (refuted by Dennison in a Minority Report) and for some years it seemed to work that way. As we shall see in chapter 7, as the years went on other factors intervened and extensive subsidy arrangements only served to produce other problems.

In the meantime, however, from the point of view of land-use planning, the Agriculture Act and the Town and Country Planning Act of the same year were complementary. The latter dealt in effect primarily with control of land use in urban areas; the former gave primacy to the countryside for agriculture. Planning policy was (and has remained) based on effecting a clear distinction between town and country; sprawl had to be avoided. The countryside was a farmed environment; its landscape would thereby be protected; and Development Plans would ensure that towns and cities were contained within tight boundaries. The neatness of the arrangement would ultimately break down, but the post-war planning objectives had been established.

Housing

There was an uncomfortable split between the ministries of Town and Country Planning, and Health, regarding the planning of residential neighbourhoods. The responsibilities of the former extended to the broader aspects of layout; while the interests of the latter concerned the selection of housing sites, the layout, design and equipment of dwellings, and standards of accommodation. In the *Manual* of 1944 the Ministry of Health had advised on the provision of three-bedroomed two-storey houses. In the *Housing Manual*, 1949, the ministry advised on a greater variety of house types. The standard size of all dwellings was increased: 900–950 sq. ft. for three-bedroomed dwellings as opposed to 800–900 sq. ft. in the 1944 *Manual*. Further advice was given on site planning and the grouping of buildings in a harmonious landscape setting. Standards of internal accommodation were prescribed to the smallest detail. As with Tudor Walters in 1918, the state put forward a national house style in design and layout – a new vernacular architecture eminently suitable for standard components and layouts set by cost targets.

Transport

A committee set up by the Ministry of War Transport in April 1943 reported in 1946. Its recommendations formed the basis of the post-war design and layout of roads in built-up areas. It established norms for the country's urban road pattern, confirming the radial and the ring in the form of a spider's web, advocated by Alker Tripp (1942) and shown by Abercrombie in his *Greater London Plan* as the model to emulate. It also provided guidelines for local authorities for road design, down to the detail of road intersections and pedestrian crossings.

Alfred Barnes, Minister of Transport, announced a ten-year national road plan in 1946 (Starkie, 1982). There would be three phases. During the first two years emphasis would be placed on the backlog of road maintenance. The next three years would tackle some major works, including some new roads for the Development Areas and certain improvements to relieve city traffic congestion. The last five years would see a comprehensive reconstruction of the country's principal national routes, for the most part constructed as motorways, roughly 800 miles in total length. Complementing the motorways was a series of improved general purpose highways radiating out of London, the longest being the Great North Road. Financial restrictions soon led to the abandonment of that expenditure and the country waited for a further eleven years before a national road building programme was once more announced – intriguingly very similar to its predecessor.

It is impossible to underestimate the importance of the period 1945–51 in the twentieth-century history of town and country planning. It was in these years that the hopes of the pre-war enthusiasts were met, and when a Cinderella profession was propelled into post-war reality with legislative backing and a statutory system within which to act. The period was a bridge, almost literally, in the middle of the century, between two very different experiences: previously town planning had been largely a matter for enthusiastic amateurs, a handful of consultants, and the pressure of a garden city lobby; afterwards it became institutionalized and the concern of bureaucrats and professionals in the corridors of local government power. This is a huge over-simplification but there is sufficient truth in the point to justify making it.

The Attlee administrations (and Silkin in particular) put in place the fundamental elements of the post-war planning system. With only a few exceptions they have proved remarkably robust. The machinery was established by a government which set out with an interventionary programme of social and economic measures in which an enlarged role for town planning fell naturally into place. The new activity had fertile soil in which to grow and the political consensus ensured no years of drought. War-time legislation was readily built upon and new statutory machinery was provided effortlessly. By the time of a change of government the new framework was firmly set and, with the exception of the financial provisions of the 1947 Act, continuity was readily secured. Even the formerly miniscule town planning profession found it possible to cope, surviving an official inquiry chaired by Sir George Schuster (1950) into the education and qualifications of planners, the findings of which helped the Town Planning Institute in its search for independence from the three professions out of which it had been born (architecture, engineering and surveying). The stage was set for a bright post-war future.

But Attlee's policies received a varied response. Some argued that Labour's policies were certainly radical when seen in today's terms, but they are consensual now; they did not take the government beyond what was already in place. Correlli Barnett for instance takes a somewhat hostile view of the period for constraining 'British dreams and British realities'. His book *The Lost Victory*, for example, seeks to explain how it was that between the ending of the Second World War and the outbreak of the Korean War Britain let slip a unique and irrecoverable opportunity to remake herself as an industrial country while her rivals were still crippled by defeat and occupation.

Another of Barnett's books, *The Collapse of British Power* (1972), traces the resulting diplomatic, strategic and financial dilemmas from the 1920s up to the nemesis of 1941–2. It argued that one root cause of this débâcle lay in the nature of the British governing elite between the wars. It accused this elite, the small-'l' liberal product of a late-Victorian upbringing, of seeing international relations too much in terms of romantic ideals and moral purpose, too little in power and strategic calculation. *The Audit of War* (1986, the second in the series) showed that, behind the deceptive façade of victory, and the propaganda of the 1960s and 1970s, the ideals were already present in war-time; in short the book made special reference to the British failure for a century adequately to educate and train the nation for industrial success. It was this yearning that was encouraged and given shape by just the small-'l' liberal idealists, these evangelists of the 'Brave New World' of the welfare state.

The Lost Victory projects the major thesis of *The Collapse of British Power*: that of global overstretch – political, strategic and financial. It describes how, eagerly taken up by the Labour government in 1945, it condemned Britain to remain a third-rate world power, and one whose economy was kept going by borrowed dollars. Correlli shows 'that British total strategy between 1945 and 1950 was shaped less by the realities of Britain's postwar plight than by the nation's dreams and illusions' (1995, p. xiii).

7 State Planning in Operation

In this chapter we review a pattern of events covering nearly a quarter of a century, during which time the state maintained a prominent interventionary role in economic and social affairs. Keynesian orthodoxy was applied to the management of the economy, and the objectives of welfarism were extended to many quarters of British social life. The beginning and end dates of the period concerned are indicated by the general elections and changes of government in 1951 and 1974, but the dates in themselves are not all that important. The real significance of the period lies in its internal coherence and the broadly common way in which successive governments, Conservative and Labour, dealt with economic and social affairs between the beginning of the 1950s and the mid-1970s. Rival ideologies of state collectivism and the market were played down; conformity to the assumptions of a common mind-set prevailed; and pragmatism governed responses to external circumstances.

At the outset a Conservative administration took over the planning machinery set up during the Attlee years, while relaxing the burden of controls and encouraging the private sector in key areas. By the beginning of the 1960s the Conservatives found it necessary to resume certain planning initiatives, and add to others. These were swept into greatly strengthened planning programmes when Labour returned to office in 1964. The 1960s saw a considerable revival of planning after the relative quietude of the 1950s. Between 1970 and 1974 another Conservative administration, in spite of early indications that it might not maintain the broad consensus, did in fact do so, though the planning enthusiasm of the mid-1960s had by now gone. However, the post-war settlement was on the point of breaking down and during the second half of the 1970s it finally dissolved.

We begin with a reminder of the ideological consensus concerning the role of the state during this period. We then sketch the political chronology from 1951 to 1974 in economic and social affairs. Thirdly, we consider the operation of town planning and related matters during this time.

The Ideological Consensus

Between 1945 and 1951 political opinion across the parties converged on Keynesian orthodoxy. We might recall its tenets. Keynes' analysis of the inherent instability of industrial accumulation led him, in a liberal collectivist perspective, to advocate limited forms of regulatory state intervention, while leaving the market-based capitalistic structure of the economy intact. This enabled both major political parties to assimilate his recommendations within their own policy positions (Martin, 1989).

The objective of Keynesian state intervention was neither large-scale public ownership of industry nor the planned direction of economic development. Rather it was the intermittent use of expansionary fiscal measures and investment by the public sector in infrastructural schemes so that occasional counter-cyclical nudges might be applied when the economy failed to provide full employment. As an example, regional policy was Keynesian inspired: the problem was seen not as one of productive capacity but rather as localized employment arising from spatially maldistributed demand, which would be solved by a redistribution from one part of the country to another, such as from London and the Home Counties to the north-east or Scotland.

In short, Keynes advocated government intervention to make the market work more efficiently. The technique for this was 'demand management'. When the economy slowed down, output fell and unemployment rose, the economy would be stimulated by a combination of increases in public expenditure, an expansion of private consumption through tax cuts and the easing of credit controls. If necessary, governments would adopt the principle of deficit financing – the spending of more of their income and meeting the difference by borrowing or expanding the money supply. Alternatively, when the economy overheated, with symptoms of rising inflation, shortages of labour and higher imports, the policy would be reversed. Demand would be cut by reductions in public spending, increases in taxes and credit restrictions. Keynesian economics therefore rested mainly on fiscal policy, involving taxation, public expenditure and demand management. The assumption was that normal market forces would take care of the supply side, including investment, the take-up of new technology, measures to increase productivity and the supply of an appropriately skilled workforce (Farnham and McVicar, 1982).

Both major political parties were attracted to forms of indicative planning implicit in Keynes' approach. It implied a dialogue between government and industry, both public and private, so that a framework could be established within which both government policy and company decisions could be made. In 1951 the Conservatives were confident that the 'middle way', as outlined by Macmillan in 1938, would bring prosperity and contentment, and like the Attlee government before them, they assumed that their task was the successful management of the economy in order to maintain full employment and optimize the use of national resources. Partnership between government, industry and labour, and a plan for the continued recovery of Britain after the war, seemed axiomatic. Manifesto slogans in 1955 and 1959 reveal this party perspective particularly well: 'Invest in Success' (1955) and 'Conservatives give you a better standard of living – Don't let Labour ruin it' (1959) (Letwin, 1992). In 1964 Labour persuaded an electorate that they would manage the economy more successfully and bring about a growth in national prosperity through planning and the application of scientific technology. Emphases may have been different, but the ideology was the same. The administration which followed, under Edward Heath, was scarcely dissimilar.

By 1951 some 20 per cent of Britain's industry and commerce was in the hands of the state, and the remainder, though privately owned, was subject to a variety of government rules and regulations. As we shall see, Churchill's government in 1951 made no great move to change this inheritance. Continuity of policy was almost assured when some very powerful officials served successive administrations. Sir Ernest Bridges was head of the civil service from 1945 to 1956 and Sir Norman Brook was secretary of the Cabinet from 1947 to 1962. Lord Roberthall served as chief economic adviser to both Labour and Conservative Chancellors of the Exchequer between 1947 and 1961 (Kavanagh and Morris, 1989).

Yet changes in emphasis did take place. For much of the 1950s there was a marked diminution in enthusiasm for some of the inherited institutional arrangements that Labour had introduced (Seldon, 1981). An early indication was the fate of the Economic Planning Board within the Treasury. Set up in 1947 to promote contact between government and the private sector, it had declined in importance even by 1951. After that it was largely ineffectual and withered away by the end of the decade. Another example of change concerned the control of raw materials. The Labour government had taken the decision that control should be entrusted to those departments responsible for each particular industry. Accordingly, in the case of cotton, it was decided that the bulk purchase and distribution of raw cotton should be given to a non-departmental body, the Raw Cotton Commission. A break from this central mechanism occurred when the Conservatives reopened the Liverpool Cotton Exchange and removed restrictive controls. Finally the Ministry of Materials was wound up in 1954, giving encouragement to enterprise in markets which had for many years been under a system of state control.

The general disposition of the Conservative governments in the 1950s was to adhere to the broad principles of Keynesian demand management and the welfare state measures, while pragmatically 'fine tuning' the various instruments of planning, taken over from the Attlee years as and when the situation demanded. The downgrading of the notion of detailed central planning continued when, in conditions of full employment, the main emphasis of the Ministry of Labour and National Service shifted to industrial relations. Under a highly successful minister, Sir Walter Monckton, its role moved to conciliation in the settlement of disputes. On another front, to all intents and purposes, regional planning was quietly shelved. The regional offices of the old Ministry of Town and Country Planning were closed, and while unemployment remained low in the former hard-hit regions, regional economic policy was accorded a low priority.

During the 1950s, then, many of the planning instruments of central control were removed or given diminished status. Peter Thorneycroft as President of the Board of Trade (1951–7) proclaimed a new objective: that it was not the task of government to regulate or intervene in industry, rather to lay down the ground rules within which industry might make its decisions. As we shall see, over the next twenty years public policy would vacillate around this point of principle, and Thorneycroft's liberalism was not maintained for long. Around the beginning of the 1960s the Conservatives were sucked into a range of centralist planning initiatives in response to deteriorating economic situations, and to cope with new pressures thrust upon them. Arrangements associated with the post-war collectivist state, dormant or ineffective for some time, were reactivated. What the Conservatives redeployed, Labour maintained and strengthened, as far as circumstances permitted, after 1964. Finally, a further return of the Conservatives under Heath in 1970 changed remarkably little.

Opposition to the dominant collectivist stance was limited. Economic liberals were thin on the ground; Hayek left Britain for the University of Chicago in 1950 and Robbins was no longer prominent in the movement to which he had subscribed. Two 'ginger groups', however, emerged within the Conservative Party, which developed a distinctly anti-socialist philosophy: the One Nation Group (founded in 1950) and the Bow Group (1951). Members of the former, particularly Enoch Powell, took the lead in exploring new approaches. They repeatedly contrasted the rigidity of socialism with the flexibility of the market and pointed to the mistakes made by central planning. Powell emerged as the most prominent economic liberal in the new post-war generation of Conservative MPs (Cockett, 1994). He resigned with Chancellor Thorneycroft and the rest of the Treasury team in January 1958 in protest against what they saw as excessive public expenditure by Macmillan's government. In time, however, he was regarded by many in his party as a dangerous maverick. After his 'Rivers of Blood' speech against immigration in 1968 his views on other issues were increasingly ignored and his brand of economic liberalism was sullied.

Meanwhile, within the Labour Party there were signs of intellectual movement away from previous positions. Anthony Crosland (1956) in *The Future of Socialism* dismissed the need for wholesale nationalization. He argued that the mixed economy under Keynesian management could secure social justice and equality by the reallocation of resources and wealth, governed by judicious public spending. This 'revisionist social- ism' later coloured the approach of Harold Wilson's governments.

Powell's views received strong support from the Institute of Economic Affairs. Founded in November 1955, the IEA became one of the main bodies through which the post-war consensus was attacked and an almost dormant philosophy reinvigorated. Directed by Ralph Harris and with Arthur Seldon as editor, it modelled itself on the Fabians and the early socialists by treading a path of long-term intellectual persuasion. For many years in the political wilderness, it yet developed a coherent body of free-market ideas, applicable to all areas of the economy. It acquired the reputation of advocating policies then held as unthinkable: freeing the exchange rate, removing rent controls, charges on pollution, vouchers for education, contracting out and charging for public services. It took twenty years for economic liberalism seriously to penetrate Conservative thinking to the extent of breaking the post-war consensus, but in the conversion process the IEA's role was remarkable. As early as 1968 its influence was noted by the Fabians: in the Society's Tract 387, *The New Right: a critique*, David Collard labelled the IEA's philosophy the 'New Right' and the term stuck. The Institute's ultimate achievement was to create a public platform in Britain for the rehabilitation of Hayek and the introduction of the American guru Milton Friedman. The consequences of this would be seen after 1974.

The Sequence of Events

The period 1951–74 shows a consistency of approach towards economic and social matters by governments of different persuasion. The post-war consensus held though there were variations of enthusiasm for planning and state intervention. General elections in 1955, 1959, 1964, 1966 and 1970 provide some natural breaks within the period, and the stance of Conservative administrations from 1951 to 1964 and from 1970 to 1974 can be distinguished from that of the Labour administrations between 1964 and 1970. Overall, however, there was a continuity of purpose in observing the orthodoxy of economic management and in pursuing the objectives of the welfare state laid down both during the war and up to 1951. As we examine in the next section, the period provided conditions which were remarkably conducive to the furtherance of town planning. But before we describe the development of this activity, and its burgeoning of influence during this time, we must provide the background context of political change.

The 1950s have been judged a period of wasted opportunities and failed leadership (Hennessy and Seldon, 1987). In 1951 the Conservatives won with an overall majority of 17 but Churchill's return to power marked no break, rather a remarkable continuity from the past. The ending of controls and rationing continued. The iron and steel industry was returned to private ownership (in line with manifesto promises), but Richard Thomas and Baldwin's [a steel company] in South Wales remained under public ownership and an Iron and Steel Board was set up to supervise investment in the industry. Road transport was also denationalized, but the Transport Commission was allowed to keep much of its long-distance lorry fleet. There was little change elsewhere: aid for industries and depressed areas remained and the support system for farmers was retained. There was no legislation on industrial relations and little change in education or social policy. Finance remained the restraint that Attlee's government experienced. The one area of departure was the shift of resources to housing; Macmillan, as the incoming Minister of Housing and Local Government, meeting the pledge to build 300,000 houses per year. By the mid-1950s a start was made on a massive slum-clearance programme.

An interesting story unfolded during the Churchill government which illustrated the strength of public feeling against public acquisition of land and support for the sanctity of private property: this was the Crichel Down affair. In 1937 the Air Ministry compulsorily acquired some land near Crichel Down in Dorset as an experimental bomb site. In 1950 the ministry decided that it had no further use for the land. In normal circumstances it would have been offered back for re-purchase to the original owners or their heirs, but in this case the Ministry of Agriculture intervened and decided that since the land was already Crown Property, it would like to retain it. The initial decision in favour of retention was taken by the Labour minister, Tom Williams, but his Conservative successor continued to defend it. An outcry ensued. An enquiry under a QC found against the ministry and in favour of the daughter of the original owner. The enquiry report was sharply critical of a number of named civil servants and, under the doctrine of ministerial responsibility, Sir Thomas Dugdale resigned. His two junior ministers Richard Nugent and Lord Carrington offered resignation but Churchill refused to accept their offer.

In the early spring of 1955 Churchill resigned, to be succeeded by Anthony Eden, for long the heir-apparent. In the May general election the Conservatives had an overall majority of 58 (the Conservatives had 344 seats and Labour 277). Eden's government was bedevilled by the ill-fated Suez adventure in 1956 and by his own ill-health. He resigned in January 1957 and was succeeded by Macmillan, who, when he went to the country in 1959, was returned with a 100-seat majority. Labour at this time was in internal disarray over Clause IV of the party's constitution and nuclear disarmament.

A surge in consumer credit did much to ensure Macmillan's success. The outward shape of British life began to change, with a widening array of consumer goods an indicator of rising prosperity. But there were other portents of change, including race riots in the summer of 1958 at Nottingham and Notting Hill, London, which would lead to heavy state involvement in immigration and social policies; also the beginnings of increases in regional unemployment in the winter of 1958/59 which reawakened regional policy questions. A national motorway programme at last got underway, with the opening of the Preston bypass, to meet the accelerating increase in the number of annual car registrations.

Macmillan's triumph was short-lived. The economic boom was not sustained and the national mood quickly changed. Michael Shanks (1961) caught the sense that Britain was lagging behind European rivals and had become a 'stagnant society'. A major sterling crisis developed in 1961 as imports surged and a dangerous trade deficit resulted; Chancellor Selwyn Lloyd introduced an emergency budget in July. The 'pay pause' became part of 'stop-go' policies. Two new institutions designed to plan for steady economic growth were announced: the National Economic Development Council (a forum of government, unions and employees for considering ways of promoting faster economic growth) and the National Incomes Commission. The Macmillan government proved fully capable of pursuing state *dirigisme* in total commitment to the post-war consensus. Macmillan successfully converted his Party to indicative economic planning and sought to persuade the unions of the need for incomes policies.

An exceptionally cold winter in 1963 led to widespread lay-offs, and the unemployment figure peaked at 900,000 in the February of that year, the highest figure since the (equally severe) winter of 1947. Long-term regional development once again became fashionable with plans announced for Central Scotland and the North East. The Board of Trade was reorganized to become the Ministry for Industry, Trade and Regional Development. Strategic planning returned to the national agenda in a big way, with a resumption of a new towns programme to supplement the local authority housing drive which was then in full swing, and the expansion of the motorway network. Attention was given to the future of the country's railway system; in 1963 the Beeching report, *The Reshaping of British Railways*, proposed to cut uneconomic branch lines in an attempt to reduce the BR deficit. University expansion was already underway; Sussex opened in 1961 and authority was given for new universities in York, East Anglia, Essex. Kent, Lancaster and Warwick. The Royal Commission on Higher Education (1961–3), chaired by Lionel Robbins, was accepted by government; containing a set of recommendations for escalated state involvement and expenditure, the report 'would have been anathema to most of his former Mont Pelerin colleagues' (Cockett, 1994, p. 121).

The turning point came at the Labour Party Conference at Scarborough in 1963 (Ben Pimlott, 1992). Wilson's speech was 'a commitment to science as the agent of social change. The Party Leader argued that the planning of science was the essence of modern socialism' (p. 302). It called for a revolution in education – the eleven plus would go and there would be a dramatic expansion of universities. The Ministry of Science would sponsor research, which would be lined to planning. Through planning, there would be government-fostered new industries. There would be an uncompromisingly *dirigiste* theme: Labour would use state power to modernize industry, plan the economy and end privileges; it advocated government intervention in almost every aspect of the nation's economic life. Planning was a central directorate to a new administration based on science, statistics, professionalism and purpose. Labour's 1963 conference was a triumph; the Conservative one a shambles – Macmillan absent, in hospital because of a prostate operation, and the government fatally wounded by the Profumo affair.

During this period the government's record on the home front appeared satisfactory: between 1959 and 1964 the economy grew by an average of 3.8 per cent per year, unemployment averaged 1.8 per cent, inflation stood at 3 per cent and investment in manufacturing industry rose by 26 per cent. But, relatively, Britain fell behind. In the same period while the British economy grew in real terms by 18 per cent, other equivalent figures were: Belgium 29 per cent, Netherlands 31 per cent, France, West Germany and Italy 32 per cent and Japan 89 per cent. The dollar value of the British exports grew by 33 per cent, but the performance of France was 59 per cent, Netherlands 61 per cent, West Germany 62 per cent, Japan 93 per cent and Italy 104 per cent. Another indicator was the British share in the value of world exports of manufactured goods: standing at 25.5 per cent in 1950 it was 16.5 per cent in 1960 and had fallen to 13.9 per cent in 1965 (Pinto-Duschinsky, 1987). While the national standard of living continued a steady rise, with money channelled into consumer spending, housing and social services, investment required for industrial modernization failed to keep pace.

Meanwhile the Labour Party, under a new leader, Harold Wilson, after Gaitskell's death, prepared policies for economic expansion derived from planning; the modernization of the economic infrastructure and new programmes which required large increases in public expenditure would be paid for from the fruits of sustained economic growth. Macmillan's illness in 1963 meant a change of leader; disclaiming his peerage, Alec Douglas Home, became prime minister. But, in a general mood of discontent, he lost the general election of October 1964, though it was a close-run thing, Wilson gaining a four-seat majority overall.

Wilson ushered in a period in which there was a revived faith in central planning. The efficacy of government economic intervention would arrest decline and Britain would recover from being the sick man of Europe. Electorate expectation of success led to his paper-thin majority being turned into a comfortable margin in 1966.

Wilson's grand plans were presented in 1964 from the point of view not of doctrinaire socialism but as a popular party of the Left. His ideological baggage was remarkably unspecific. Labour's manifesto undertook to re-nationalize iron and steel (which it proceeded to do in 1966) and also to reorganize the country's water supplies (on which no action was taken). Policies for industrial investment and productivity were enabling measures, rather than designed to promote public ownership. An Industrial Reorganization Corporation was established in 1966 to stimulate industrial mergers. The Selective Employment Tax was introduced to influence the distribution of employment. The Shipbuilding Industry Act, 1967, aimed to rationalize shipbuilding. The Industrial Expansion Act, 1968, enabled government to buy shares in private industry, its purpose being to provide risk capital for research and development.

The early Wilson years marked a huge expansion in public sector investment; they were the high-watermark of a period from the late 1950s to the late 1960s when public expenditure surged (broadly speaking a period from 1957 when Macmillan became prime minister to 1967 when Roy Jenkins became Chancellor and imposed a new regime of austerity). The New Towns programme, higher education, roads (both urban improvements and motorways), and hospital building all absorbed government spending at historically high levels. To be fair, Wilson inherited general expectations of the probability of expanding public expenditure. In 1963 the newly established Public Expenditure Survey Committee had projected real annual average increases of 4.1 per cent to 1967–8, the spending rising in line with growth in output. In fact public spending grew faster than output, both in central and local government.

The setting up of a Ministry of Technology and the Department of Economic Affairs, and the installation of Regional Economic Planning Councils, indicated the seriousness of the intent to engage in economic policy. 'Planning' would be a distinctive approach, as seen in George Brown's National Plan (1965). This had three prongs: an industrial policy to boost investment and productivity, an incomes policy to hold wages in line, and an array of new and ambitious social programmes financed from the anticipated increase in national production. The plan aimed to secure a 25 per cent increase in real gross domestic product between 1964 and 1970, equivalent to an increase of 3.8 per cent per annum. Spending on trade and industry surged; by the end of the decade subsidies to private industry amounted to nearly £1 billion per year, equivalent to more than 6 per cent of central government expenditure. But this was overreaching national capacity. The increase in GDP turned out to be 14 per cent (not 25 per cent as anticipated), equivalent to 2.2 per cent per annum. The National Plan was abandoned and the Department of Economic Affairs itself was wound up in 1969. The failure of indicative planning was followed by a return to economic orthodoxy. The period 1967–9 was one of deflation using traditional Keynesian techniques: the devaluation of the pound and an incomes policy operated through the National Board of Prices and Incomes. The expectations in the government's capacity to manage economic growth simply dissolved.

There was no machinery in central government to manage the style of economic planning that had been envisaged. In particular the control of public expenditure proved increasingly difficult. Yet the structure of the corporatist state flourished. The minutiae of national life was investigated by the National Board of Prices and Incomes. Harold Wilson (1971) praised the 'fearless' reports of its chairman, Sir Aubrey Jones, but a subsequent critic has ridiculed its activities: 'The Board pronounced on the marketing of soap powder, the productivity of baking and of brewing, the working practices of busmen employed by the Corporation of Dundee, the fees of solicitors and architects, the need for overtime in banks, and, altogether, 170 similarly arcane matters' (Jenkins, 1987, p. 11). Elsewhere there were institutional creations of grandeur, as in the setting up of the vast Department of Health and Social Security, and proposals for local government reform in England and Wales (the Royal Commission chaired by Redcliffe-Maud), which would have created new large unitary authorities, met with support. Local government expanded as professional ambitions soared; social work received a fillip after the Seebohm Report (1968) on Local Authority and Allied Personal Services, and sport, leisure and tourism received increased attention. The setting up of the Ombudsman, the Parliamentary Commissioner for Administration, and the introduction of public participation into town planning also enlarged the state's role in national affairs.

Wilson went to the country in 1970 in a general election which he expected to win. But the Conservatives under Edward Heath were returned to office. Leader since 1965, he had developed three themes: to secure a greater importance for private enterprise, a reform of the welfare state and Britain's entry into the Common Market. There was every impression of a decisive shift being made away from the 'middle way' when, to plan for the coming election, the Shadow Cabinet met in conference at the Selsdon Park Hotel, Croydon (Letwin, 1992). Certainly, on election, the Heath government appeared to challenge the post-war consensus with the promise of trade union reform, a reduction in state intervention in the economy, avoidance of a formal prices and incomes policy, cuts in public spending and a move to greater selectivity in welfare (Hennessy and Seldon, 1987).

The intention to stand aside from industrial matters was honoured when the travel firm, Thomas Cook, and the state-owned brewery houses in Scotland and Carlisle (a throw back to the First World War) were denationalized. The Prices and Incomes Board was dismantled. The regional employment premium was phased out and Benn's Industrial Reorganization Corporation was abolished. But the nationalized status of the steel industry was accepted and policy reversals were soon apparent. Heath had promised less government and of a better quality, but the government's *dirigisme* was reasserted. Beset by growing inflation, strikes, rising wages and falling productivity there was no stomach for cutting public expenditure. Ailing enterprises were rescued: when the Rolls Royce company fell and attempts to rescue it failed, the aero engines division was nationalized in 1971. Later that year the collapse of the Upper Clyde Shipbuilders led to restoration of massive government subsidies. In 1972 the Industry Act gave the new Department of Trade and Industry extensive power to support industrial projects with cash injections. Later that year legislation empowered government to freeze pay, prices and dividends. As a Conservative MP, (Bruce-Gardyne, 1974), would later write 'Whatever happened to the quiet revolution?'

Edward Heath's managerialist instincts were well exemplified by the setting up of the Central Policy Review Staff (CPRS, the 'Think Tank') in 1971 (Blackstone and Plowden, 1988). The White Paper, *The Reorganisation of Central Government*, was published in October 1970. Proposing a major reorganization of the machinery of central government, it promised less but better government, improved analysis, greater clarity about objectives, priorities and strategy. The means to these ends included the merging of government departments into new, larger units, new ways of analysing government expenditure programmes, and a new centrally located review staff – 'a small multidisciplinary staff in the Cabinet Office', in the words of the White Paper. The CPRS had in fact been long in gestation, dating from the time Lloyd George succeeded Asquith as Prime Minister in 1916. Temporary huts in the garden of No 10 (dubbed a 'garden suburb') formed the accommodation for an embryo Cabinet secretariat, which survived even after the huts were demolished in 1922. The new impetus came in 1968 when Heath asked a small working group of former civil servants, chaired by Baroness Sharp (Permanent Secretary, Housing and Local Government) to review the machinery of central government. The CPRS was the answer to the alleged weakness of Whitehall's central planning and co-ordinating capability.

In February 1974 Heath went to the country in response to an outside challenge by the miners to government policy, and lost. The belief at the time was that if he had gone three weeks earlier he might have won. But since October 1973 his government's problems had multiplied as a result of the outbreak of war in the Middle East, which resulted in the Arab states cutting their oil supplies and quadrupling the price. The effect on western economies was profound, but chickens were coming home to roost anyway; at the end of 1971 Chancellor Anthony Barber announced a £600 million public spending boost on specific programmes, but boom was followed by bust. Somehow it was all depressingly familiar.

Developments in Town and Country Planning

The period from the beginning of the 1950s to the middle of the 1970s proved to be one of sustained expansion for town planning, and, although inevitable associations with bureaucracy produced local irritations – a suicide case incensed Churchill apparently (Ward, 1994, p. 124) – the activity had a fair political wind. The profession boomed and its Institute received the Royal Charter in 1970 (Cherry, 1974). Its footing both in central and local government grew secure. It could scarcely have been any other given the nature of the post-war settlement which we have described. In 1951 town planning was feeling its way, having just embarked on the task of preparing development plans for the whole country; by 1974 the activity was fully fledged in one of the great departments of state, and local authorities had presided over a period of urban renewal which had transformed the face of Britain's towns and cities. This period was a high-watermark for town planning achievement and for its reputation world-wide.

A post-war planning system was built on the back of legislation framed largely to deal with war-time issues; in particular the resolution of the compensation and betterment problem required a comprehensive framework for the preparation of obligatory plans and the day to day control of development. Quite what the system would secure was a matter of conjecture; no coherent statement of objectives was ever drawn up, but at least by the beginning of the 1950s a number of explicit aims could be discerned.

There would be a veto on sporadic building in rural areas (the scourge of the 1930s) and the economic and social base of the countryside would be protected by a revivified agriculture. The urban spread of towns would be contained; sprawl would be avoided, and the London green belts showed the way. Towns and cities would be redeveloped; the scars of war would be healed and the squalor of old building replaced by new. Overcrowding would be eased in a process of moving population out to a combination of peripheral estates and new towns. Over time, built-up areas would be reconstructed according to new principles of layout and design; order would replace disorder, amorphous residential areas would be transformed into planned neighbourhoods with social and other facilities, and the various land-use components would be neatly separated. Overall, qualitative improvements in urban living conditions would be effected. The country's assets of scenic heritage would be protected in National Parks. All these matters became the conventional wisdom of post-war planning, the collectivist state being the steersman to a brighter, nobler future for its citizens.

There were reasonable grounds for thinking that it was possible. The research section of the Ministry of Town and Country Planning had worked out the methods and techniques local authority staff would need to handle the problems of reconstruction, and advice was given on such matters as zoning, density control, road layout and design. A unified set of ideas formed a common 'cook book' for the professions which would be responsible for the redevelopment of urban Britain. The Ministry of Town and Country Planning assumed the role of teacher and guide for the local planning authorities in the technical application of their task.

Meanwhile the important task of preparing development plans had been embarked upon, as required by the Town and Country Planning Act, 1947. Duncan Sandys' 1954 Ministerial Annual Report (1955) acknowledged that the preparation time for development plans had been extended in the case of 126 out of 148 planning authorities, but by the end of 1954 all but five plans had been submitted and 54 approved. In the circumstances this record of achievement was as much as could have been expected, but it provided a foretaste of the immense scale of the obligatory system of plan preparation (of various kinds) followed by the appeal system, ministerial approval, incorporation of amendments and the subsequent five-yearly review, all with a built-in capacity for delay and bureaucratic overload. By the time of Henry Brook's 1959 annual report (1960) twelve plans were still outstanding and there was abundant evidence of a central system becoming clogged with administrative action on County and County Borough Plans, control of advertisements, minerals, preservation orders, inquiries and appeals.

By the early 1960s professional opinion came to the view that the Unitary Development Plan itself required an overhaul. Richard Crossman, Minister of Housing and Local Government set up a Planning Advisory Group in 1964, chaired by a civil servant, I. V. Pugh. Its report, *The Future of Development Plans*, published in 1965, recommended that planning proposals would better fit a range of different types of plans, in place of the land-use maps that had prevailed to date. The recommendations found their way into the Town and Country Planning Act, 1968 (later consolidated into the 1971 Act), which established a two-tier system of plan making. Structure plans became statements of intent and broad policy concerning spatial development, housing, employment and traffic; they would now provide the context for a variety of local plans to show detailed proposals for small areas. Structure plans would continue to be approved by the Secretary of State, but local plans would be adopted by the local authority. A further refinement dealt with the widening of community involvement in the plan-making process. In the hope of limiting or eliminating the confrontation evident in appeals at the time of development plan exposure at a public inquiry, the structure plans would be considered in open debate at examinations in public. Public participation in the planning system was encouraged in the report of a government-appointed committee chaired by Arthur Skeffington MP, *People and Planning* (1969).

This strengthening of the statutory planning system was undoubtedly necessary. But it was still capable of incremental adaptation, by conferring new land use control powers on local authorities, as two examples from this period suggest. One concerned green belts. In 1950 the ministry prepared a green belt map for London, based on that of Abercrombie, for the guidance of local planning authorities in the region. When preparing their development plans, county councils in the London area included this green belt, and between 1954 and 1958 as the plans were approved, London acquired its green belt through statutory procedures (Thomas, 1970). But this was not the case elsewhere and in 1955 the minister, Duncan Sandys, issued Circular 42/55 which invited local planning authorities in England to make proposals for clearly defined green belts, where appropriate. By 1963 the first round of green belt submissions had been made and controls were in operation around most major English cities. During the Labour years of 1964–70 the designatory device fell from favour, but was rehabilitated with the return of the Conservatives and the new Environment Minister, Peter Walker; it became an effective strategic land-use tool in shaping big city growth (Elson, 1986).

Duncan Sandys was also the source for a second initiative which utilized the statutory planning system to the full. He promoted a Private Members' Bill which came to the statute book as the Civil Amenities Act, 1967. This legislation provided for the designation of Conservation Areas, notable for their special architectural or historic interest. In the higher standard of planning control which would be applied to these designated areas, special consideration would be given to their aesthetic character. The act has proved a popular weapon in the local authority armoury of control powers, with an estimated 8,000 Conservation Areas now designated.

By the time the new generation of structure plans and local plans were being prepared, a new local government map was in place. The changing population geography of Britain had thrown into prominent relief the outmoded local authority boundaries which obtained, particularly around the big cities. During the 1960s ad hoc modifications saw some large municipal boroughs, such as Luton and Solihull, become county boroughs (and hence planning authorities in their own right); the heart of the West Midlands was restructured into six county boroughs; and new county boroughs were created at Teesside and Torbay. The London County Council was enlarged and internally restructured to become the Greater London Council in 1966. There was a predominant view that greater efficiency in local government would be derived from greater size and additional resources – a notion which extended to all units of administration including schools and hospitals.

The mood was taken up in country-wide reviews. The Royal Commission on Local Government in England, chaired by Sir John Redcliffe-Maud, reported in 1969. It recommended the creation of a relatively small number of all-purpose, single-tier authorities, while for the conurbations there would be a two-tier metropolitan county structure. In a memorandum of dissent one commissioner, Derek Senior, recommended a pattern of city regions with a large number of second-tier authorities.

Wales was considered separately, by the Local Government Commission for Wales; so too was Scotland, by the Wheatley Commission.

The Labour government accepted the broad outline of the Maud proposals; the incoming Conservative government did not. The new Secretary of State for the Environment, Peter Walker, favoured a two-tier structure, based on counties and districts, for England and Wales and this took effect from 1974. Scotland's new structure, based on regional councils, was put into place in 1975.

Meanwhile the town and country planning 'system' had received its biggest change much earlier: during the 1950s the financial provisions of the 1947 Act were dismantled, and the nationalization of development rights abandoned. Under the 1947 Act, a sum of £300 million would be distributed among landowners whose interests were depreciated by the provisions of the act; by late 1951 the Treasury estimated that admitted claims already totalled £350 millions. In the meantime the government alleged that Silkin's scheme was not working. Sandys' 1954 ministerial Annual Report (1955) observed that, 'the difficulties associated with the financial provisions had become formidable. They were succeeding in their object, which was to enable the use of land to be controlled without fear of compensation; but they were acceptable neither to land owners nor to developers' (p. 82). Landowners were unwilling to sell at the 100 per cent betterment charge and the developers saw the charge 'as a hindrance to development and a tax on enterprise'. Behind the bland words of a ministerial Annual Report lay another story. Cox (1984) records antipathy to the act on all sides: by the estate agency, valuation and legal professions, by officials in the Treasury, Ministry of Health and Ministry of Town and Country Planning, and by local authorities in their relationships with the Central Land Board. The Town and Country Planning Act, 1953, abolished the development charge and repealed the provisions in the 1947 Act for the distribution of the £300 million.

The Town and Country Planning Act, 1954, introduced new financial provisions which had the effect of restricting compensation to loss of development value which had accrued up to 1947, but not thereafter. In effect there was now a dual market in land: private sales were conducted at the current market prices, while compensation for certain planning restrictions and for compulsory purchase was paid on the basis of existing use, plus any admitted 1947 development value. This was a situation which could not last, and the Town and Country Planning Act, 1959, restored fair market price as the basis of compensation for compulsory acquisition. The restoration of the open market valuation for land compulsorily acquired removed one of the planks in the immediate post-war arrangements for the state regulation of national resources, in this case wealth derived from the operation of the land market.

There was another attempt, however, by the Wilson government. In a renewed attack on the problem of compensation and betterment the Finance Act, 1967, introduced a capital gains tax. In the same year the Land Commission was set up with two objectives in mind: to secure land (either by agreement or compulsory purchase) for the implementation of regional and local plans, and to ensure that it was to return a substantial part of the development value to the community by means of a betterment levy fixed at 40 per cent. These measures were entirely in tune with the greater enthusiasm for state planning during the two Wilson administrations.

The Heath government withdrew the new scheme, abolishing the Land Commission in 1971. Just 2,800 acres had been purchased for the intended 'land bank' and £46 million of betterment levy collected. Party political incompatibility with regard to land and property was once again amply demonstrated. The adversarial basis of British politics rather than consensus had prevailed. In fact despite the slow start and the initially high administrative costs, the Land Commission was beginning to be successful. Cox (1984) concludes that in the long term the commission would not have been a technical failure, but it was bound to fail politically.

Other Aspects of the Planning System

The provisions of the 1947 Act and successive legislation of similar title related to the plan making and development control powers which represented 'town and country planning'. But the notion of 'land-use planning' or 'physical planning' extended far beyond this to include such matters as new towns, national parks, housing (location, layout and design, clearance, improvement and redevelopment), roads and transport, and regional economic planning. It also included mineral extraction and land restoration, and would soon come to include waste disposal and a raft of environmental protection issues. It is an indication of the outreach of the state in mid-twentieth century Britain that town and country planning absorbed so many functions. During the period 1951–74 developments under many of these headings assumed considerable importance and governments of different political persuasion gave them much attention – so much so that during that time a minor Ministry of Town and Country Planning mushroomed into a huge Department of the Environment, and from headquarters in a modest office in St James' Square to three tower blocks in Marsham Street.

New towns

The first generation of new towns ended with the designation of Corby in 1950. Dalton, the new Minister of Local Government and Planning (as the new ministry was called in 1951), had already initiated a draft bill designed to secure an alternative means of enabling overspill population to be rehoused away from the overcrowded parent cities, to operate alongside the new towns programme. The method was 'town development' whereby voluntary arrangements would be entered into between the big cities (the exporters of population in housing need) and small country towns in surrounding shires (the receivers). Houses would be built with subsidy assistance by the receiving authorities, while the exporting authorities would nominate the tenancies. Macmillan, from 1951 the Minister of Housing and Local Government (as the new ministry was now called), soon introduced a similar bill, and the Town Development Act received the Royal Assent in August 1952.

Because the act did not apply to Scotland, it became necessary to turn once more to new town procedures to deal with Glasgow's mounting housing problems. Macmillan had fought off a sustained Treasury attack on new town costs, and Stuart, Secretary of State for Scotland, faced a fairly easy task in advocating a second new town for the Scottish city. Glasgow's overcrowding was such that 48,000 families there were living at more than two persons per room. Housing unfitness was chronic, and the city's housing programme was expected to grind to a halt by 1958 because of a shortage of sites (Cullingworth, 1979). Cumbernauld in Dunbartonshire was designated a new town in 1956 – after Corby the only new town in Britain in the 1950s, London County Council's scheme to build a new town at Hook (LCC, 1961) in Hampshire coming to nothing.

But by the early 1960s a potentially problematic situation was developing. A continuing rise in the birth rate, coupled with immigration from overseas, pointed to a large population increase and consequent housing demand over the next twenty years; additionally, substantial population movements within certain regions would result from the operation of planned overspill from the conurbations. The big cities including Liverpool, Manchester and Birmingham, were known to be running short of housing land, and Town Development Act provisions had not so far been all that productive. Henry Brooke, Minister of Housing and Local Government, succumbed to resurrecting a new towns programme as early as March 1960 (Cullingworth, 1979). The conversion was dressed up in the guise of a 'modern' settlement and employment policy, but privately there was despair at the failure of the local authorities to solve their housing problems without further state intervention. The ministry did not relish continuing the intermediary role between the large county boroughs and the surrounding shires in the search for overspill sites: Manchester had already been refused permission to develop at Lymm in Cheshire, likewise Birmingham at Wythall in Worcestershire. The government's inclination to follow the post-war norm of using state powers to resolve national housing problems was restored.

The new generation of new towns began at Skelmersdale, designated in 1961 for the relief of North Merseyside. It was followed by Livingstone (1962) for Glasgow overspill, but so located as to create a new focus of industrial activity in East Central Scotland. Successive ministers at MHLG, Charles Hill and Keith Joseph, kept up the momentum: Dawley (later expanded and renamed Telford) followed in 1963 and Redditch in 1964, for the West Midlands, and Runcorn (1964) for Merseyside. 'Growth poles' were now in fashion, and Lord Hailsham, 'government representative' for the north-east, gave support for the designation of Washington (1964) located between South Tyneside and Sunderland.

By the time of the defeat of the Conservatives in October 1964 six additional new towns had reached the designation stage. A further two had been agreed (Irvine and Warrington) but for various reasons designation had been delayed. Moreover, a White Paper, *London – Employment: Housing: Land* (1963), made a commitment to examining the need for further new and expanded towns, and ministers considered the implications of the proposals contained in *The South East Study* (1964). A new problem was unfolding; whereas Abercrombie had dealt with the distribution of an existing population and its employment, the question now was the distribution of growth in both population and jobs. A population increase of 3.5 million was forecast for the south-east region in the twenty-year period 1961–81, the majority in the form of natural increase; employment growth was also accelerating. A strategy of developing centres of growth, alternative to and well clear of London was advocated, and locations were suggested. A White Paper, *South*

East England (1964), made no commitment to any particular method of implementation (new town or town expansion) but the minister, Joseph, had no doubt that the development schemes should be organized on the basis of 'public ownership of the land, in the hands of public agencies empowered to see that the necessary development takes place as it is required, whether carried out by private developers, by local authorities or by the agencies themselves' (Cullingworth, 1979, p. 205).

Between 1964 and 1970 the Labour government continued the new towns programme. Advanced by successive ministers, Richard Crossman and Anthony Greenwood, the following were designated: Milton Keynes (1967) in North Buckinghamshire, Peterborough (1967), Northampton (1968), Warrington (1968) and Central Lancashire (1970), embracing Preston, Chorley and Leyland. In Scotland there was Irvine (1966) and in Wales, Newtown (1967) designed to re-vitalize mid-Wales. In Northern Ireland, Robert Matthew's Belfast Regional Survey and Plan led to the designation of four new towns – Craigavon, Antrim, Ballymena and Londonderry, all between 1965 and 1969. But the programme of designations had almost run its course and as population forecasts began to down-turn once more, schemes for new towns at Ipswich and Llantrisant in South Wales were withdrawn.

The Glasgow overspill problem remained acute, however, and the Conservatives (1970–4) made one last designation order, for Stonehouse (1972). This really was the end, for after the building of the first houses the project was abandoned, in 1976. Thus concluded a remarkable piece of state planning. The Town and Country Planning Association remained resolutely propagandist about the realization of Ebenezer Howard's dream, and Frank Schaffer (1970), a former official in the Ministry of Town and Country Planning and latterly Secretary of the Commission for New Towns, wrote of the imagination and enthusiasm that had inspired the new towns. Cullingworth's Official History (1979) tells a rather different story of pragmatism, uncertainties over public expenditure and difficulties with local councils. Aldridge's (1979) broad assessment is of 'a programme without a policy', marked by incrementalism and haphazard decision-making over a period of 30 years.

It remains to consider the fortunes of the town expansion programme. Government maintained pressure on local authorities to use the 1952 Act, the Treasury always mindful of the lower costs involved compared with new towns. In spite of a slow start, after 20 years or so (the agreements were terminated in the later 1970s) a significant contribution had been made to the national housing programme and a material input made to decentralization policy. A total of 55,000 dwellings were built for London's overspill in as many as 32 towns including Basingstoke, Swindon, Huntingdon, Thetford, Haverhill, Wellingborough, Andover, Witham, Aylesbury and Houghton Regis. Birmingham negotiated 13,600 dwellings, particularly at Tamworth, Daventry and Droitwich. Other cities made smaller arrangements, Manchester, Salford, Liverpool, Newcastle and Bristol all involved. In Scotland (after a Town Development Act for Scotland was enacted in 1957) Glasgow negotiated 42 reception areas, the major schemes being at Linwood, Johnstone, Erskine and Kirkintilloch.

National parks

In one sense a change of government in 1951 was of little consequence for the national park movement. The National Parks Commission, set up under the 1949 Act, continued with the designation programme begun under Labour. The Pembroke Coast and North York Moors National Parks were designated in 1952, the Yorkshire Dales and Exmoor in 1954, Northumberland in 1956 and the Brecon Beacons in 1957 (Cherry, 1975; Blunden and Curry, 1990). At that, with a total of ten national parks in England and Wales, covering an area of 5,258 square miles, equivalent to 9 per cent of the land area, a halt was called, only the South Downs and the Broads still excluded from Hobhouse's list drawn up in 1947. There were other things to do: from 1956 attention was given to an expanding list of areas of outstanding natural beauty and the question of long-distance footpaths.

But one result of the change of government was that the Labour die-hards in the national park movement (Dalton in particular) were replaced by those less given to the populist outdoor recreation lobby. On the question of the administration of the parks the Conservatives adopted a more pragmatic line (though there is no telling that Labour would not have modified its stance had it remained in power). The 1949 Act provided that where a national park lies within the area of more than one local authority, the park should be administered by a Joint Board. Boards for the Peak and the Lake District were established; the former had its own planning officer, but in the case of the latter the local resolution was to suffice with the shared services of the planning officers of the three counties concerned, for a trial period. Dalton insisted on a joint board for Snowdonia, but Macmillan gave way and accepted a joint advisory committee in its place, again for a trial period. In the case of Dartmoor (wholly within one county, Devon) the question of a joint board did not arise, but the issue of membership of the park committee did: the county got its way with the (alleged) extent of local as opposed to national representation. No more joint boards were created, and as another sign of ministerial lack of enthusiasm for the former hard line, the Quantocks were omitted from the designated area of the Exmoor National Park in deference to Devon and Somerset county councils' objections.

By the late 1950s the government's record on national parks was not all that good: in spite of ten designated areas, the commission had proved weak and was running out of steam, and Treasury parsimony had prevailed. Moreover, the state was proving to be a very unsatisfactory guardian of national amenity, as developments within national parks at Milford Haven (an oil refinery), Trawsfynydd (a nuclear power station) and Fylingdales (a Ballistic Missile Early Warning Station) suggested.

By the early 1960s (as with new towns) rapidly rising population forecasts created a new situation; in the case of national parks the issue shifted from scenic heritage and its preservation to a response to a more general pressure for outdoor recreation from increasing numbers of people, largely car-borne. The focus slipped away from the designated parks to alternative countryside recreation sites. Successive Countryside Conferences in 1963, 1965 and 1970, under royal patronage, alerted ministers to the need to take effective action on rural change, while American experience suggested Britain was embarking on a leisure boom. Sir Keith Joseph showed himself alive to the need for new legislation and was keen to introduce a new National Parks Bill, but he was held back by his Permanent Secretary, Dame Evelyn Sharp.

In the 1964 election manifesto the Conservatives promised a Countryside Commission with resources to care for the countryside and coast. Labour proceeded to establish it. In 1964 a new department, the Ministry of Land and Natural Resources, assumed responsibility for national parks. Before it was abolished, and its functions reintegrated with the Ministry of Housing and Local Government, the minister, F. T. Willey, had issued a White Paper (1966) on leisure in the countryside outlining new arrangements for countryside enjoyment in areas additional to national parks. Anthony Greenwood proceeded with the Countryside Bill, a measure for maintaining the national parks, while introducing a new facility, 'country parks'. Passage through Parliament was uncontentious. A Countryside Act for Scotland had been passed in 1967; the act for England and Wales followed in 1968. The National Parks Commission was abolished; instead Britain had two Countryside Commissions.

A flurry of activity followed with the establishment of country parks and picnic sites around the major centres of population. But national parks were not to be removed from the political agenda; indeed they could not be left in the uncertain position to which the 1968 Act had consigned them (A. and M. MacEwen, 1982). The Report of the Royal Commission on Local Government in England (1969) recommended that national parks should be the responsibility of planning boards, not the new unitary authorities it proposed. But the Conservatives did not follow Labour's acceptance of Redcliffe-Maud, and in its White Paper (1971) said that little change was needed in the planning and administration of national parks. Once again there was more than a hint that the Conservatives were content to demote the status of national parks from the level provisionally accorded by Labour. In 1971, an under-secretary, Lord Sandford, was appointed to chair a government committee to consider whether national parks had fulfilled their purpose, and to make recommendations for future policies. The committee, reporting in 1974, took a strong management line, pointing to the relative failure of statutory development plans and structure plans to achieve much without follow up. But Sandford was overtaken by the local government changes taking effect in 1974. The Boards for the Peak and Lake District were reconstituted; elsewhere each park would have its own committee with an appointed National Park Officer, with the duty of preparing a national park plan.

In some ways the national park story had run its course. In 1972 the Secretary of State for Wales declined to approve a Cambrian Mountains National Park because of opposition from local farmers and residents. In 1976 the commission's proposed East Anglian Broads National Park was withdrawn, again in the face of local opposition. It took until 1989 for the Norfolk Broads to be given national park status, and even then the standard administrative machinery of a park board acting as a planning authority was omitted. In 1992 the New Forest was designated the New Forest Heritage Area, with national park status, but again with reduced administrative functions.

Housing

It fell to Macmillan, minister of the newly named Ministry of Housing and Local Government, to implement the Conservative manifesto promise in 1951 to build 300,000 dwellings a year. Seldon (1981) is of the view that the shift of resources towards housing 'was not so much a reflection of underlying philosophical differences . . . as an astute gamble by the Conservatives for electoral gain' (p. 422). Labour had underachieved in this sphere, but the balance was soon redressed: in 1953 the figure of 319,000 was reached, followed by 348,000 the next year. More generous subsidies and a general stimulus to private building succeeded in breaking the barriers.

These achievements almost obscure the fact that for a decade the principal feature of the housing situation was a gradual diminution of the role of the state (Donnison and Ungerson, 1982). The proportion of houses built for private owners rose from 15 per cent in 1952 to 63 per cent in 1961. The 1957 Rent Act removed rent restrictions for the most expensive houses and raised rents for the remainder in a further gesture to the operation of a free market. Council housing programmes for the general waiting list were reduced and switched to slum clearance, or (in part) specifically targeted on old people. Housing subsidies were reduced for general needs in 1954 and totally abolished two years later.

However, government would be sucked in to an enlarged role once more. Housing need refused to go away; the early 1960s showed an alarming increase in population forecasts, and there was continued evidence of 'household fission' whereby the number of households was increasing at a faster rate than the population itself. Moreover, the slum-clearance machine was now in full swing, requiring its own replacement provision. Rising rents squeezed the stock of dwellings available to those on low incomes, while an additional shortage factor was caused by immigrants from Commonwealth countries. The situation in London rapidly worsened, where an additional problem was the competition for housing land from office developers. (Years later one local conflict over land use was celebrated as 'the battle for Tolmer's Square', Wates, 1976.) The unscrupulous activities of slum landlords caused public outcry (the Rachman affair achieved notoriety). A call for larger council houses and improved standards had been made by Parker Morris (CHAC, 1961). Subsidies for general needs were reinstated in 1961, but a deteriorating situation led to rising land prices and office substitution for housing – issues which were well represented in the 1964 general election.

Labour implemented the 'minimum standards' recommendations of Parker Morris (CHAC 1961); they were mandatory on all council houses built after the beginning of 1969. London's housing problems were investigated by a Committee of Inquiry (the Milner Holland Committee), 1965. *The National Plan* (1965) incorporated an annual output of 500,000 houses in its growth predictions. A faster rate of progress in clearance programmes was called for, followed later by an ambitious grant-aided improvement programme. The grandiose expansion plans collapsed as the domestic economy could not sustain the growth that was required. Renovated housing became a preferred option, on cost grounds, to new construction.

A down-turn in population forecasts helped to reduce the need for the continuation of the public sector house building programme at its 1960s level. The private sector was looked at again to play a larger role in housing supply, with owner occupation a declared virtue. The Conservatives' Housing Finance Act, 1972, attempted to redistribute the different burdens of local authorities' housing debts, to rationalize rents, to reduce total housing subsidies and concentrate them more effectively on those in greatest need. But as the burden of housing subsidies continued to grow, the act was held to have been a failure and was repealed when Labour was returned in 1974. Housing policy remained a political football, but the playing field had been remarkably level for a quarter of a century; the differences had been in the relative enthusiasms for a public sector role, not whether there should be one at all.

Meanwhile the very appearance of British towns and cities had been been strikingly altered in a 20-year period of clearance and rebuilding between the mid-1950s and the mid-1970s which cut across party political lines. The 1951 census showed the poverty of the national housing stock: one-third of the dwellings of England and Wales were more than 80 years old, and 37 per cent of all households lacked a fixed bath, 8 per cent a WC (and another 13 per cent were required to share) and 6 per cent a kitchen sink. Renewal could not be left to the private sector; the answer lay in subsidies for clearance and rebuilding. In the period 1955–74 a total of 1,165,000 houses were demolished or closed; in Scotland a further 296,000 were included (Cherry, 1976). In a massive programme of compulsory purchase local authorities considerably extended their council land-holdings and tenanted housing stock, to the extent that by 1971 nearly a third (31 per cent) of all dwellings were in public sector ownership.

The years of greatest building activity was the period 1966–72, largely reflecting the organizational drive under Labour. In the collectivist enterprise there were many beneficiaries: professionals, local political parties and the house building industry. Overall housing standards rose to the obvious advantage of some of the ill-housed, but precipitate community disruption was adversely commented upon, as in the study of Bethnal Green by Young and Willmott (1957); insensitivity in the process of redevelopment was demonstrated as in Liverpool by Muchnick (1970); and conflict between a local community and a city planning department was analysed by Davies (1972) in Newcastle. By the early 1970s there was hardening community resistance to slum clearance, described by Dennis (1970) in Sunderland, and regret at the passing of identity and the prevalence of buildings no longer of human scale, by Taylor (1973) in respect of London.

House improvement grants had long been available. As the cost of the clearance programme mounted, the Ministry of Housing and Local Government was glad to turn to renovation of properties as a cheaper option (Thomas, 1986). The Denington Report (CHAC, 1966) recommended more generous levels of grant, and these were put into effect in the Housing Act, 1969. It also introduced the idea of General Improvement Areas, shifting the focus from the individual house to a whole area. The improvement programme was taken over by the Conservatives, and an increased level of grant came with the Housing Act, 1971. The principle of targeting was refined in the Housing Act, 1974, which introduced Housing Action Areas. The number of grants made surged in the first half of the 1970s, but even at the end of the decade neither the General Improvement Area nor the Housing Action Area had made much of an impact on the overall housing situation.

Government was also influential in matters of the design and layout of dwellings, continuing an advisory role in housing, seen since 1918. The mixed development of multi-storey and tower blocks came to dominate the visual scene (Horsey,1988). Post-war architects set their own fashions, inspired by peers in Scandinavia or by the Corbusian tradition seen in pre-war German or Dutch architecture, but the Ministry's *Flats and Houses* (1958) encouraged uniform designs of four-storey blocks and flats. Government grants for building high undoubtedly contributed to the surge of tall building, particularly in the 1960s. Local authority housing programmes were severely pruned by the early 1970s, but not before a number of big cities had produced some spectacular developments: Manchester's Moss-side, Sheffield's Park Hill estate of 'streets in the sky', Birmingham's Castle Vale on the site of a former airfield, Newcastle's Byker Wall and Glasgow's highest blocks in Europe at Baldornock. London's performance in 'quality' high-rise was always better, as Glendinning and Muthesius (1994) have demonstrated. The public sector in alliance with the construction industry, fed on a variety of professional interests, gratified civic boosterism and inflated local political egos. All too often, ten or twenty years later the achievements degenerated into a new clutch of environmental and social problems.

Over a quarter of a century governments had presided over ambitious programmes of building, demolishing and improving the national housing stock. They had advised on design and layout and on standards of accommodation. Through subsidy arrangements they had greatly expanded the number of dwellings rented from public authorities. Both Conservative and Labour had trumpeted their achievements, each claiming when the occasion demanded that the welfare objectives of the post-war settlement were safe with them.

Roads and transport

It took some years for the questions of road traffic and improvement to British roads to climb the political agenda. There are few signs that the parties thought of the car in any terms other than economic or financial. The long-held assumption was that car ownership could never become universal or even general. It was not until the end of the 1950s that cars were seen as more than middle class luxuries (Plowden, 1973). The Ministry of War Transport's (1946) report on the design and layout of roads in urban areas still echoed the conventional wisdom of road patterns conforming to the shape of a cartwheel (radials and ring roads). Within the framework of that strategy, local design detail favoured precincts, as seen in the shopping square at Stevenage New Town, in the central area of Coventry, and as advocated in Holden and Holford's (1951) City of London Plan. As far as a national road system was concerned, Alfred Barnes' ten-year plan announced in 1946 was soon abandoned and no revision was forthcoming for a decade.

The 1950s were well advanced before the government found it necessary to respond to events. Traffic volumes were rising: in 1957 the number of cars using British roads had doubled from 2 million in 1949 to 4 million, and by 1961 had trebled to 6 million. By the end of the 1950s one and a quarter million new vehicles were being registered every year. Pressure for road improvements mounted from a persuasive constituency of interests: professional lobbies, motor manufacturers and traders, the TUC, keen to attract more spending to safeguard employment, local authorities to promote their redevelopment plans, and the British Road Federation which represented road construction interests. The road building lobby, popularly supported it has to be said by an increasingly motorized British public, proved successful in getting government to take an increasing interest in road planning and investment at national and city levels.

The return of the Conservatives in 1951 brought little immediate change (Starkie, 1982). Expenditure on new roads up to 1953 continued at levels no higher than those achieved by Labour between 1948 and 1950. For Labour, Alfred Barnes had been Minister of Transport for six years; in the same length of time the Conservatives had five different ministers. There was indifference to road transport, and for some time parliamentary debates moved little from the concerns of traffic accidents. When the government was in a position to prepare schemes for road construction, it simply reverted to elements in Labour's motorway plan of 1946.

In 1957 Harold Watkinson, Minister of Transport, announced a programme of large projects that were all expected to start within four years. These were: the reconstruction of the Great North Road with five bypasses of motorway standard; a motorway from London to the north-west (in effect a continuation of the London–Birmingham motorway already announced); better roads to the Channel ports; a route from London to the west; and better communications between the Midlands and South Wales. These projects echoed many of the 1946 proposals. An interesting deviation was the inclusion of what became known as the Ross Spur motorway – an alternative to a more costly Severn Bridge, thought necessary to placate the Welsh in view of the fact that decisions had already been made to go ahead with a Forth Bridge for Scotland. The M50 remains to this day one of Britain's lesser trafficked motorways, and in any case the Severn Bridge opened in 1966, only two years after the Forth Bridge.

Even before the initial leg of the first motorway opened (the Preston bypass in 1958, suitably inaugurated by the prime minister) steps were being taken to advance the road programme beyond the quintet of projects already announced. Proposals emanated for motorways from London to Crawley New Town, from London to Basingstoke, an extension of the M1 towards Leeds, and a central section of the M62; all these had appeared on the 1946 plan. An additional proposal, from

London to Bishop's Stortford, was new; it could scarcely be justified on traffic congestion grounds, but the proposed line ran close to a large war-time aerodrome called Stansted.

After the opening of the Preston bypass, the first 72 miles of the M1 were completed in 1959. The Lancaster and Maidstone bypasses followed, together with the Ross Spur motorway. Meanwhile there were improvements to the trunk road network, particularly on the Great North Road (by 1963 160 out of 280 miles between London and Newcastle had been dualled). In 1960 the Ministry of Transport published the first of its 'rolling programmes' whereby roads expenditure was fixed five years ahead and rolled forward each year. The road building programme became voracious and was accelerated.

Inter-urban roads formed one aspect of the Ministry of Transport's concerns. The other was intra-urban roads, and local councils in the big cities kept up a constant cry for funding to improve roads and build new ones to relieve congestion. The Road Traffic Act, 1956, permitted the installation of parking meters and the Roads and Road Improvement Act, 1960, introduced the traffic warden. But these measures, together with traffic management schemes, were palliatives. The removal of congestion spots and the partial speeding-up of traffic flows by themselves would not cope with a situation rapidly getting out of hand because of the surge in numbers of cars. Birmingham succeeded in commencing its inner ring road (the Smallbrook Ringway leg) in 1957, but this was due as much as anything to the particular influence of Herbert Manzoni, the magisterial city engineer; during the long history of the scheme, powers of land acquisition became available in a local act judiciously obtained in 1946 (Cherry, 1994).

Ernest Marples, a new Minister of Transport, dramatically advanced the prospects of increasing intervention by public authorities in matters relating to urban traffic. In 1961 he established a working group in the ministry 'to study the long term development of roads and traffic in urban areas and their influence on the urban environment'. The leader was Colin Buchanan, a former inspector in the Ministry of Housing and Local Government, and the author of an influential book *Mixed Blessing* (1958) which called for a fresh approach to urban planning to cope with the new situation created by the motor car. A steering group, chaired by Sir Geoffrey Crowther, was appointed to act alongside the working group and give independent advice on recommendations as they emerged. The result was the Buchanan Report, *Traffic in Towns* (1963), one of the major planning documents of the post-war era.

Buchanan's premise was that there are absolute limits to the amount of traffic that can be accepted in towns and that in order to retain a civilized environment society will have to face up to the payments necessary for the physical changes required. If we were to have any chance of living with the car, then a different type of city design and structure was needed, for which the report outlined a set of principles and indicated how they would work in particular instances, described in case studies.

But there was in fact no wholesale reconstruction of British cities to cope with the new car situation. The forecast rate of traffic increase did not materialize, incremental adjustments to road improvements, some new relief roads (including urban motorways) and a Treasury inability to fund at the required level, took the heat out of the situation. But perhaps the biggest factor was the increase in public resistance to measures of urban destruction in order to accommodate the car. A number of *causes célèbres* during the 1960s suggested the extent of concern. A proposed tunnel under Bath and a relief road across Christ Church Meadow, Oxford, produced furious local comment. The M4 viaduct out of west London (the Westway) was regarded as alien to the amenities of those who lived in the shadow of it. Urban motorway schemes, often blighting many hundreds of homes, provoked local outrage in many cities including Cardiff (Hook Road), Portsmouth, Southampton (the Portswood link) and Nottingham.

But perhaps the most celebrated example came in the early 1970s when the Panel of Inquiry into the Greater London Development Plan (DOE, 1973) pared down the road proposals which the GLC had advanced. Two of Abercrombie's intermediate inner ring roads were removed, leaving the major features, the M25 (largely outside the GLC area of responsibility) and, controversially, the inner ring (Ringway One). The London Labour Party adopted an anti-motorway stance and when they won the 1973 GLC elections, London's inner motorway plans were abandoned. Ringway One, as Hall (1980) observes, ran through key constituencies at the border of working-class and middle-class inner London. There had been strong Labour support for the London roads policy to date. The East Cross Route of Ringway One was planned by the old LCC and completed without much opposition. When the plans threatened middle-class London they ran into trouble and to capture these areas Labour reversed its policies.

This was the first occasion when roads policy breached the party political consensus. The policy on trunk roads was in fact featured by remarkable longevity. During this time party politics played very little part in the direction of policy and at election time both Conservatives and Labour parties promised much of the same. In 1959 it was a case of a bigger road programme; in 1964 it was to give consideration to Buchanan's proposals; in 1970 an expanded inter-urban roads programme was offered; and in 1974, juggernaut lorries having been a recent issue, a policy of lorry routing was highlighted. A bipartisan consensus had prevailed, during which time successive governments had been in thrall to an alliance of sectional interests. The questions of traffic restraint and the competitor, public transport, had scarcely arisen.

Regional planning

The Labour government between 1945 and 1951 had embarked on a kind of regional economic planning; it also retained a regional presence in the machinery of town and country planning, though the 1947 Act, by greatly reducing the number of planning authorities, limited the need for organization on a regional basis. From 1951 the Conservatives continued the dual agenda; however, the take-up was inconsistent as policy driven entirely by response to changing circumstances. During the 1960s, and particularly between 1964 and 1970, both regional perspectives were given greater attention. After 1970 regionalism lost the importance recently accorded to it.

Regional economic planning was always the more specific of the two approaches. With the return of the Conservatives the provision of factories and industrial estates by the Board of Trade remained the principal aim of regional policy; in the meantime Treasury loans and grants were of limited significance (McCrone, 1969). This kind of pump-priming provided 45 million sq. ft. of factory space, resulting in further employment for 201,000 workers in the development areas, between 1945 and 1960. But the bulk of this provision had come in the first half of the period; the very success of the policy in the immediate post-war years meant that it was accorded a lower priority thereafter. Industrial Development Certificates became readily obtainable for new development in the south-east and the Midlands, and the booming of the traditional industries elsewhere meant that regional policy fell into abeyance during the middle of the 1950s for much of the rest of the decade.

But economic changes were already taking place. The pace set by the traditional industries could not be maintained. International competition hit shipbuilding and coal, and textiles to a lesser extent. On the domestic front deflationary policies after the investment boom of 1954–5 bore heavily on the old problem regions. Regional policy attracted a new interest, leading to spectacular interventionism on the one hand, fine tuning on the other. In 1958 the prime minister determined the future of a new strip mill for the steel industry. Originally to be located in the Midlands, Macmillan decided on a split, one mill to go to Llanwern in South Wales and the other to Ravenscraig, Scotland, economic implications overruled by political and social considerations. The Distribution of Industry (Industrial Finance) Act, 1958, modified the Development Area 'map' by including additional places based on unemployment criteria. Viewed in retrospect the decade was one of lost opportunities. Government measures were at best half-hearted and at most quixotic. Meanwhile long-standing problems were not addressed: investment and restructuring, the failings of management and unbridled labour disputes.

The 1960s, under both Conservatives and Labour, saw much greater attention given to regional economic policy. The Local Employment Act, 1960, abolished the old development areas and replaced them with development districts; defined with reference to high unemployment rates, they could be scheduled and descheduled as circumstances changed. Unemployment, however, was no measure of an area's economic potential for investment, and (as unemployment rose and fell) constant changes to availability of government support was disruptive. But these limitations to the new act were met with fresh initiatives which placed a new emphasis on stimulating viable growth. The Toothill Committee (Scottish Council, 1961) had emphasized the need to promote faster economic growth in Scotland. A subsequent White Paper on Central Scotland (1963) delineated eight growth areas. In the north-east high unemployment levels had resulted in the appointment of Lord Hailsham as minister with special responsibility for the region. A White Paper on the north-east (1963) likewise proposed a growth zone, in a similar strategy.

The 1960 Act was concerned with the control of a new industrial development. But office employment, particularly in London, was already growing rapidly, and the Conservatives, late in their parliamentary span, brought it into regional policy. The Location of Offices Bureau was set up in 1963 to encourage offices to move from the centre of London, at least to the periphery.

Labour expanded and strengthened what the Conservatives were doing. In 1966 they abolished the development districts (established in 1960) and replaced them with new development areas. The Industrial Development Act, 1966, now scheduled virtually the whole of Scotland, the northern region, Merseyside, much of Wales and Cornwall and North Devon. Forty per cent of the land area of Britain was now available for regional aid – no longer dependent on unemployment criteria, and with a choice of locations available within the regions to accord with industrialists' preferences. A modification in 1967 introduced special development areas as priority heartlands within, but this seemed to revert to an unemployment-based focus rather than the grander sweep of growth zones. A further modification came with intermediate areas, to blur the distinction between inclusion and exclusion from the development areas.

Together with greater and additional loans and labour subsidies to promote development, Labour's regional policy attempted to tighten the control measures. The Industrial Development Certificate, previously required for development above 5,000 sq. ft. was extended to factory building in excess of 1,000 sq. ft. The exemption limit was later raised to 3,000 sq. ft. and restored to 5,000 sq. ft. outside the Midlands and the south-east. With regard to offices, Board of Trade permission was soon required for all new office development in London; in 1965 legislation introduced the Office Development Permit, required initially for the London Metropolitan Region and extended subsequently to other parts of the country.

On their return in 1970 the Conservatives both relaxed and tinkered with the regional policy measures. Industrial development certificate controls were eased, and office development limits were raised in Greater London and removed in the Midlands. On the other hand, in 1971, the number and size of special development areas was increased as a gesture to rising unemployment. The Industry Act, 1972, abandoned tax incentives and reverted to grant payments – a reversal of traditional Conservative measures. Intermediate Area status was applied more widely. The continuity from Labour was also marked when service industries were brought within the scope of regional policy.

If we turn to the other aspect of regional planning (though it becomes increasingly difficult to separate the two) we see a similar pattern of take-up, from indifference to enthusiasm in response to changing circumstances. During the 1950s the vestiges of war-time regional administration were abandoned and the Ministry of Housing and Local

Government had closed its regional offices by 1958. But there were rising pressures for a return to a regional awareness. We have already noted the deteriorating economic conditions in the early 1960s which led to attention being given to Scotland and the north-east, but it was the alarming population forecasts and the implications for housing demand in the south-east and around the big cities that drew the government once more to consider regional programmes across England.

The South East Study (MHLG, 1964) prepared the ground for the region's second generation of new towns (later to be implemented at Northampton, Peterborough and Milton Keynes) and for a renewed burst of development in town expansion schemes. The revived interest in regional planning was taken further with Labour, particularly in association with the strategic objectives of the new Department of Economic Affairs. Regional economic planning councils (and boards) were set up for Scotland, Wales and the standard regions in England, but they were concerned as much with 'physical' planning as economic planning. The department was abolished in 1969 but this regional structure was retained until 1979. Regional studies proliferated, alongside some 30 sub-regional studies (Wannop and Cherry, 1994). Transportation studies were commissioned for the large conurbations, and expansion plans were prepared for the major estuaries of the Severn, Humber and Tay. In Scotland a new agency was launched in 1965, the Highlands and Islands Development Board.

By the time of the Conservatives' return in 1970 population forecasts had become less expansive and the pressures for regional studies were easing. The final complement of English regional plans was initiated, but after publication they largely withered on the vine. In Scotland there was more of an afterlife: the West Central Scotland Plan (1974) proposed an economic development corporation for Strathclyde, and this was implemented by Labour in the form of the Scottish Development Agency. Regionalism in Scotland also benefitted from local government reorganization in 1974 whereby the Conservatives retained the recommended system of regional authorities for the greater part of the country. In England and Wales the only equivalent regional gesture was the creation of regional water authorities from a mass of small water boards, but even then the Water Act, 1973, set up the Water Space Amenity Commission to provide a measure of national co-ordination in the field of outdoor recreation.

During the post-war settlement Labour proved more inclined to follow a regional perspective than the Conservatives; they installed and worked through forms of regional administration (always appointed, not elected). But the Conservatives in the early 1960s found it convenient to prepare regional plans and in the early 1970s they retained the Regional Economic Planning Councils set up by Labour. Pragmatism proved stronger than ideological preference for much of the time.

8 The Consensus Breaks, 1974–9

Party political turbulence during the mid- and late-1970s marked the break-up of the ideological convergence which had characterized the previous 30 years. As the Conservatives moved to the right and Labour to the left, the discontinuity in political affairs contributed to a decade which was 'discontented, quarrelsome, unsteady, ineffective, self-defeating' (Beer, 1982, p. 1). It provided a new context for the furtherance of town planning activity, but there were few immediate consequences to affect the performance of the statutory machine; rather, as we shall see, it affected attitudes and perceptions. It was largely in the inner circles of the professional body of town planners (the Royal Town Planning Institute) that the impact of sharp political controversy was felt: from a particular section of young, left-inclined members the Radical Institute Group, which urged a more explicit political stance to planning action. The chief characteristic of the period however was that town planning fell prey to the critique of the social sciences.

This chapter deals with the political upheavals of the period, the radical departures from past attitudes to state engagement in social and economic affairs, and developments in town planning itself.

The period is dominated by two factors. The first was the rupture in the post-war 'settlement'. As Marquand (1987) reminds us: 'The central, dominating reality of post-war British history is that for thirty-odd years – starting with the commitment of the 1944 Employment White Paper to a "high and stable level of employment" after the war, and finishing with James Callaghan's speech to the 1976 Labour Party Conference, warning that deficit finance breeds inflation – party differences were argued out, and government policies settled, within a framework of common commitments and common assumptions' (p. 319). The crucial commitments, three in number, threaded a consistent path from the mid-1940s to the mid-1970s. They covered full employment and Keynesian demand management; a range of welfare reforms; and prosperity via 'the mixed economy'.

The second factor (and it was related to the first) was the growing dissatisfaction with Britain's poor economic performance amongst the industrialized nations. Government bore the blame. Two parties had shared common aims since the war, to restore and expand the British economy. They failed in this task; the economic decline which they inherited was not arrested, rather it accelerated. During a period of thirty years the role of government in the direction and management of the economy had become paramount. Intervention had multiplied to the point of assuming responsibility for the functioning of the entire national economy. Difficulties had been encountered in periodic times of economic stringency, the challenge of heightened social expectations and the problems of demographic change, but sustained economic decline could not be concealed.

By the mid-1970s it seemed that too much had been attempted and too much hoped for. As Calvocoressi (1978) observed:

> Governments had been in charge and had failed. Whether failure came from ineptitude or bad luck or a mixture of both, the verdict remained adverse and it was easy, if not entirely logical, to go on to judge that governments had taken on what they did not know how to discharge and had better get out of the business again. They had bitten off more that they could chew. (p. 112)

Vaizey (1983) makes a similar point: the ideals in which the post-war world had reposed confidence, had proved wanting. He selects Gaitskell, MacLeod, Titmuss, Crosland and Boyle – five men who helped to shape a generation – and concludes that 'their shared ideas and ideals made up the common currency of a quarter of a century and they were for the most part wrong' (p. 2). They believed that the tools of the welfare state and nationalization would bring about social change in Britain. They repudiated market mechanisms in education, health and social welfare. But in office they were not radical; there was no trade union reform for example. The basic problem of Britain's precarious post-war industrial structure was not tackled. The question of poor managerial performance in nationalized industries was avoided. In the early/mid-1970s their generation stood at a crossroads – the path of east European style socialism or that of a freer market – and an increasing sense of lost opportunities was in the air. Many reasons were adduced for this failure. One cause, the collectivist polity, was seized on by the right, and used to hasten the demise of the left. Beer (1982) has been one to argue this analysis very strongly:

> I do not find the source of the trouble in the ignorant multitude, oppressive capitalists, selfish trade unionists, arrogant bureaucrats, egotistical politicians, misguided ministers, fuzzy traditionalists, or isolated elites. Indeed, in my version of the story there are no villains. Britain, I say, has been turned against itself by 'the political contradictions of collectivism'. (p. xiv)

Edward Heath's U-turn, early in his period of office, from neoliberalism back to the consensus, suggests the power of the collectivist polity; the early 1970s may have been too early to break the mould, but later in the decade much stronger pressure was mounted. The irony is that the people who framed the programmes of the collectivist polity utilized the ideas of Keynes and Beveridge, but Keynesian and Beveridgean thought did not necessarily require the centralized, planned corporatist state which emerged during the 1940s and was used subsequently by both Gaitskell and Macmillan. Come what may, by the middle 1970s radical challenges were mounted to the inherited political and collectivist assumptions. The New Right launched its assaults and Labour fell in disarray.

Joseph and the New Right

The post-war consensus had lasted a surprisingly long time. As we have already seen, the organized form of the individualist counter-revolution against the century-long drift towards collectivism had started as long ago as 1947 with the meeting of economists at Mont Pelerin, and had received a national fillip with the foundation of the Institute of Economic Affairs in 1957. But the individualist case made little headway against the seemingly successful post-war settlement in which a reconciliation between capitalism and socialism appeared to have been struck. Cockett (1994) asserts that no more than fifty people were engaged at the outset of the counter-revolution to turn the tide of political and economic thinking.

The consensus began to disintegrate when in the early 1960s 'arm's length' management of Keynesian social democracy shifted to 'hands on' intervention. The departure which bridged political eras from Macmillan to Wilson, was clearly seen in the new attempts made to plan the national economy. Inevitably this implied a growth in corporatism: industry had to be governed with the consent and participation of organized business and the trade unions. The consensus eroded further when evidence suggested that the post-war settlement had scarcely been successful in economic terms anyway; Britain had achieved a persistently slow per capita growth compared with its competitors. Finally, the whole notion of governance on the lines of Keynesian social democracy came under critical scrutiny.

With Enoch Powell now a peripheral figure (he left the Conservative Party in 1974), Keith Joseph became the standard bearer of the message of the Institute of Economic Affairs. Socialism, the middle way and all forms of collectivism had to be abandoned. From more than one source collectivism was identified as the corroding culprit for both economic failure and moral decay. In March 1974 the Centre for Policy Studies was founded – a new body in which free-market ideas might be developed outside the usual party apparatus – and Joseph used it to the full. A little later, in 1976, the Adam Smith Institute was founded on the bicentennial of the publication of *The Wealth of Nations*. This was an important additional centre for the dissemination of what would shortly become the new orthodoxy.

The Centre for Policy Studies was launched at a public meeting in Upminster (Essex) in June 1974 when Joseph gave 'the most celebrated speech of his career' (Cockett, 1994, p. 240). He drew comparisons between Britain and those countries that practised more market-oriented economics:

> Compare our position with that of our neighbours in north-west Europe – Germany, Sweden, Holland, France. They are no more talented than we are. Yet, compared with them, we have the lowest pay and the lowest production per head. We have the highest taxes and the lowest investment. We have the least prosperity, the most poor and lowest pensions. We have the largest nationalized sector and the worst labour troubles. (p. 241)

This speech was followed by one at Preston in September where he identified the commitment to full employment as the error from which poor performance flowed. He also addressed the problem of inflation. By this time macro-economic management had acquired an inflationary reputation and, alleging that inflation was caused by governments, Joseph specifically advocated a monetarist counter-inflation policy. Thus it was that monetarism and market economics found their way into the mainstream of Conservative thinking, building on a party tradition of political and economic individualism and offering a direct challenge to the drift towards collectivism. In due time Margaret Thatcher would be the leader of this radical departure from the post-war settlement, but in preparing the ground Joseph 'had played the Baptist's role' (Jenkins, 1987, p. 61).

Keynesian policies came under mounting attack. The theory of the carefully-managed growth economy withered and died in the 1970s as new economic experiences revealed difficulties to which the orthodox analysis apparently offered no solution. There were differing views amongst economists as to the direction of post-Keynesian policies for the attainment of high employment and stable prices (Kavanagh and Morris, 1989). Neo-Keynesians wished to pursue economic growth, but would curb inflation by an incomes policy. The Cambridge School called for import controls in order to protect an uncompetitive home market. But the most influential response came from a school of monetarists, centred in Chicago, inspired by F. A. von Hayek and a new leading exponent, Milton Friedman, author of *Capitalism and Freedom* published in 1962. Their argument was that the key to reducing inflation was to control the money supply. Joseph went further, arguing that government should also adopt 'supply side' measures to restore the enterprise economy. It should cut direct taxation, encourage work incentives, promote labour mobility through lower welfare benefits and weaken the powers of trade unions.

There was mounting criticism of the post-war growth of the state. Bacon and Eltis (1975), for example, argued that the growth of the public sector was crowding out investment and employment in the market sector. This argument, popular at the time, lost its force later, but conveniently swayed opinion which was increasingly open to ideas which ran counter to orthodoxies which had prevailed for 30 years and more. The restoration of market mechanisms and the break-up of the rigidities of collectivist control were the new targets. The end of the Keynesian era was in sight, eroded by a return to market liberalism and the adoption of monetarist economic policies. The idea of the role of the state being to compensate for market failure changed to a recognition that state interventions created more problems than they solved. The state was alleged to be overloaded, a view developed by political scientists in their thesis of 'ungovernability'. The philosophy of big government was attacked, encouraging policies for denationalization, transfer from government to the private sector, reduction in the size and influence of bureaucracy, restoration of competition and a radical reorganization of welfare services to introduce choice. The floodgates of political alternatives had opened.

In a time of reappraisal some key figures in the Conservative Party readily embraced new outlooks though the managerialist 'middle way' tradition lived on, not least in Edward Heath who was succeeded by Margaret Thatcher as leader in 1975. Outside the party long-standing party political affiliations were reconsidered. Paul Johnson, latterly editor of the *New Statesman*, was one who turned against the unions and the Labour Party after 1975 (nearly 20 years later he would rejoin it). He came to the conclusion that the state was an inefficient instrument for the allocation of resources and the taking of mercantile decisions. He went further: the state was not merely inefficient, but prodigal, breeding parasites. He wrote (1980): 'The overwhelming imbalance of our age has been caused by the huge increase in collectivism. The power of the state has increased, is increasing and ought to be diminished: there, in a sentence, is the great redressment problem of our time' (p. 5).

In this context the pros and cons of the free market were looked at again. The post-war era had preferred to recognize the deficiencies of economic liberalism, and a raft of arguments was well understood. A free market merely legitimized the actions of the powerful, its distributional effects led to inequalities, failures in the system imposed costs on the weakest, and unfortunate welfare effects were to be seen in unemployment. But the experience of the post-war years suggested that certain counter-arguments were stronger. Economic actors (producers, entrepreneurs and consumers) made the best economic decisions, provided that they were given the freedom to do so. By comparison, governments and large corporations protected privileges and the status quo, while those involved in the machinery of administration will always demand extensions to bureaucracy. Free markets will punish complacency and inefficiency and encourage enterprise and change. Free markets also constitute the best information system for an advanced economy.

Collapse of the Keynesian Order

Labour moved to the left in the 1970s. Anthony Crosland's *The Future of Socialism* (1956) had argued that the market economy under Keynesian management had no need to approach socialism by means of a command economy; instead, social justice and equality could be achieved by the reallocation of resources and wealth (in other words by public spending) provided that resources overall expanded at a sufficient pace. There was certainly no need for wholesale nationalization. In May 1975, as environment secretary, he instituted tight controls on expenditure by local authorities telling them that 'the party is over'. It did not help, of course, when the quadrupling of world oil prices by the Organization of Petroleum Exporting Countries (OPEC) in 1973–4 caught Britain unprepared, and an acceleration of inflation exacerbated historically high price levels. But Crosland's world in the early 1970s was already collapsing around him. By the time of his death in 1977 the world economy had changed out of all recognition and his political assumptions could no longer be sustained.

The public service bureaucracies had burgeoned. Between 1961 and 1975 employment in central government increased by 27 per cent, and in local government by 70 per cent. Meanwhile Britain's economic growth failed to provide the wealth that Crosland took for granted. During the 1960s Britain's economy grew at an average of 3.75 per cent, while the rest of the industrialized world managed 5.5 per cent. Over the whole of the 'long boom' (1950–73) Japan averaged a 9.7 per cent annual growth, Germany 6 per cent, France 5.1 per cent and Britain 3 per cent. Another telling statistic was that while Britain's share of world export trade in manufactured goods was 20 per cent in 1953, during the four years between 1973 and 1977 it fell to an average of 9 per cent (Jenkins, 1987).

In Labour's move to the left Crosland's bible of revisionist socialism was attacked in favour of a return to explicit socialist policies. For example, Stuart Holland, in *The Challenge of Socialism* (1975), argued that the mixed economy and the Keynesian techniques of demand management no longer represented a feasible option for Britain. In a world now dominated by multinational corporations, national controls could be avoided by multinational managers, so undermining government policies on employment and investment. Holland reverted to the need for public ownership and control of the dominant means of production, distribution and exchange, reasoning that without this control, the state would fail to manage the strategic features of the economy in the public interest.

Meanwhile, Labour in opposition worked up an ambitious economic strategy. In 1973 the party resolved to take over the leading financial institutions and 25 major companies. The 'planning agreement' was devised as a crucial instrument of socialist policy. The 100 largest companies would be obliged to enter into such an undertaking with the government, and a Ministry of Planning was envisaged for the purpose. As a condition of state investment, they would be required to involve their work-force, through their unions, in the planning process. Another aspect of state planning would be import control, seen as the answer to the balance of payments crisis.

In government, however, things turned out rather differently. Public ownership was extended only to the aerospace and shipbuilding industries – and these were already in receipt of substantial state aid anyway. The National Enterprise Board, established in 1975 with power to make voluntary planning agreements with firms, and extend public ownership, never became the great institution for economic revival which Anthony Wedgwood Benn desired; it did little beyond grant-aiding firms in financial difficulties, including British Leyland and Chrysler.

In 1975 Benn was removed from the Department of Industry and given a new home in the Department of Energy. His outburst of radicalism was a spent force. The Wilson government beat a hasty retreat from nationalization plans and large public-spending programmes. The pressures of inflation and a collapsing confidence in the currency were followed by developments in 1976 which clearly indicated the demise of post-war conventional approaches to economic affairs. James Callaghan's government capitulated to the International Monetary Fund, Chancellor Dennis Healey's budget took the decisive steps towards monetarism (introducing control of money supply, cash limits, and cuts in current rather than future expenditure) and Callaghan told the Labour Party Conference that autumn of the death of Keynesian economic policies which had dominated the post-war years. Under the weight of inflation, unemployment and the industrial disorder which accompanied it, the Keynesian consensus broke down.

Callaghan's party conference speech was prepared for him by his son-in-law, Peter Jay. One section is worth repeating at length:

> For too long, perhaps ever since the war, we postponed facing up to fundamental choices and fundamental changes in our society and in our economy . . . For too long this country . . . has been ready to settle for borrowing money from abroad to maintain our standards of life, instead of grappling with the fundamental problems of British industry . . . The cosy world we were told would go on forever, where full employment would be guaranteed at the stroke of the Chancellor's pen, cutting taxes,

deficit spending – that cosy world is gone . . . We used to think that you could just spend your way out of recession to increase employment by cutting taxes and boosting Government spending. I tell you in all candour that that option no longer exists and that insofar as it ever did it worked by injecting inflation into the economy. (quoted in Cockett, 1994, p. 187).

The Labour government struggled on, responding to the force of events. The recognition of the need for change, expressed by Callaghan, and the financial stringency adopted by Healey, came from no ideological conversion (as was being worked out in parts of the Conservative Party), rather it was an economic response thrust upon them. The government ran into increasing problems, failing to obtain adequate backing for a counter-inflation policy. Finally it found it difficult to arrive at an appropriate target for the 1978–9 pay round: it feared that failure to improve on the 1977–8 guidelines would appear defeatist, but if too low a figure was set, the whole policy might collapse. This danger in fact materialized and the 'winter of discontent' ensued. It was a miserable end to a well-meaning but flawed chapter in British politics and to the planning experiment. As Skidelsky (1988) puts it: 'The era of Keynesian social democracy (ended) with garbage rotting in the streets, hospitals closed, and grave-diggers refusing to bury the dead' (p. 12). The government fell on 28 March 1979, the first to be defeated on a vote of no confidence for 50 years.

Against this political scenario, Heath's initiative in setting up the Central Policy Review Staff, designed to remedy the weakness of central management structures in Whitehall in relation to strategic planning and the co-ordination of the various activities of different departments, was continued by the Labour government. It will be recalled that the CPRS (the 'Think Tank') was set up in 1971 and was first headed by Lord Rothschild. He resigned in 1974 and was succeeded by Sir Kenneth Berrill, an academic economist, previously Head of the Government Economic Service; he later resigned, in 1980, and there were other appointments before the organization was abolished immediately after the 1983 general election.

At the beginning of the 1970s the remedies for Britain's economic (and other) ills included an enhanced capacity for planning aided by improved machinery of government, and a capacity for research, analysis and strategy formulation. By the early 1980s this particular nostrum seemed irrelevant. Wilson and Callaghan both used Heath's creation and a decade's experience of strategic planning can usefully be recounted at this point. After all, the post-war settlement included a belief in planning and established the machinery of planning for a variety of purposes both in central and local government and through a range of public authorities. The experience of the 1970s served to cast doubts about the capacity of governments actually to plan, while the rediscovery of the virtues of the free market suggested to some that as a matter of principle governments should not try to do so. The failure of the Callaghan government was not unrelated to failure about objectives, priorities and strategy – the very qualities concerning which the CPRS was established to ensure greater clarity. The ultimate demise of the CPRS tells us something about the nature of planning, and its limitations in a British setting.

The historians of the Think Tank (Tessa Blackstone and William Plowden, 1988) conclude that in principle, at least, there is still a strong case for ensuring that somewhere in government there is a capability to undertake the tasks originally given to the CPRS. The problem initially addressed – the 'hole in the centre' – remains unresolved. But the whole process of policy analysis and review in government remains weak. The reason for this may be that this simply reflects the British political culture coloured as it is by the nature of the training and experience of civil servants, an inherent pragmatism, the desire to avoid confrontation, and the ready adoption of forms of crisis management. There is also the nature of the relationship between subordinates (officials who are permanent) and those at the top (politicians are therefore almost by definition temporary); typically ministers are laymen on the subject matter of their departments. Equally important, however, is the reality of the nature of government bureaucracies. They are large, well established and hierarchically organized. They have their own implicit sense of priorities and value systems. Their attitudes and values become strongly entrenched. With their own strengths and weaknesses, they become locked into relationships. It follows that strategic planning and the co-ordination of various activities of different departments becomes a very difficult exercise.

Blackstone and Plowden (1988) make a telling point from their experience of the CPRS which goes to the heart of the planning activity. They assert that the reality is that governments

> in all forms of regime in all parts of the world, are pluralistic, divided, under-informed, short sighted, only partly in control of their own processes, and unable to guarantee the outcomes which they promise. There are enormous gaps, and sometimes no linkages at all, between realities, perceptions, decisions, actions, and consequences. The collective interest is too often dominated and distorted by sectional interests;

'rational' decisions are distorted by political considerations; there is an excessive focus on the short term. The responses to new problems are incremental rather than radical. Individual decisions are often inconsistent with each other, with existing policies, and with any overall objectives that the government may have defined. (p. 12)

This sober assessment was as accurate in 1978 as it was in 1988, and indeed at any other time, except perhaps when a nation's energies are focused by war. As the Keynesian era came to an end it is not to be wondered at that government performance came under intense scrutiny and the long-proclaimed virtues of planning were called into question. A return to the free market offered less reliance on government, greater freedom from planning and a withdrawal from the collectivist state.

Town Planning and the Social Sciences

During the 1970s town planning was strongly influenced by the social sciences. Its traditions so far had been derived largely from the professions of the built environment, including architecture, engineering (civil and municipal) and surveying. Henceforth these formative influences would be at least shared by those of the social sciences, notably geography, economics, sociology and political science. The profession and practice of town planning came under strong pressure to widen a remit, up until then based on land, design, layout and spatial distribution, to one more concerned with people, communities and their needs, and questions related to justice, discrimination, poverty and privilege in cities. The challenge, designed to turn an activity which had been place-based into one which was people-based, was one which neither the profession nor the statutory planning system found easy to handle. The source of the assault on British planning was in part American, inspired from US experience of city problems during the 1960s and the output of American commentators, notably H. J. Gans (1968), but it also echoed new issues emergent at home, particularly those stemming from the consequences of urban renewal and the wholesale dislocation of (often disadvantaged) communities.

Another destabilizing factor came from the demise of two, previously dominant, theoretical underpinnings to town planning. The subject field had always borrowed heavily from other disciplines (it still does) and during the 1930s both geography and sociology (largely expounded from the United States, primarily from centres in Chicago) strongly influenced the norms of British planning, particularly in relation to urban form and structure. From geography came notions of ideal cities, notably in terms of size, internal spatial structure and processes of change. They came to provide a coherent framework of land-use objectives for British cities, and indeed the wartime and early post-war plans were predicated on them: containment of urban spread (ringed by a green belt if necessary), an internal package of different land-use parcels, and a target for future population size. From sociology came the new orthodoxy of neighbourhoods, self-contained islands for particular communities, a collection of which would give a pattern of meaning to a larger urban area.

These lessons of geography and sociology together provided a working model for town planning: planners had a spatial picture of what reconstructed cities after the war should look like. But by the 1970s, a model from nearly 50 years before no longer sufficed. British cities could not be contained and neatly packaged, as the magisterial review of the containment of cities in England by Hall et al. (1973) clearly showed; a static model had to be replaced by one which admitted far greater dynamism and a capacity for change to futures which were unknown and unknowable. Moreover, the complexities of urban life could not be contained in the simplicities of pre-ordained neighbourhoods. City planners were caught unprepared and intellectually ill-equipped to deal with the need to change traditional outlooks.

A critical onslaught came from a number of observers, largely outside the profession. Practitioners in the Royal Town Planning Institute (the Royal prefix was granted in 1970) were not unaware of the new circumstances facing their profession; Cherry's (1970) *Town Planning in its Social Context*, suggested as much, at least. But generally speaking their training made it difficult for them readily to respond to the criticisms they faced. Furthermore, as the servants of a local government machine they were expected to operate a state statutory planning system which itself was resistant to change. Independent academics in planning schools often practised as planning consultants, and were disinclined to enter the new fray. Non-planners, though close observers for all that, had a field day. The target must have been embarrassingly easy.

Harvey (1973), a geographer, and Pahl (1970), both a geographer and a sociologist, in providing a focus on the urban condition, stimulated developments in urban social theory, which became an academic growth industry during the 1970s. They focused on the processes associated with the incidence of poverty, racial discrimination and the ills of an urban society, and pointed to the need for forms of planning which dealt with immediate social issues rather than ideal, long-term futures. Pahl (1970) observed thus:

> The crucial lesson for British planners is to learn their limitations, and to make these limitations more widely known. The public, seeing, for example, the physical environment in decay, mistakenly assumes that the solution lies in physical renewal alone. However, the planner finds that the amelioration of one problem brings about a deterioration in another sphere, for he is dealing all the time with symptoms not causes . . . The planner cannot be the *deus ex machina* of the urban condition. (p. 193)

British planners had so far seen cities as physical entities with physical problems; they had now to see cities as social entities, the product of a particular society at a particular time.

Harvey (1973) wrestled with the notions of geographic space and the nature of urbanism. He concluded that:

> Created space . . . reflects the prevailing ideology of the ruling groups and institutions in society. In part it is fashioned by the dynamics of market forces which can easily produce results which nobody in particular wants. Created space is an 'ethnic domain' in only a very limited sense. Yet created space is an integral part of an intricate sign-process that gives direction and meaning to daily life within the urban culture. (p. 310)

Planners were now told that cities were rather different from what they had imagined, there could be no certainty about city futures, and that planning was an altogether different exercise from what their training had led them to believe. Moreover, in Harvey's case, he had drunk copiously from the cup of Marxist vocabulary; new terms and concepts bewildered many in the planning profession.

This then was the period when the long-held promise of physical planning lost its allure and yielded to the siren song of social, economic and welfare planning. Earlier definitions and approaches to town planning, forged during the first decades of the century and made the bedrock of the post-war statutory system, were reassessed. Criticism mounted of a profession slow to change. Simmie (1974), a local authority planner turned academic, concluded that interest-specific professions and local government departments were a hindrance rather than a help to the discharge of new tasks.

Social scientists insisted that city problems were societal problems, and therefore the methods of town planning had to change. Simmie (1974), for example, argued that:

The real, immediate issue facing town planners, and indeed all institutions of welfare at the present time, is the fair, equitable and just distribution of the current equipment, income and wealth of society. This will not take place if, for example, town planners continue to believe that various parts of society are organically and functionally related, nor if they continue to believe that all the groups in society share a common set of values and interests. (p. 207)

This echoed the views of Blair (1973), an American sociologist and Professor of Planning at the Polytechnic of Central London:

Urban planning, like other forms of planning, is a multi dimensional political act. It sets values in motion towards specified ends and benefits. It also involves ordering the relationships among socially differentiated populations, spaces and productive forces. Planners and architects are not outside the play of social forces; they are part of the continuing patterns of conflicts and cooperation involved in the competition for space and access to the benefits of urban society. (p. 26)

The Marxist approach was the theme of Castells (1977), who argued that a critical revision of the traditions of the urban social sciences was required. He found new tools of enquiry in the Marxist tradition, with an analysis of society as a structure of the class struggle. Marxian concepts were adapted to the urban sphere, using in particular the reading of Marx given by the French philosopher Louis Althusser. Castell's position was that

a concrete city (or an urban area, or a given spatial unit) is not only a unit of consumption. It is, of course, made up of a very great diversity of practices and functions. It expresses, in fact, society as a whole, though through the specific historical forms that it represents. Therefore, whoever wishes to study a city (or series of cities) must also study capital, production, distribution, politics, ideology, etc. Furthermore, one cannot understand the process of consumption without linking it to the accumulation of capital and to the political relations between the classes. (p. 440)

Left-inclined academics responded warmly to this sort of analysis. The social science wing of town planning gained a dominant influence in the profession, but the statutory framework of the activity remained unaltered. The irony was that the intellectual debate was being conducted almost without reference to the political arguments elsewhere which were concerned with the rediscovery of the merits of the free market and a re-examination of the claims of planning.

One immediate result of the new insights to be gained from geography and sociology was the recognition that cities, both as physical artefacts and as forms of social organization, were constantly in flux. Town planning therefore was an activity concerned with process and the management of change towards uncertain futures. The profession had almost been led to believe that it was engaged in some heroic act of deliverance whereby it would rescue cities from an insensate, industrial nineteenth century and propel it towards an enlightenment fashioned in its own image. Instead, a new reality showed that town planning was in the much more sordid business of having to undertake an activity in the complex shadowy world of competing interests and power relationships, and with no definitive rule-book to guide it. One specialist branch of planning would benefit enormously from this – planning history, which embarked on the reinterpretation of the circumstances both in which and whereby planning events in the past had actually taken place. The Planning History Group, beginning as a small network of (largely) academics in 1974, is now the International Planning History Society, and planning history has become an important specialist interdisciplinary area in its own right.

Meanwhile, the social sciences continued to broaden the context of town planning. From a number of perspectives came repeated emphasis on social issues. Community-action programmes in US cities offered models for community involvement in Britain; the meeting of social needs through architectural determinism was rejected in favour of citizen participation which was lauded as a new technique for mobilizing social interaction. 'Planning for People' (the title of a monograph by Broady, 1968) became a watchword of the time. It was only a short step to fierce criticism by sociologists and political scientists of a failure by local authorities to engage with social sensitivity in their planning operations, particularly urban renewal. Davies (1972), in his study of the revitalization of the Rye Hill district of Newcastle, accused the city planners there 'of being very foolish *before* the event and only a little less so *after it*,' with the 'same obsession with technology and the same belief that it can somehow be regarded as independent of the socio economic system into which it is intruded' (p. 218).

Housing issues loomed large on the planning agenda. Government had for a long time played an interventionary role in housing matters: in the production of dwellings, determination of design and layout, provision of facilities and in establishing rent levels. Town planning traditionally had a close association with housing affairs, largely in the technical considerations of provision, layout and distribution. Social science questions forced town planning to address new issues, however – not on the bricks and mortar of building but on the needs of the communities. The housing problem assumed a new definition: it was concerned with the processes of social change – the gentrification or downward spiral of neighbourhood composition, tenure aspirations, poverty and homelessness. In Cullingworth's (1973) review of the problems of an urban society, housing figured prominently, and planning would form part of the solution.

Of all these related social questions none was more intractable than race. It was already clear that 'coloured immigrants' (to use the then fashionable term) were confined to the inner cities and run-down working-class districts where they occupied the worst and the oldest of the housing stock. Widely discriminated against in the council house sector, hit by the decline of private renting, and with difficulties experienced in becoming owner occupiers, this particular sector of the community figured extensively in the new emphasis on discrimination and social justice, to which planning was inevitably drawn.

During the 1970s planning was clearly recognized as an activity affecting issues much wider than the concerns with which it had been earlier associated. Both the profession of town planning and the statutory machine established during the 1940s found this a mixed blessing. Eversley (1973), once an economic historian and demographer but captured by the Greater London Council to be its Chief Strategic Planner, 1969–72, observed that:

> 'The Planner' has become a monster, a threat to society, one of the most guilty of the earth-rapers. Suddenly he has become a breaker of communities, a divider of families, a promoter of neuroses (first noticed as 'New Town Blues'), a feller of trees and bringer of doom by noise, visual intrusion and pollution, a destroyer of our natural heritage, a callous technocrat razing to the ground a large proportion of Britain's historic buildings. He is regarded as a dictator, a technocratic law unto himself, outside the process of democratic control. (p. 14)

Eversley argued that the profession was simply out-of-date, dominated by those for whom the social sciences did not exist and for whom planning had no political connotations. It was imperative that the planner be occupied more effectively with the ills of society and engaged in a task of arbitration between conflicting priorities. It was all very different from the world in which the first post-war generation of practitioners and teachers were given their shared assumptions. As Peter Hall (1974) observed, in a widely-read text of the time, planning in practice was far removed from the earlier notions of the theorists: 'It involves conflicts of values which cannot be fully resolved by rational discussion or by calculation; the clash of organized pressure groups and the defense of vested interests; and the inevitable confusions that arise from the complex interrelationships between decisions at different levels and at different scales, at different points in time' (p. 293). These were the realities which neither Abercrombie's *Greater London Plan* nor the framers of the 1947 Town and Country Planning Act dreamed of addressing.

The widening frame of planning was certainly daunting. In the 1970s the range of concerns assumed the definition which came to characterize the last quarter of the twentieth century. The British economy experienced recurrent bouts of recession with unemployment reaching figures not seen for 40 years; a sustained contraction in manufacturing and a partially commensurate rise in service sector employment produced a new spatial planning agenda. Meanwhile the fruits of economic growth fed the consequences of affluence seen in rising car numbers and substantial additions to the housing stock. But there were worrying aspects of social change associated with a profound discontent with the achievements and products of post-war Britain: a surge in divorce rates, increase in crime and the relatively new phenomenon of violence (crowd behaviour at football grounds first became a concern in the 1970s). Vandalism of public property, when seen for example on council estates, became linked with allegations that bleak estate layouts bred crime and encouraged neighbourhood disorder. The term 'defensible space', originating with Newman (1972), entered the vocabulary of town planning and architecture at this time.

Town Planning in Operation

It was against this background – of challenge to established certainties and changes in society which posed additional questions – that town planning was conducted. The machine of statutory plan-making and land-use control was by now powerfully entrenched through legislation and a battery of circulars and statutory instruments. Town planning was a key function of a powerful Department of State (Environment) and, following the reorganization of local government effective from April

1974, all the new districts set up planning departments in their own right. (The 1960s had seen only a slow and reluctant creation of separate planning departments by some of the old county boroughs.) Town planning was called on more and more to take on co-ordinating roles in the management of government activity, and its tentacles spread into sport, leisure, tourism, transportation, economic development, environmental protection and other areas. The practice of town planning responded to the new remit set by the social sciences, grafting additional areas of involvement on to an established statutory base. The newly required structure plans came on stream and at first they were hugely ambitious in covering a range of social, economic and other issues. Government advice later directed local authorities to focus on a limited range of key issues. The over-arching, co-ordinating role to which town planners aspired also beckoned in the new management fashion of corporate planning, advanced as a rational approach to intra-corporate organization, programming and budgeting (Friend, Power and Yewlett, 1974). Town planners became key figures in local authority management teams and some became chief executives (a new office replacing the former town clerk). In another area, however, the expanding reach of town planning received a set back: road-building programmes were curtailed and while public transport enjoyed a revival (favoured by town planning), the creation of a new, separate Department of Transport in 1976, hived off from Environment, weakened the hopes still residing in the notion of an integrated planning/transport system.

During the mid- and late-1970s, then, town planning built on the advantages derived from local government reorganization in terms of an enlarged power base, and basked in the opportunities presented to it by a widening remit of activity. Its statutory foundations remained unchallenged, even though in wider political arenas the ideological underpinning of planning as a state activity was under severe challenge. The town planning machine was too firmly established and by this time had a momentum of its own; it continued its functions without interruption. Indeed two particular developments seemed destined to give yet more power and influence to town planning: a new attempt to control the land market and a fresh initiative regarding inner cities.

The leftward lurch of the Labour Party in the early 1970s encouraged a renewed attempt to control speculation in the land market. A property boom and its precipitate collapse during 1972–3, marked by company failures and bankruptcies, provoked widespread disquiet and encouraged radical solutions. Ambrose and Colenutt (1975), for example, academics with community-based planning associations, exposed the mechanics of the property boom (particularly in office development) and concluded that the defects of the system demanded radical new policies, including the public ownership of all land and buildings. In 1973 the Conservatives had proposed a development gains tax, and this was enacted by Labour in 1974. But the new government's initiative came with a Community Land Scheme, the brainchild of John Silkin, Minister for Planning and Local Government under Anthony Crosland at Environment. He was the son of Lewis Silkin who had introduced the 1947 Act, with its financial provisions concerning compensation and betterment.

The scheme envisaged the public acquisition of areas of land ('land banks') at current use value so that the community would have land provided in those places that were in fact required, with the public facilities needed at prices that could be afforded. This was a return to 'positive planning', a phrase much used at the time. The scheme rested on two acts. The Community Land Act, 1975, gave local authorities both opportunities and duties to acquire development land by compulsion at existing use value. The Development Land Tax Act, 1976, introduced a new tax on land value increases, initially set at 80 per cent, but intended to rise to 100 per cent. The scheme fell victim to restraints on public expenditure as well as considerable disinclination on the part of Conservative councils to participate; there were few practical achievements. Andrew Cox (1984), in his scholarly assessment, describes the record as 'abysmal', and the 1975 Act was quickly repealed by the Conservatives on their return. In one sense it may be seen that positive land planning was sacrificed on the altar of monetarism, but it was unlikely that Silkin's assault on the free operation of the land market could ever have succeeded on a permanent basis, given the adversarial politics which had dictated its introduction.

The initiative on inner cities proved of longer significance. The new towns programme came to an end with a ministerial announcement in 1977. In strategic terms, the outer city which had benefitted from massive public funding for 30 years in the form of peripheral housing estates, expanded towns, new towns and an accompanying range of facilities, now had to be accorded reduced priority in favour of the regeneration of the older, inner areas of British cities. This switch was most readily seen in the allocation of resources to the renewal of inner Glasgow when Stonehouse, the most recent new town designation, was aborted in 1976. From the middle 1960s, as shown in chapter 7, there were insistent tell-tale signs of a creeping malaise: the collapse of a manufacturing heartland, selective out-migration of population which left typically residual communities of multiple disadvantage, racial tension and creeping environmental decay. Initiatives to combat emergent problems had been underway for some years. In 1967–8 Education Priority Area programmes were specifically area-based, and targeted on the inner city and other deprived areas. In 1968 an urban programme was established under the Home Office. The Community Development Programme began in 1969 with local projects established in deprived neighbourhoods (not necessarily inner city). In 1972 Peter Walker, Secretary of State at the DOE, commissioned studies of inner Liverpool, Birmingham (Small Heath), and London (Stockwell); they reported in 1977, a common thread being the need to see urban renewal, in terms of a close association with employment policies, housing and co-ordination of local services – a far cry from the former approach of clearance and rebuilding. By this time the inner city had become well-trodden ground for academic analysis and prescription, the Social Science Research Council setting up a Working Party in 1977 to establish future research directions (Hall, 1981).

A new policy framework was sketched in the Inner Urban Areas Act, 1978. The key was partnership in designated areas. Local authorities in England and Wales (Scotland followed its own procedures) with severe inner-city problems were given additional powers to engage in social projects and industrial, environmental and recreational matters. The areas identified for help were carefully selected and prioritized. First, the partnership areas were Birmingham, Gateshead, Liverpool, London (seven boroughs in all), Manchester, Newcastle-upon-Tyne and Salford. Second districts with Inner City Programmes included a further 15 authorities. Finally, a further 19 authorities (including five in Wales) also benefitted. Economic regeneration soon became the most important feature and loans and grants were available to all these areas for industrial building and the creation of Industrial Improvement Areas.

Thus the state interventionary role of town planning remained well to the fore. The existing machinery proved robust and well-entrenched. An expansively-minded profession and an ambitious bureaucracy in both central and local government found it easy to secure political support from a Labour administration for further schemes and projects. But the ideological radicalism which was washing away many of the inherited precepts of the wider notions of planning would soon break on the shores of town planning itself. During the 1970s the storm was deflected, but Keith Joseph (1974) was already critical of this overblown outreach of the state. In a paper to a joint conference of RIBA and the Civic Trust he argued: 'Clearly it is right that we should try to protect our environment and we cannot do that without a measure of planning . . . But do we really need the immense apparatus that we have at the moment – the arbitrariness, the bureaucracy and the expense?' Town planners then came under attack:

> It is not only that the pursuit of town planning aims intensifies land shortage, prolongs delays, increases devastation, imposes rigid lifeless solutions; it is not only that the ambitious system of town planning leads to long administrative delays with heavy concealed costs all round on top of the visible costs of a big bureaucracy; it is not only that any system leading to such wide disparities of land values must offer temptation to corruption; it is that town planners and architects are as fallible as the rest of us and the more power we give to them the greater the errors that will be made when they are wrong.

For a quarter of a century town planning in post-war Britain had secured almost unqualified support. It ran into popular opposition in the later years of slum clearance and rehousing from those who bore the brunt of draconian policies. It fell foul of academics from the social sciences who ridiculed an intellectually light-weight profession. Meanwhile the town planning system delivered its statutory requirements and expanded into other areas. But as new political judgements were formulated, a new era was dawning in which town planning would be seen against very different criteria.

9 The Post-war Settlement Remade: from 1979

The consensus was already broken when Margaret Thatcher swept to office in May 1979 with a majority of 44 seats. The Callaghan administration had rejected orthodox Keynesianism in a return to financial rectitude; it had presided over the demise of an incomes policy; and mass council house building had come to an end. The Conservatives, pushing at a door already ajar, confirmed the fracture. They established ideological bridgeheads on three fronts: politically (the state was over-mighty); financially (a high tax economy spelled decline); and morally (the people should get what they deserved) (Hennessy and Seldon, 1987).

The immediate focus was on the reach of the burgeoning state. In 1979 the state-owned sector accounted for 10 per cent of national GDP, 15 per cent of national investment and 7 per cent of employment. The scale and cost of the nationalized industries was enormous: the total subsidies to them amounted to £4.6 billion in that year, and, added to the total borrowing by those industries (£2.5 billion), the aggregate sum came close to equalling the entire cost of servicing the national debt (£8.4 billion in the fiscal year 1979). Moreover, these sums were being spent, not on growing industries, but on old, declining manufacturing concerns. The growth of the public sector was well illustrated in its employment statistics. In 1979, of more than 25 million people employed, between a quarter and one-third (7.45 million, or 29.3 per cent) were employed in the public sector. The civil service (at 738,000) was twice as large as it had been in 1939. The National Health Service employed 1.5

million people, more than three times the entire number of personnel in the armed forces. The nationalized industries employed more than 2 million; local authorities employed 3 million (Letwin, 1992).

This chapter looks initially at the very different course of British politics during the post-consensus era, and the changing context of social and economic affairs. Changes in town planning are then assessed against this background together with the developments in planning-related matters which accompanied them.

The Changed Course of British Public Policy

The outcome of the 1979 general election signalled a clear repudiation of Labour. But that party had shown an impressive capacity for electoral recovery during 1978, and the Conservative victory was widely regarded as possibly little more than a short-term swing in political fortunes. At the time few saw the election necessarily as a turning point in political history. It could still be asked whether Margaret Thatcher would prove to be as radical in government as she had promised. Would the slogan, 'Rolling back the frontiers of the state', be articulated in a set of policies which met the instinct of the New Right?

In fact 1979 did turn out to be a watershed year. The building blocks of the post-war settlement finally collapsed. Changes within the Labour Party hastened its demise; activists moved to the left, arguing that the government wing of the party had failed, and in March 1981 four prominent Labour politicians (Roy Jenkins, David Owen, William Rogers and Shirley Williams) left to set up the Social Democratic Party. But the undermining and ultimate destruction of the consensus owed its origins to wider forces of change. The post-war reliance on consultation with interests, an acceptance of incremental change, and the ability of important pressure groups to veto change amounted, by the time of the 1970s, to nothing less than political inertia. Kavanagh (1987, p. 8) has called the style 'directionless consensus' – one of make-do and mend, sacrificing long term objectives for the short term. In contrast, Thatcher promised a no-nonsense style of leadership and a hostility to the premium derived from gaining agreement by a negotiated consensus.

The break that took place in the 1970s, and given a defining date in 1979, appears all the more significant when seen in a century-long perspective. Middlemass (1980) argues that the first half of the twentieth century saw the emergence and institutional growth of central bodies representing management and labour; they established positions which enabled them to take shares in the running of the modern state. Beginning in the 1890s, seen again in the period 1911–14, and encouraged by the events of the Great War, the role of bargaining with government took on a modern form. Initially the objectives were to overcome agitation, settle strikes and defuse social unrest. Later, the emergent corporate bias sought to further a mixed economy. Ultimately a whole range of interests could support the new collusion because it allowed those not directly represented in the formal democratic system to share in the operations of the state, thereby fulfilling the various aims of the many constituents.

The settlement during and after the Second World War had this background. It was 'conceived initially as a balanced, harmonious set of remedies for outstanding grievances from the inter-war years, and planned with increasing vigour as the great emergency receded' (Middlemass, 1986, p. 1). The hostile economic climate immediately post-war required a modification of the settlement, but then through the 1950s (increasingly affluent years) it was maintained without much difficulty. A brief revival during the early 1960s saw the two main political parties moving towards similar positions on industrial issues: a tripartite forum for discussion was set up, there were radical changes in state-owned industries, and new methods of planning for sustained growth were established, with the French mechanism of the Commissariat du Plan viewed with favour. The 1970s saw the break-up of the settlement, as described in chapter 8. Both the style of government 'characterised by institutionalised consultation between government and the major economic actors, including notably the trade unions' (Kavanagh and Morris, 1989, p. 3), and the range of policies pursued by governments of both parties between the late 1940s and the mid-1970s, based on Beveridge and Keynes, were finally abandoned.

Thatcher's election in 1979 marked the demise of welfare capitalism and the mixed, or managed economy – both terms used to describe the Keynesian social democratic elements of the post-war consensus. Those policy options – which for over 30 years had been regarded by both political figures and civil servants as politically acceptable, economically affordable and administratively practicable – were rejected. Years later, Gray (1993) remarked that:

comprehensive economic planning was an epistemological impossibility, demanding of the socialist planning institutions knowledge – of relative resource scarcities and consumer preferences – that they could not possess; and that the attempt to institute comprehensive planning and to suppress market pricing could only issue in a calculated ted chaos whose practical upshot was impoverishment. (p. vi)

The new Conservative government would no longer expect to own significant sections of industry, to negotiate its policies with employers and the unions, nor necessarily maintain full employment if that were to mean subsidizing inefficient industry. Collectivist, egalitarian values would be replaced by individualism and freedom.

However, Thatcher's first administration actually set modest goals. It aimed to restore the recently nationalized shipbuilding and aerospace companies to the private sector, review the activities of the British National Oil Corporation and National Enterprise Board, and relax the licensing system of bus companies. There was as yet nothing to anticipate the scale of privatization that followed. But the dimensions of Thatcherism were soon established even so. These embraced a general suspicion of government activity and this led to hostility to much of the public sector, to nationalized industries, the incidence of high taxation, and a reliance on subsidies and public spending. The role of government as the manager of economic affairs, as provider of welfare and planner of social change was systematically diminished. Nonetheless there would be a strong state, with a government resilient enough to resist being manipulated by self-seeking interest groups and lobbies. Law and order would be emphasized, buttressed by traditional moral values. Money supply would be strictly controlled in the attack on inflation, and in the interests of a stable currency and a free economy.

Thatcher's impact stemmed from the fact that she presided over a change of attitudes (Jenkins, 1987): individualist rather than collectivist, private rather than state ownership. Her government's article of faith was that private enterprise could run things better than the state. Election victory was the opportunity not simply to halt the advance of collectivism, but to reverse it. The bastions of Labour's power – the trade unions, the council estates, socialist local authorities and the nationalized industries – provided immediate targets. This was a government whose telling political experiences were forged, not under mass unemployment and the shadow of war (as had been the case of all previous post-war leaders) but under socialist rule at home and the threat of the cold war abroad. The profound generational difference highlighted the ideological change. The 1980s proved a roller-coaster decade, plunging from economic recession to boom and back again, with a government buoyed by electoral victories and a leader triumphant against all rivals, but finally ousted by her own colleagues.

In the early years Thatcher presided over a reduction in manufacturing output reminiscent of the early 1930s, her own exchange rate policies at least contributing to, if not causing, the collapse. Between the first quarter of 1980 and the second quarter of 1981 Britain's gross domestic product fell by 3.7 per cent, industrial production by 9 per cent, while unemployment nearly doubled to 2.5 million. In the middle of all this, Geoffrey Howe's 1981 budget was the antithesis of Keynesianism – a massive deflation in the middle of a recession. By the time of the 1983 general election some commentators were taking the view that the government had lost its radical cutting-edge, but with Labour in disarray and led by an unappealing leader (Michael Foot), Thatcher was returned to office in the aftermath of the Falklands War. It was a landslide: the Conservatives won with a majority of 144, the largest of any party since 1945. In her second administration the low point was 1986 when she was beset by a number of difficulties – the Westland helicopter affair which prompted the resignation of two members of the Cabinet (Heseltine and Brittan), the privatization of Leyland, and the odium incurred through Britain's support for the US raid on Libya. But the 1987 general election was won comfortably enough, though with a reduced majority. After that her personal fortune plummeted, beset by problems on Europe, differences of opinion with Chancellor Nigel Lawson and the ill-fated poll tax. Her Cabinet support eroded and she was defeated in a leadership election in November 1989.

John Major became prime minister, and to most commentators' surprise won the next general election in April 1992, albeit with a small working majority. Plunged into financial turmoil on withdrawal from the European exchange rate mechanism, and struggling to come out of another deep recession, he presided over a querulous party, riven by different views over Europe (Eurosceptics versus Eurofreaks) and the pace of market reforms (the left and right wings of Conservative thinking), while the Labour Party stole into middle-ground politics under the leadership of Tony Blair. By the summer of 1995, when Major himself experienced a leadership challenge, he was being accused by Lady Thatcher of not being Conservative enough. He won, and relative peace was restored to his party.

Although the two periods, 1979–89 and 1989–96, were very different in character, they can be regarded as one in that the break with the old consensus, apparent in the later-1970s and confirmed with Thatcher's premiership, has continued. Indeed it may be argued that a new consensus has been entered into. Thatcher's enduring contribution to British politics has been that she has framed a common agenda once more for all political parties. Major's consensual style of management (both of his party and national affairs) brought no return to Keynesian social democracy.

So overall we can recognize a clear set of Conservative achievements. The power of the trade unions to constrain the market has been reduced by a radical reform of industrial relations law. Housing legislation has been equally radical, particularly in extending tenant choice and in reducing the scale of local authority control. In local government the Greater London Council and the Metropolitan Counties in England were abolished in 1986. New units of local government in Wales and Scotland have been established, and new boundaries drawn in England (for 1996). There has been a break up of the bureaucracies of the welfare state and their replacement by quangos, private agencies and a range of intermediate agencies (the so-called 'third sector' governance). Privatization has extended to the nation's telephone system, gas, water and electricity, the largest airline, airports, steel, coal and rail. Monopolies have been broken up: of solicitors over conveyancing and of opticians over prescribing spectacles, for example. In the Health Service and education an internal market has been established. Local authority services have been put out to tender: to begin with, refuse collection and hospital catering and laundry services, but now extending more widely as local government is exposed to the rigours of market forces. In Whitehall, most national government public services, administered by the civil service, are now managed through operational agencies.

Throughout public service provision American-derived concepts of business organization have been introduced. New terms such as 'customer care' and 'total quality management' have entered business parlance in a new business culture of competition, performance and service delivery to customers. The revolution of corporate life in America spread to its local and national government. The 'tax revolt' which started in California in 1978 with Proposition 13, which cut the state's tax base by 25 per cent, obliged local government in that state to choose between making draconian cuts to their programmes and obtaining other funding alternatives. Strategies adopted combined two approaches: the finding of new ways to combine public and private finance in meeting public objectives, and the restructuring of local government to incorporate new business methods. The result was the delivery of 'more for less', as it was known in the US, or 'value for money', the British equivalent.

Increasingly the model for government has focused on the development and management of policy, not the delivery of services. Politics and management had become incompatible. The answer to the problem was to reduce the functions of government by means such as privatization and contracting out, thereby decreasing the fields in which government is open to public criticism. Most services can be delivered better by non-governmental agencies, notably the private or voluntary sectors, and that competition between service providers is essential if value for money is to be secured. Where contracting out to the private or voluntary sectors is not possible, internal markets are necessarily created to ensure competition between public service providers. These new forms of entrepreneurial government can be seen in the Citizen's Charter whereby citizens are empowered through their redefinition as customers with choice and provided with performance information.

These constitute the winds of change which have swept through British governance. State planning of the old kind has gone, and with it many of the institutions and practices of state delivery. The market is now seen as the better distributor of rewards and resources. Arguments of 50 years ago have been stood on their heads. Privatization, externalization and deregulation have replaced a former reliance on state bureaucracies. Local government is no longer the provider of free services. The citizen is a purchaser of services, individually priced. Town planning in the closing years of the twentieth century is conducted against a very different background from that which obtained in the 'settlement' years of the post-war era.

However, in spite of these fundamental changes in outlook, the actual implementation of new Conservative policies has been uneven. Marsh and Rhodes (1992) in their audit assert that 'the Thatcherite revolution is more a product of rhetoric than the reality of policy impact' (p. 187). They consider that only in the area of housing did her government achieve its policy and political aims. Elsewhere, in areas of industrial relations, privatization and local government, a great deal was accomplished in terms of legislation, but rather less in terms of outcomes. Meanwhile it is necessary to recognize the down-side of government performance: the huge rise in unemployment in two deep recessions, the surge in homelessness and repossession of mortgaged properties, and gyrations in economic and fiscal performance. Moreover, Audit Commission Reports (1995) still find too many local government officers inefficiently employed, large numbers overpaid and few councils functioning adequately: the management revolution has some way to go yet. Nonetheless much has happened in terms of style and direction of government. The initial objectives set out in 1979 (reducing the role of the state and the size of the public sector, strengthening the operation of market forces and transforming the post-war consensus) still remain, and their pursuit, however faltering and at times uncertain, has established new conditions for public policy.

Town Planning: New Directions

During the late 1970s it became commonplace to highlight alleged failures in urban policy matters across a wide front. For example, McKay and Cox (1979) observed:

> Among the more important criticism are claims that state housing provision is characterized by social and spatial inequalities; that land use planning policies have resulted in urban blight and decay and have aggravated the disparities between inner cities and suburban and New Town locales; that land values policies have failed to stem land price inflation; that transport policies have done little to halt the environmental damage wrought by the rising tide of motor vehicles; that policies designed specifically to improve the lot of the urban disadvantaged are hopelessly underfunded and possibly based on false empirical assumptions; and finally that governments of all shades and at every level are unresponsive to citizens' demands and needs. (p. 14)

Many of these shortcomings reflected performance in town planning and related policy areas. If they were well-founded a new, incoming administration with a very different outlook on the role of state intervention in urban and regional affairs might be expected to engage in a radical review of planning objectives. In this section we consider policy changes in the area of town planning.

The reassertion of the primacy of the market over state direction, and the importance accorded to individual freedoms over bureaucratic control, made it inevitable that changes would be sought in the planning system. The government's vocabulary changed: the term 'strategy' had no place and notions of 'comprehensive' planning were discounted. Michael Heseltine, Secretary of State for the Environment, blew the

Thatcherite trumpet in proclaiming the spirit of free enterprise. The Local Government, Planning and Land Act, 1980, set the first scene by repealing the Community Land Act (though the Land Authority for Wales survived in a more market-oriented capacity). The introduction of money charges on planning applications illustrated the determination to dispel the concept of a state funded by taxation. The main focus of attention however was on the setting up of Enterprise Zones and Urban Development Corporations.

Enterprise Zones (EZ), foreshadowed in Geoffrey Howe's 1980 budget, had first been advocated in non-political circles, at a town planning conference, by Peter Hall, as experiments in non-regulation where enterprise might flourish. In practice EZs were designated in run-down areas where a much simplified planning regime was agreed upon. Ten-year exemptions from local taxes and full capital allowances against national taxation represented the financial bonuses which would stimulate development. The experiment turned out to be a rather cautious one and not all that much new development (as opposed to firms simply changing location to take advantage of the benefits) was created. The first round of EZs was announced in 1981. Some were in inner cities (Salford/Trafford, Tyneside) but others were in smaller industrial towns (Swansea, Dudley). By 1985 there were 25 EZs, covering no particular spatial location, after which, under Heseltine's successor Nicholas Ridley, they fell from favour.

Urban Development Corporations proved of greater significance. These new planning agencies had their objective in urban regeneration, achieved in ways that bypassed local government. Based on nominated, not elected membership they had similarities to the New Town Development Corporations, but the resemblance ended there because the intention of the UDCs was to promote private development, not to seek an extension of state enterprise.

The London Docklands Development Corporation set up in 1981 responded to a fact of changing economic geography: the progressive down-river drift of dockside trade and related industry and the changing nature of shipping practices which favoured containerization. Over many years the locally controlled councils had failed to prepare adequate plans for the area's regeneration. The LDDC swept aside the restrictive power brokering of the Thames-side authorities and opened the way to the Canary Wharf development which in time created 10.5 million sq. ft. of new office floor space. Competition with further office development in the City of London, together with continued opposition from the local authorities on the grounds that housing needs of nearby communities had been ignored, and the collapse of the property market before the project was completed, all conspired to give the scheme a fraught beginning. The developers, Olympia and York, went into receivership and the Jubilee line extension was delayed, but there has been a subsequent recovery and East London now possesses a dramatic new skyline and a commercial magnet to replace the former run-down assembly of dockside premises. Visually and functionally the result is as arresting as the new style of planning which gave it birth, but local communities suffered disadvantage as the housing needs of working-class districts were relegated to lower priorities – to the extent that Brownhill (1990) considered the development as 'another planning disaster'.

The Merseyside Development Corporation, also set up in 1981, was a much smaller scale enterprise, but it provided another test bed for further proposals in other parts of the country. In 1987 further UDCs were designated for the Black Country, Tyne and Wear, Trafford Park, Cardiff Bay and Teesside; in 1988 for Sheffield, Leeds, Bristol and Central Manchester; and in 1989 for Belfast (Laganside). In 1993 Plymouth Dockyard was designated. In the same year Birmingham Heartlands UDC replaced the city's earlier attempt to go it alone with its private company independent of government – the enterprise culture finally prevailed in this provincial bastion of local state, civic boosterism.

The Conservative government's approach to town planning was curiously mixed during the 1980s. There was no attempt to radically overhaul the system which regulated Britain's land use and development (the system itself was remarkably constant over a period of 30 years, apart from questions of compensation and betterment). No real broom of fresh thinking from a right-wing perspective was applied. An independent review by the Nuffield Foundation (1986) saw no need for any significant change, rather than improved co-ordination of planning at different levels of government and a strengthening of guidance from the centre. There was no stomach in any quarter for jettisoning the 1947 system, and the planning scene was featured by a preparedness in all quarters to accept the status quo. The planning profession fought a survivalist corner, and local authorities were content not to be harried by any prospect of change. Those inclined to run with a right-wing baton satisfied themselves with ad hoc genuflections to market-oriented policies and occasional withdrawals from public sector primacy. Any consistent agitation came from those left of centre who yearned for a return to the days when planning was all about the setting of social and economic objectives, redistributive policies, strong regional plans and the integration of the various elements in a comprehensive system. Ambrose (1986) asked 'whatever happened to planning?', while a group of radically-minded planners (Montgomery and Thornley, 1990) fell back on the collectivist ideal as the way forward.

The Conservative instinct with regard to planning was to play down the notion of a national planning system which offered strategic guidance in urban and regional affairs and aimed at an interrelated comprehensiveness. The days of regional studies and regional plans have long since gone. Local authority collaboration, as in the south-east through SERPLAN (the London and South East Regional Planning Conference), and in the West Midlands (the West Midlands Forum), maintains the regional perspective. But regional strategic considerations are now confined to statements of 'regional guidance' from government regional offices when County Structure Plans and Unitary Development Plans in metropolitan areas are being prepared. The recent proposals for the strategic development of the East Thames Corridor (or Thames Gateway as it is now called), in order to redress the east–west imbalance in the growth directions of metropolitan London, is a rare exception to the more usual 'hands off' approach.

By contrast, planning has relapsed into a set of disjointed initiatives – of which the EZs and UDCs were good examples. Grandiose structure plans were discounted. The setting up of new organizations with responsibilities previously held by state departments fitted the government's stance very well: a good example was English Heritage (the Historic Buildings and Monuments Commission for England) which took over conservation matters and historic buildings from the DOE. The notion of planning was also weakened when it was regarded as a burden on enterprise: Lord Young, Minister without Portfolio, incorporated this in the White Paper (1985), *Lifting the Burden*. Proposals were introduced for Simplified Planning Zones, with the objective of facilitating development and encouraging entrepreneurship. Meanwhile the status of approved development plans was reduced when it was indicated that in future they need not override other factors if the stimulation of enterprise was more pressing. Further, in 1987 the Use Classes Order was revised: virtually unchanged since 1948, the use classes (which determine whether planning permission is required or not for development) were relaxed, though not to any great extent. In 1988 the General Development Order was revised; this extended to permitted development rights for extensions to business premises.

These deregulative measures did not amount to very much and (as we shall see) they were largely overtaken by others, which had the effect of adding to a regulated planning system. An even greater prize of deregulation opened up in rural affairs – and was equally spurned. Attempts were made in the period 1983–4 to relax the green belt. During the 1970s the amount of land in England subject to green-belt policies increased significantly (Elson, 1986). In 1974 approved green belt land extended to 6,928 sq. km., an area extended to 15,815 sq. km. in 1984, the largest single tracts being around London, Birmingham – Coventry, West, South and North Yorkshire, also Cheshire and South and East Lancashire. In 1983 Patrick Jenkin, the environment secretary, issued draft circulars on green belt and housing land which advocated a loosening of green-belt boundaries. The conservation lobbies and the Tory shires were hostile to prospects of further development beyond the metropolitan fringes; Jenkin retreated and the published White Papers in 1984 restored the permanence to green belts. Deregulation had been thwarted. Enterprise culture had its limits, and pragmatism would prevail where other political values were at stake.

The same hesitation over how far to follow the instinct of market-led development applied to a set of proposals made by a group of private housebuilders known as Consortium Developments Ltd in the early 1980s for creating new settlements in countryside locations around London. The public sector new towns programme had come to an end, so too had town expansion, with the consequence that planned decentralization on the Abercrombie model had ceased. But pressure for building around the metropolitan fringe (and beyond the provincial conurbations too) continued unabated, with preferences for rural and semi-rural living adding to population levels in small country towns and villages in a significant way.

In the 1970s substantial private sector development at South Woodham Ferrers in Essex and at Lower Earley near Reading suggested the manner in which new communities would sustain the peripheral growth pattern in south-east England. Four proposals came from the consortium for new settlements at Tillingham Hall (Essex), Foxley Wood (Hampshire), Stone Bassett (Oxfordshire) and Westmere (Cambridgeshire). Tillingham Hall was rejected by Nicholas Ridley in 1989; it was in the London green belt at one of its narrowest points. He was minded to approve Foxley Wood, but his successor, Chris Patten, rejected it, together with Stone Bassett, in 1989. By this time a strengthened environmental lobby had to be appeased. Westmere, despite support from the county council, was rejected in 1991. The ideological commitment to enterprise and deregulation was not sustained (if indeed it had ever taken off in some DOE circles); there was a failure of nerve, and pandering to Tory 'nimbyism' and a retreat into protective green belt and countryside values won the day. By now it was clear that the biggest beneficiaries of the planning system were the special interest groups and lobbies, particularly when they were in harmony with environmental values relating to countryside protection. The fact that the same values sought to protect Conservative interests in maintaining residential exclusivity in suburban and rural locations made them extremely powerful.

The planning system had so far conferred considerable discretion upon local councils in determining applications for development, and with cases being decided on their merits (while within the general parameters of a development plan) the DOE Inspectorate bore a considerable burden of work in handling appeals. A White Paper in 1989, *The Future of Development Plans*, provided the basis for an altogether tighter planning system in which the provisions of a development plan were to be overriding in the consideration of planning applications. This 'plan-led' planning system finds clear expression in the Planning and Compensation Act, 1991: 'where, in making any determination under the Planning Acts, regard is to be had to the development plan, the determination shall be made in accordance with the plan unless material considerations dictate otherwise' (s. 26). This alters the previous presumption in favour of development. The system has been bolstered by a comprehensive set of Planning Policy Guidance Notes (PPGs) and statements of Regional Guidance.

The change in approach came from a number of objectives. If the number of planning appeals handled by the inspectorate could be reduced, the central state role would be seen to have diminished. Equally, if local authority plans had primacy in decisions on planning applications, then local councils would be seen as bearing their own responsibilities. But it did not work out like that. In slavish adherence to PPGs and Regional Guidance, local authorities are able to pass the blame for unpopular policies (e.g. housing allocations and road proposals) onto government. The result has been that the planning system is now more regulated and systemized than ever before; local initiative and enterprise is much reduced; and because of the gauntlet of public consultations, plans become reduced to the lowest common denominator of acceptability. Seen from this perspective the DOE has failed to articulate the notion of a deregulated, enterprise-oriented planning system. The department's preferred procedures show characteristics which are out of kilter with the political philosophy of the government it serves.

On the other hand, inner-city planning has embraced initiatives which do indicate a different style of planning from the norms of earlier decades. We have already noted the increased role of the private developer in Enterprise Zones and the work of the Urban Development Corporations. The major financial institutions were encouraged to invest in inner city recovery through a series of new incentives; these included the urban regeneration grant and city grant, both of which depended on 'leverage', i.e. the enhancement given to public investment through securing additional private investment. The attempts at local authority economic planning development undertaken by certain Labour councils in the early 1980s were soon overtaken by these mixed sector initiatives.

A modest return to giving greater scope to local authority direction came with City Challenge, introduced in 1991, though the comparison with inner-city planning pre-1980 was still marked. The objective this time was in competitive bidding in order to obtain funds for worthy schemes. Opponents argued that inner-city problems were such that more money should be on the table anyway and that the objectives of planning were being reached only through something akin to a lottery. But the government's point was that the competitive bidding encouraged the submission of better and more imaginative schemes, involving the private and voluntary sectors as well as the local community. In this competitive process the planning system responded to right-wing expectations.

Related Planning Matters

Housing

The colours of the new government were perhaps best seen with regard to public sector housing. No other welfare programme has been cut so substantially (Forrest and Murie, 1988). House building has been curtailed, exchequer subsidies for council tenants have been cut and council rents have risen. Council estates have been disposed of to private developers and quasi-public trusts. In the search for a property-owning democracy council house sales were promoted through a statutory 'right to buy'. Discounts on sales were progressively raised as public assets were sold at below market value. The council housing sector is now being dismantled through compulsory competitive tendering.

The disposal of council houses was nothing new, but it was not until the 1960s that council house sales became a major issue in housing policy. Since 1945 however there has been a major political divide between the two main parties. During the Second World War the sale of council houses was forbidden and refusals were maintained subsequently by Labour. In 1951 the Conservatives were committed to encourage sales and a general consent was issued in Macmillan's Housing Act of 1952, which removed the requirement that the local authority was obliged to obtain the best price.

In 1968 the Wilson Government imposed a limit on the proportion of municipal stock sold annually in the major conurbations. In 1970 the restrictions were removed, and in 1974 Labour did not rescind the general consent to council house sales. During the later-1970s Conservative councils increasingly implemented policies within the terms of the general consent and the numbers of sales rose. With the new Conservative Government, the Housing Act, 1980, conferred the right to buy. Huge numbers of sales were recorded in the early 1980s as a consequence, the total reaching more than a million dwellings by 1987, by which time the wave of selling had clearly passed. Something like one-eighth of the council stock in England was sold during this period. The sales were higher in the south-east, East Midlands, east and south-west regions, and lower in London (particularly the inner London boroughs) and the northern regions. Scotland, which had the highest level of council housing in Britain, had the lowest rate of sales. Northern urban authorities recorded low sale figures; southern rural authorities (where council housing was least common) recorded the highest. Flats (30 per cent of the total council stock) featured in the fewest sales (5 per cent, 1981–5).

British council housing is in sharp contraction, in numerical terms, relatively and absolutely. In 1979 a 60-year period was brought to a close. During this time the tenure structure of British housing was given a marked state imprint through the number of dwellings built by local authorities; and payment of subsidies to bring rents within the reach of lower income households, played a large part in welfare policies. In spite of its faults, council housing, within the range of welfare state provision, most successfully targeted the working class. But from 1979 the Conservative's housing policy was that '*some* people *need* council housing but most people *want* owner occupation' (Forrest and Murie, 1988, p. 66). Consequently, by the 1980s council housing was increasingly catering for specific groups within the working class; it became a residual service for them and for the poor, and their rents were paid through benefit arrangements. Council housing became 'social housing' catering for the needs of a residual population, denied entry on cost grounds to either the owner-occupier market or the privately-rented sector. Just as the introduction of the council house during the inter-war years and its massive expansion post-1945 had served to restructure the housing market and reorganize the welfare state, so too did its contraction during the 1980s and 1990s. Privatization by means of council house sales extended home ownership, redistributed wealth and met the government's objectives of limiting the role of the state.

During the late 1980s privatization moved into a higher gear. With individual sales falling, new methods of demunicipalization were introduced. Housing Action Trusts were formed on government initiative to take over areas of poor housing; the intention was to renovate the properties and pass them on to different tenures and ownerships including housing associations, tenant co-operatives, approved ground landlords or owner occupiers. In another initiative whole estates were sold to developers: two particularly large disposals were the GLC Thamesmead development and Knowsley's Cantril Farm Estate. Freedom of choice was extended when local authority tenants were given the right to transfer to other landlords. Finally, from the mid-1990s, the massive dismemberment of local stock was set in train through compulsory competitive tendering.

Meanwhile another bastion of centralization in the housing field had its wings clipped – the Housing Corporation. The brainchild of Sir Keith Joseph when he was housing minister, it was set up in 1964. His Labour successor Richard Crossman welcomed it (and the voluntary housing movement) as 'the third arm in housing' when 1,000 associations then owned a total of 100,000 dwellings. The Housing Act, 1974, switched the emphasis from co-ownership to rented homes, the housing association grant (HAG) was introduced, and the corporation was made responsible for the funding of the whole voluntary housing movement. Between 1964 and 1979 the partnership between the housing associations and the corporation produced more than 140,000 homes, with the peak building period in the later-1970s. Reorganization took place in the 1980s with Scottish operations moving to a new organization called Scottish Homes and a Welsh independent body created in Tai Cymru. Mixed funding and competition was introduced by the environment secretary, Nicholas Ridley. The economic recession of the early 1990s saw HAG rates reduced sharply and by the middle 1990s the corporation was no longer commanding its early high level of reputation.

By the end of the century a remarkable 20-year period will have unfolded. It is unlikely that an incoming Labour government, if elected in 1997, will reverse the steps taken since 1980 to privatize a substantial section of the public housing stock. It may halt further demunicipalization, but there is little likelihood of a return to the role of local authority house provider which saw its high-watermark during the 1970s. The arguments for the extension of tenant choice and the improvement of efficiency outside the grasp of local authority bureaucracy have gone too far, while pragmatically the constant need to reduce the public sector borrowing requirement will continue to be a determinant.

In the meantime the long-running saga relating to the hostility against tall blocks and the anti-social feeling they incurred was continued in a new level of objection. This was taken up by the Land Use Research Unit at King's College in the University of London where Alice Coleman took a determined lead (Alice Coleman, 1985). Her study area includes two of the London boroughs which contain more council flats than anywhere else (Southwark and Tower Hamlets), and also, for comparison, an out-of-town estate south-east of Oxford (Blackbird Leys), where there are some 4,000 dwellings. These features have been mapped in detail and rigorously tested to see which of them are associated with various lapses in civilized behaviour: litter-dropping, graffiti-scrawling, vandalism, pollution by excrement, and family breakdown leading to children being placed in care. These were the differences between modern problem estates and the ordinary unplanned housing of the past. The involvement of so many planners, architects, developers, housing managers, and DOE housing staff suggests a relative failure, for over 20–30 years of their collective minds in determining design. It allowed Coleman to ask the following question:

> Why should Utopia have been such an all-pervading failure, when it was envisaged as a form of national salvation? It was conceived in compassion but has been born and bred in authoritarianism, profligacy and frustration. It aimed to liberate people from the slums but has come to represent an even worse form of bondage. It aspired to beautify the urban environment, but has been transmogrified into the epitome of ugliness. Its redemption, after 40 years, is not only a matter of improving the

buildings, but also of winning the hearts and minds of those who create and control them.

Regional economic planning

As we saw in chapter 8, Labour maintained the regional aid structure, which had been a consistent feature of post-war government policy, until 1977 when regional aid was sharply reduced. Regional economic planning virtually disappeared in England, though the Scottish and Welsh Development Agencies gave new frameworks for those two parts of the United Kingdom. In Scotland the SDA gave integration and strategic direction to planning, though in Wales the WDA pursued a rather more opportunist course.

The Conservatives post-1979 did nothing to encourage the restoration of a regional economic thrust in planning circles. Regional Economic Planning Councils were quickly abolished. Planned office decentralization soon had no part to play. The Office Development Permit was withdrawn immediately and the Location of Offices Bureau abolished in 1981. The Industrial Development Certificate, a major key to the operation of regional policy since 1947, was first suspended and finally abolished in 1986. Regional aid was reduced.

Arrangements for regional assistance have been restructured. In 1984 the category of Special Development Area was abolished; the remaining two (Development Area and Intermediate Area) survived and the West Midlands was included in the coverage of the latter. In 1993, assisted status was granted to areas of colliery closures, parts of East Anglia, inner-east London and certain coastal areas. Meanwhile, the European Community's Regional Development Fund, established in 1975, has flourished and the UK has done rather well out of it. However, overall the emphasis is now firmly on selective assistance, and the regional dimension of economic planning, so beloved of the early post-war planners, has withered. Reliance on a patchwork of economic promotion has quite overtaken any notion of securing development guided by a strategic location policy. Infrastructure projects such as motorway developments, airport extensions, estuarial improvements and the Channel Tunnel have been accorded no wider regional significance. The comparison with the regional intention, if not necessarily the outcomes, of earlier governments in post-war Britain is striking. The state, local and central, is but one player in regional development; overall, the market will determine regional economic fortunes. Meanwhile local authorities will enhance their economic position through success in 'place marketing', and similar boosts to civic endeavour.

The environment

If the 1970s had been the decade when town planning was influenced by the social sciences, then the 1980s and particularly the 1990s have been the decades most influenced by environmental considerations. A flurry of speculation and concern had marked the 1970s when an increasingly vigorous environmental debate was mounted. There were warnings of landscape changes in Britain: the reduction of trees and general vegetative cover, particularly in the English lowlands, and sharp reductions in numbers and varieties of plants and animals. Huge advances in the application of science and technology to farming served to obliterate herb-rich hay meadows, drain the wetlands, reclaim moor and heath for arable land, and remove hedgerows and copses. Shoard (1980) wrote of this loss as 'the theft of the countryside'. Environmental and landscape issues came to the fore. The dragon to be slain was development in all its forms, and planning was seen as an accessory to the crime. Wider perspectives fuelled purely national anxieties. Max Nicholson (1970) expressed an international concern about the vulnerability of the natural environment and Schumacher (1973) considered the values inherent in current philosophies which applied to man's relationship with nature. Global and inevitably long-term approaches to pressing environmental problems were stressed. Amenity bodies and pressure groups came to play active roles in landscape protection (the Council for the Preservation of Rural England (CPRE) for example) and the wider issues of environmental management in its various aspects, particularly traffic restraint (Transport 2000 for example).

In 1979 the environment was not a priority on the government's agenda. However, it inherited Labour's Countryside Bill, introduced in 1978, which fell with the general election of May 1979. Michael Heseltine reintroduced the measure, now the Wildlife and Countryside Bill, in November 1980; believed to be a non-controversial piece of legislation, the bill's passage commenced in the House of Lords, yet it attracted a record of 1,120 amendments and it took longer to negotiate in Parliament than any other bill that session. The bulk of the controversy centred around those animals and plants which were to be protected (indicative of widespread environmental and wildlife concerns). But the act (it received the Royal Assent in October 1981) was primarily concerned with the control of the conflict between agriculture and wildlife, and landscape. The previous Labour government had wrestled with the problem of moorland ploughing in the Exmoor National Park (so transforming the very landscape feature that had justified Exmoor's designation as a National Park). The new farming practice could not be stopped as it was exempt from planning or indeed any form of public control, and Labour's bill sought to give National Park authorities power to make conservation orders. Heseltine's measure resisted compulsory reserve powers and relied on voluntary management agreements.

The government would be drawn further along the road of landscape protection, through the designation of Environmentally Sensitive Areas (ESA). Originating as a British policy initiative, they were introduced by the European Community in 1985 and implemented in Britain by the Agriculture Act, 1986. Six were designated that year, covering a range of environmental conditions: grazing marsh (Somerset Levels and the Norfolk Broads), grassland (Pennine Dales and South Downs), small-scale field system (West Penwith) and afforestation (Cambrian Mountains). With further additions to the programme, a total of 2.5 million acres are now covered by ESAs where farmers are given financial inducements to manage and enhance traditional countryside landscapes.

Towards the end of the 1980s there was a perceptible quickening of environmental concerns in planning circles. One factor was the report of the United Nations' World Commission on Environment and Development, *Our Common Future* (1987). Chaired by the Prime Minister of Norway, Mrs Brundtland, it popularized the notion of sustainability, or the proper stewardship of the environment in the interests of future generations. Within a few years the word 'sustainability' could scarcely be kept out of the planning vocabulary. Another factor was the discovery by geographers and the scientific community of global warming through increases in so-called greenhouse gasses. Mrs Thatcher lent her personal authority to governmental pronouncements of concern.

A sympathetic secretary of state, Chris Patten, brought out an environmental White Paper *This Common Inheritance* (1990). Promising strengthened and integrated environmental policies it recorded:

> What we are doing already and what we plan to do to make our air and water cleaner; to preserve the beauties of our countryside and historic buildings; to improve the quality of life in our towns and cities; to promote more research and public information as to the foundations of good environmental policy; to develop a more open and constructive dialogue with industry, local government and voluntary groups; to develop the

institutions that monitor and regulate environmental quality; to explore new ways of using economic pressures to achieve environmental goals; to play our full part in the environmental diplomacy that will dominate the international agenda in future decades; and much else. (para 139)

This document of nearly 300 pages, containing no fewer than 350 proposals, spoke a new planning language for the 1990s. The Environmental Protection Act, 1990, soon followed to give substance to some of the undertakings.

10 Town Planning and the Planning Ideal

Some concluding reflections can now be offered, drawn from the history of twentieth-century town planning which has been sketched in earlier chapters. First, the successive phases through which British town planning has evolved over approximately the last 90 years are summarized; the detail is stripped away, the essential features highlighted. In like manner, the course of the rise and fall of the planning ideal (the socio-political framework against which town planning itself has unfolded) is also charted. Second, the implications for present-day town planning are drawn. As a new century is approached, where stand the principles and practice of town planning? What are its likely directions over the medium-term future?

Recapitulation: the Past Retraced

Two themes have been addressed: the twentieth-century development of town planning (the circumstances of its genesis, its years of high expectations and its relapse into regulatory administration) and of planning as a state activity in economic and social affairs (its rise, its blossoming and its fall). The two themes interconnect, though only imperfectly; they came together most obviously during the middle years of the twentieth century when town planning was propelled into a high profile role on the back of a much widened interventionism by the state. In the last 20 years there has been a curious, partial divergence: the role of the state has withered in substantial areas, yet the activity of town planning has been maintained, embedded in the inertia of governmental structures and the attendant bureaucracy.

The birth of town planning (chapter 2) can be dated to the years between 1895 and 1910, though an even wider span from 1885 to the outbreak of the Great War still provides a recognizable period in which the formative features may be seen. During these years town planning took shape, fed from at least six critical directions. One, attempts were made to secure improved housing conditions for the labouring classes, through philanthropic experiments. Two, evidence was presented that, for the poor and the ill-housed, urban conditions in late-Victorian Britain were prejudicial to national health, fitness and morality. Three, a new solution was advanced: the development of garden suburbs for low density housing, and of the garden city for urban dispersal in accordance with a decentralist strategy. Four, experiences were shared with other industrially-advanced countries which had rather different responses to urban problems. In the event, Britain's preferred model not only suited British conditions but also proved internationally attractive. Five, town planning took root in the institutions of government, education and the professions. Six, once established it proved adept in quickly developing a broader agenda and building up an integrative corpus of knowledge drawn from many disciplines relating to 'urban affairs'.

The infant town planning rested on an activity which revolved around a need (and the means) to secure lasting improvements to housing and the environmental conditions in British cities for those (insofar as could be arranged) to whom these things would otherwise be denied. The parameters of its birth were set by the socio-political crucible of late-Victorian and Edwardian Britain. Town planning stood for an extension of public control over private interests in land and property. Its case was that such an extension was justified in the public interest – health and fitness – and it was also able to claim moral supremacy in its appeal to the virtues of art and design and of equity. It was in tune with its age, and a middle class and professional elite recruited political sentiments to its ideals.

After the hiatus of war, town planning gained a foothold in national affairs between 1919 and 1939 (chapter 4). In many ways it had to make a new start, but there were a number of factors in its favour, particularly town planning's close association with housing and the demands of post-war reconstruction. There were important developments in statutory planning; 'town planning' was widened to 'town and country planning' and by 1939 the preparation of schemes was being undertaken (if not advanced very far) by the majority of local councils. Moreover, the exercise of regional planning was widely in evidence. State involvement in new housing and, later, clearance and rebuilding, proved of great significance; over one million council houses were built between the two wars, and standards of working-class accommodation met many of the ambitions of the early twentieth-century reformers. The core of the town planning activity continued to widen, elusively in matters concerning roads, rather more obviously with regard to countryside affairs, where a rural protection, anti-urban stance became a feature. Outside Britain, particularly in continental Europe where the Modern Movement and the Corbusien model of workers' apartment blocks spoke a language which British vernacular traditions scarcely recognized, alternative town planning styles were being advanced. Britain, however, remained relatively aloof and intellectually unchallenged on its home ground, though its town planning promise had still to come to fruition.

The situation changed abruptly between 1939 and 1945 (chapter 5). Town planning, its aims endorsed uncritically as in the public interest, became part of the war effort; ambitious plans were prepared for reconstruction and policies for the post-war era were prescribed. New legislation gave sweeping powers. An enthusiasm for economic and social planning in national affairs swept town planning along, its technical prowess accepted as expert guidance, and its claim to represent 'higher interests' as yet unsullied.

The Attlee years from 1945 to 1951 (chapter 6) gave town planning the secure governmental framework to which it had aspired. The elements of the post-war statutory system were put in place; legislation in 1947, crucial in this regard, provided the obligatory development plan and made arrangements for the control of development by local councils, unencumbered by the burden of compensation. The subjugation of private interests in land and property by the state was taken to new levels. Legislation in respect of new towns, national parks, industrial location (with its implications for regional policy) and agriculture, together with official action on such matters as housing provision and transport, enhanced town planning's integrative aspirations.

During the next quarter of a century the system which had been put into place proved a secure base for the aggrandisement of town planning (chapter 7). These were years when political sentiment amongst the political parties favoured interventionist state roles, and town planning was given repeated openings to prove its worth, particularly under the Macmillan and Wilson Governments. The expansion of town planning during this time forms the high-watermark of its post-war reputation. The system provided by the 1947 legislation proved remarkably robust and, with the exception of the compensation and betterment issue which became a political football, the fundamentals remained unchanged; nothing was taken away, many new features were added. Town planning presided over an era in which critical elements of post-war Britain were put in place: new towns, national parks, a protective hand for the countryside, green belts, a massive housing expansion, urban renewal, town centre redevelopment, road improvements, and schemes of regional development. By the mid-1970s town planning was administratively entrenched in central and local government. Meanwhile its rapidly growing profession had secured the royal seal of approval, and while its claims for omnicompetence were unrivalled, its language was now more of the secure bureaucrat than the free-wheeling visionary of old.

But the tide was turning. During the later 1970s serious doubts about the town planning advance were pressed home (chapter 8). Social science critiques proved wounding and there was mounting dissatisfaction with the seemingly mundane concerns of old-style 'physical' planning at a time when social and welfare problems were more acute. But town planning was still able to take advantage of an enlarged power base in a reorganized system of local government and it succeeded in widening its remit in corporate management. Meanwhile the statutory town planning machine had a momentum of its own; a regular diet of plan-making and the routine of development control ensured a high profile for the activity in local affairs.

Throughout the 1980s and into the 1990s town planning maintained its entrenched statutory position, but its importance markedly diminished (chapter 9). Grandiose strategic plans were disavowed, local authority housing programmes came to an end, regional economic planning declined to insignificance. However, there was no dismantling of the inherited town planning system, and in certain regards, because of the introduction of national policy 'advice', it was conducted on a more systematized basis than ever before. Meanwhile the new-found awareness of environmental matters raised a new agenda for town planning; it promised to revise the town planning agenda, with new questions for its twenty-first century remit.

A number of salient points arise from this historical sketch. The first lies in the factors which attended the very origins of town planning. It is worth emphasizing that these focused on housing and the layout of residential land. The improvements which were advocated met a perceived public interest, and the argument was therefore advanced that it was legitimate to seek to regulate private interests by public control.

This initial focus was later widened to include broader concerns related to the use of land, and the case for control to be exercised to meet public interests was hugely extended as the century unfolded.

The second point is that once established as a profession, the boundaries of town planning proved to be elastic. Its claim for comprehensiveness, and the demand to be seen in full integration with other spatial or thematic phenomena, proved irresistible in the halcyon days of the post-war era. At best this was pragmatic adjustment to changing circumstances; at worst it led to overweening pretentions. Lack of definitions do not help; there is an uncomfortable truth in the remark that 'town planning is what town planners do'. At a time when circumstances encouraged a wide engagement, this is precisely what was sought.

A third observation is that what stands for town planning at any one time (its power, its targets, its weight) is shaped by current socio-political conditions. Town planning was weak between the wars because its powers were circumscribed, and its objectives limited; it shot to prominence in the 1940s when it was called upon to be part of a national programme of reconstruction. It maintained an important place in the affairs of the country because governments of opposing political sentiment found that it was part of a convenient post-war settlement; and it is now held in less regard because its public sector sympathies run alien to political outlooks which prefer market-oriented perspectives. Town planning has its myths: one of them is that the activity represented a long march forward to enlightenment from nineteenth-century urban philistinism. A proper reading of town planning history soon dispels that view. The adoption of town planning in its various capacities throughout the century has been no uniform course of progression. Governments up to 1939 conferred powers sparingly; it drifted into town planning, at best it was provoked into it. In the 1940s it was convenient for government for town planning to be encouraged to add a visionary dash to the language of reconstruction. In recent years political sentiment has seen town planning as much less grandiose, rather in the style of short-term managerialism.

The parallel history of the planning ideal, which forms a backcloth of the town planning account, opens with the early twentieth-century rise in state involvement in economic and social affairs, sharply extended (but only temporarily) by the impact of the Great War. The case was made in ideological terms for a further extension in the 1930s, but it required the war to actually bring this about. A broad political consensus made it possible for some basic features of economic and social planning and the institutions of the welfare state to be maintained until the late-1970s. Thereafter, as the merits of the market were rediscovered, the various features of state interventionism were gradually removed.

The collectivist advance had already been signalled before the close of the nineteenth century, though the encroachments into private property interests were gradual (chapter 1). However by the turn of the century, and certainly by 1914, a trend was already clear. A system of modern local government was established with the help of a professional administrative class, and expanded to supervise the delivery of social welfare programmes, as in education and housing. Meanwhile measures were progressively put in place to regulate the provision of urban infrastructure, and a number of services (typically gas, electricity, water and transport) were provided by municipal councils.

The adoption of collectivist forms of state organization continued; after 1918 housing was one particular area where private interests were breached. The slow and uncertain trend was actively pushed by transformed political sentiment (chapter 3). The Fabian Society was an early advocate and New Liberalism made a break from the old Gladstonian stance. The Conservatives had their own tradition of using the state to secure social reform. However, it was a rejuvenated Labour Party in the 1930s that took the lead in outlining a programme of socialist economic planning under central direction. Meanwhile the views of J. M. Keynes commanded increasing support: economic mechanisms had broken down and interventionary policies from the centre were needed. An active state was necessary to revitalize industry and stabilize the western world. Political control over economic institutions would replace a fickle market by administrative efficiency.

The advent of the Second World War created a new situation which was conducive to the practical application of the theoretical speculation of the 1930s (chapter 5). The role of government in Britain's affairs was massively augmented; a corporate state was effectively established. Between mid-1940 and the end of 1941 the country had a command economy and huge advances were made in the structures of a collectivist state. The Coalition Government became a radical, reforming administration. State planning prospered.

The new Labour Government, elected in 1945, used the Coalition's machinery of government to discharge a socialist programme (including nationalization) of state regulation of economic, social and related matters (chapter 6). All three main political parties were committed to using the state for economic reconstruction and social redistribution. The dimensions of consensus politics had been set, resting on a subscription to Keynesian economic policies and the provisions of a welfare state in matters of housing, health and national insurance.

The broad orthodoxy of the consensual political settlement extended throughout Labour and Conservative governments until the first cracks appeared in the mid-1970s (chapter 7). There were shifts of emphasis within the period: diminished enthusiasm for instruments of planning during the 1950s may be contrasted with a new interest in them in the 1960s. Economic expansion, particularly under Harold Wilson, to restore Britain's flagging industrial performance, would be planning-led. Edward Heath gave signs of making a definitive shift towards private enterprise, yet his government reasserted forms of managerialism.

During the middle 1970s the post-war consensus finally broke with clear signs of impending departures from long-standing arrangements for state regulation in economic and social affairs (chapter 8). Collectivism was seen as one important cause of Britain's economic decline; the New Right offered the alternatives of monetarism and market economics to combat Keynesianism, inflated public service bureaucracies, and an overloaded state. Callaghan's government ran into increasing problems and, after partial attempts to follow post-Keynesian policies, was finally defeated on a no-confidence motion.

Under Margaret Thatcher the slogan 'rolling back the frontiers of the state' was articulated in policies which signalled the abandonment of the post-1945 settlement (chapter 9). The objectives were that collectivism would be replaced by individualism, and state regulation by personal freedoms. The private market in its many forms was looked to in preference to the state (central, local or ad hoc public bodies) for the distribution of resources. During the 1980s and 1990s state bureaucracies gave way to alternatives secured by privatization, externalization and deregulation. New managerial approaches have emphasized 'value for money' in public spending.

Implications for Town Planning Today

Prior to 1939 developments affecting town planning were largely the product of influences *within* the boundaries of the activity itself. These included intellectual advances, methodological sophistication, legislative and administrative progress and dominant fashions in the disciplines of the built environment, notably engineering and architecture. After 1945 the formative influences upon town planning have in the main been derived from sources *outside* the boundaries of the activity. They have been essentially those of a political nature revolving around the limits of state involvement in the planning of social and economic affairs. The salient fact for town planning at the present time is that from the late 1970s British governments have taken conscious steps to limit the outreach of the state and restore large sections of the market system. As the twentieth century draws to a close societal expectations from town planning, and its place in the national scheme of things, are inescapably reduced as the planning ideal itself has atrophied. There is a particular problem for town planning's professional idealism. Traditionally it has focused around notions of public service. It now finds it hard to transfer its affections from a system where local government was all about service provision to one where services are purchased competitively.

Post-war British town planning has experienced extremes in fortunes. The first 20 years provided a strong backing of professional encouragement, government support and (by and large) public endorsement. The last 20 years have seen that support increasingly weakened as the state collectivism on which so much depended became unworkable. State planning in economic and social spheres collapsed under its own weight, as Hayek prophesied it would. But other changes were also underway: top heavy, corporate structures typical of 'Fordist' mass production broke up, in due time financial markets were deregulated, and it became apparent that the global economy was beyond the reach of national governments. The comprehensive *dirigisme* that planning aspired to, and which town planning echoed in its wake, could not be sustained. This by itself did not invalidate the practice of town planning but it severely weakened its intellectual credentials and reduced its operational activities.

The break-up of the post-war consensus during the late 1970s, confirmed during the first Thatcher Administration, soon led to speculation as to how the 1980s would turn out. The years of transition were marked by uncertain party political directions. One attempt 'to break the mould' was the creation of the Social Democratic Party in March 1981, but it led to no drastic departure from the past consensus, rather an earnest attempt to enlighten it with the lessons derived from the experiences of the 1960s and 1970s. One observer at the time, Beer (1982), envisioned five probable futures. Two were collectivist: toryism and socialism. It was possible that Tory collectivism would continue, in admiration for the paternalistic statecraft of Harold Macmillan, and for the policies of his regime; this would imply a corporatist economy managed by a technocratic elite, suitably moderated by party government and parliamentary democracy. On the other hand, socialism, building on the centralized bureaucratic state, could lean more towards a planned economy with egalitarian social programmes.

The remaining three futures were all post-collectivist: neo-liberalism, neo-socialism and neo-radicalism. Beer argued that neo-liberals would seek to move the burdens of social choice from government and politics to the market; the number and complexity of questions that government has to decide would be reduced. On the other hand, neo-socialists and neo-radicals would leave these tasks in the public sector, attempting by participatory reforms to resuscitate the political system in order to mobilize consent.

In fact, the administrations of both Margaret Thatcher and John Major have followed the neo-liberal line, so providing a definitive political backcloth to the years since 1979. In the middle 1990s it is again pertinent to speculate about likely political scenarios for the short- and medium-term future. The socio-political context for town planning will be framed by their parameters. The options probably revolve around whether, and the extent to which, post-collectivist neo-liberalism reverts to neo-socialism. In purely party political terms the Conservative Party, either standing alone or as the most powerful element in a coalition, has held power for 70 out of the 100 years since 1895. This encourages Seldon and Ball (1994) to conclude that 'its very pragmatism and adaptability will allow it to overcome the severe internal and support problems it faces in the 1990s, and will in all probability ensure that the cycles of Conservative dominance will be repeated well into the twenty-first century' (p. 65). Those optimistic about the future of right-wing ideas see no dead-end for the Conservative agenda, rather that public attitudes throughout the western democracies favour continued shifts in this direction. High taxes are resisted; higher standards of public service are demanded at the lowest possible public cost. Highly regulated and centrally managed bureaucracies should be bypassed in favour of a new model of government which is pluralist, decentralized and entrepreneurial. There is a tide of political and managerial sentiment, internationally, running in support of such forms of twenty-first century governance – a massive reversal of the broad endorsement given to the collectivist agenda in the years following 1945.

Somewhere between the two positions it may be argued that while too much had been expected of governments in the post-war period, ascribed as they were with a wisdom and an efficacy denied to other human institutions, it would be equally wrong to expect too much of the market. Gray (1993) asserts that it would be an error 'to suppose that market institutions, if only they are left alone, will achieve a sort of natural co-ordination among human activities, which only the exogenous forces of government intervention disrupt' (p. x). The market is as fallible and imperfect as any other human institution, and therefore what is needed is not a minimum state, rather a limited or framework government, with significant positive responsibilities. This may be the pendulum around which British electoral sympathies might settle.

On the other hand, political support may incline to the left. There is distaste for the social polarization, political authoritarianism and the economic weakness which has marked the greater part of the period since 1979, sentiments which Tony Blair's New Labour has exploited. The 'supply-side' reforms of the Thatcher and Major governments have scarcely resulted in higher economic growth or better welfare, while inequality between the private and public sectors in education, housing and health is just as, or even more marked than hitherto. A return to Keynesian economics is urged by Hutton (1995) in a book which lays the intellectual foundations for the Blair revolution, a function which Michael Shanks' *The Stagnant Society* (1961) performed for Harold Wilson's revitalized Labour Party over 30 years ago.

Such speculation does not rest on the outcome of the next general election, nor the performance in office of the party which wins it. The thesis is more concerned with the broad canvas of trends in political economy and the way they are seen by the electorates in the western social democracies. In Britain it seems likely that the directional changes which have marked the 1980s and the first half of the 1990s will continue to unfold: a rejection of the post-war collectivist state, adoptions of decentralized and pluralist forms of governance, and greater reliance on the market for the distribution of rewards and resources. A new post-collectivist consensus is emerging around which the major political parties can cohere. It implies a withering and a sustained diminution of the twentieth-century notion of the planning ideal. It does not imply the rejection of town planning within that context, but it does suggest that it will be expected to perform a very different set of tasks.

We might expect that town planning will retreat from the commanding heights it reached immediately post-war and enhanced in the Macmillan–Wilson–Heath eras. The jobs it will have to do will be in the main relatively low key, short term project-based, and incrementalist and managerial in style, rather than long term and strategic. We live in a transition period to post-collectivism and the future institutional map is admittedly not yet clear, but it seems likely that state planning will play little part in it. For an activity which has relied so much on state interest (at least) and support (sometimes), town planning is now in the position of not being able to rely on either. Practitioners are faced with the antithesis of their own ideology, namely that the idea that man can shape the world around him according to his wishes is a 'fatal conceit' (Hayek, 1988).

In the mid-1990s town planning has a socio-political context within which to operate, which is less sympathetic to its objectives and provides conditions less conducive to their realization than for nearly 60 years. In the quarter century or so after 1945 governments took responsibility for the economy and for welfare, and town planning both in its regulatory and redistributive aspects fitted well into the scheme of things. That is not the situation now. No party forming a government today would contemplate the large-scale state interventions in social and economic affairs, practised even as recently as the late 1970s; the very language of planning has been diluted to virtual non-existence. Town planning is neutered; its visionary, financially naïve excesses are absent from contemporary agendas. It is tolerated in Whitehall as a harmless low-key activity which keeps local authority performance broadly under control; and may well be marginally beneficial as a useful balancing ploy among contending aspirants in environmental protection. Britain may have been run during the war by means of a successful command economy, and socialist planning after it may have promised popular results. But 50 years on a peacetime economy is best run by allowing the market to allocate resources; state commercialism with its bureaucracies is much less efficient. Recent years have seen the dismantling of state-run enterprises in most advanced countries and it may well be that we are to embark on the privatization of a large part of state welfare. Our foreseeable political future is governed by the eclipse of collectivism and the retreating tide of the state; the only variable is how far the ebb flow will proceed. The market is to be relied upon as the appropriate mechanism for allocating resources and the emphasis is to be on individual choice.

All this has been reasonably clear for many years, but as yet there has been no adjustment of town planning in either its objectives or its means of operation to fit more appropriately the political and institutional parameters against which it is obliged to work, and the dominant ethos that will govern its directions. The critical issue before British town planning today is to address the problem of 'political and institutional fit'. The basic arrangements for the operation of town planning were fixed in the Town and Country Planning Act, 1947; amended, added to and codified since, they are institutionalized through a Whitehall mega-department and local councils. Long-espoused policies governing development and the use of land proclaim the monopoly of public wisdom over these matters: urban areas are contained as much as possible and the countryside is protected through a system of designation (green belt, areas of outstanding natural beauty etc.). The present system (though it has not always been so) emphasizes the importance accorded to the plan: proposals for development which do not accord with the plan receive short shrift. The Department of the Environment is content with this, because it reduces the number of appeals to the Secretary of State while at the same time (through Planning Policy Guidance Notes and Regional Guidance) allowing them to dictate broad policy thrusts. Local authorities find their position a secure one. And the major players in the system (volume house builders, major property interests, residential and amenity groups) find they can use it to their benefit. Major controversy is conducted via consultations, inquiries and examinations in public.

All this produces a surprise-free, highly regulatory, over-systematized set of arrangements for town planning; what is missing is entrepreneurship, novelty, experimentation and creative departures from the norm which can enliven future developments. It is remarkable that this system, so much in conformity with the products of the post-war consensus, should have survived so long. Town planning represents a huge area of state direction over private interests. Some of this is justified; a good deal of it could be relaxed. Free market opportunities have not yet been opened up to the operation of town planning. For this to happen some planning policies would need urgent reconsideration against a new look at urban and rural futures. In 1945 there was a broad consensus as to what sort of cities, and what sort of countryside prevailed. Half a century on rather different futures are likely and the highly prescriptive town planning system that operates today acts more as a barrier to change than an opportunity.

One of the critical questions before town planning concerns the 'public interest' – its definition and who defines it. During the nineteenth century, over a period approaching 50 years, the supremacy of public over private interests was established in matters of urban health, housing and sanitation. Successive powers were taken by the state to provide clean drinking water, to enforce the removal of wastes and to impose minimum standards in housing accommodation. By the close of the Victorian period private interests in land and property had been successfully breached. It fell to town planning to extend markedly the precedents which had been established. The early case for town planning was that through the prosecution of Town Planning Schemes the public interest would be met by safeguarding an appropriate use of land and by ensuring that the layout and density of housing followed officially approved criteria. Town planning claimed that health, convenience and amenity were matters of public interest, and, if necessary, it was legitimate for private interests to be overridden in order to achieve them.

Throughout the twentieth century the case for town planning has rested on the claim that it is acting in the public interest and that its objectives should be underpinned by state powers when voluntary co-operation in pursuit of the objectives proved unforthcoming. Thus we have a panoply of powers to secure proper urban regulation: compulsory purchase of land and property for road-widening and new highways, or for town centre redevelopment in a comprehensive project; and for refusal of permission to develop on account of non-compliance with an approved plan – green belt, or a non-conforming use, or even by virtue of appearance and design. How far these might be legitimately considered to be in the public interest now needs to be considered very carefully. The notion of public interest is well-founded: to take steps to safeguard the health of an urban population a century ago might be equated today in terms of the measures necessary to protect an environment from pollution and despoliation of a kind that would be injurious to this and future generations, and it is defensible for public to override private interests in this regard. But the twentieth century has taken the public interest too far in town planning. It is time for the pendulum of the state bias against private interests to return to an equilibrium. Many of the things town planning sets out to achieve may be laudable and well-argued – but they are arguable and open to negotiation. We have come to the position whereby the state declares it is acting in the public interest because it has defined it so. In fact, what stands for the public interest is a bundle of self-interests and town planning is used to promote them.

Where Stands Town Planning?

Town planning enters the end of the century in a state of uncertainty. Within its not too distant history, and certainly within the memories of many of its professional members, it was called upon to play an important part in the fashioning of post-war Britain. That period has now gone and the profession now has something of an identity crisis as it accommodates new roles and new expectations.

The notion of planning on the scale and in the directions of yesteryear, which was so supportive to town planning in many of its activities and its co-ordinating functions, has all but gone and it is difficult to see any significant return in the foreseeable future. Local government, another crucible which offered opportunities for expansion, is in retreat; the externalization of planning services to other agencies (private or quango trust) is proceeding apace and compulsory competitive tendering may well be introduced. The no doubt strenuous opposition of the public sector unions may not be enough to hold the line. The bedrock of professional work, the plan making and development control functions of the statutory system, is still secure. But even here it is not implausible to envisage some scaling down, perhaps as part of sustained cost-saving programmes within local government, while some root-and-branch reconsideration of the nature of the planning system is always possible. It seems likely that the long-term, strategic and co-ordination functions in town planning offices will be reduced, while extra emphasis is given to short-term, project-oriented work, the longer horizons of plan making having relapsed already into 'rolling forward' exercises. Management may replace planning as the essence of the job to be done. This may well reopen much greater competition between rival professions, not just the old adversaries of town planning, surveying and architecture (given their traditional claims over land management and development) but other usurpers including those with backgrounds in business studies, finance and environmental science. The conclusion must be not that town planning's day has come and that it is a redundant exercise, rather that it is in a traditional period of change, as a discipline, as a profession and as an activity; the challenge before it is to accommodate that change.

The historical overview presented in earlier chapters readily confirms that the condition of town planning today stands in stark contrast with that of previous periods. For most of this century advocates of town planning could advance their claims with some assurance. Before 1939, with town planning largely untried, the promise could always be proclaimed. During the 1940s the activity made manifest common sense and there was an appealing visionary outlook about it still. Throughout the 1950s and 1960s the fruits of town planning labours were to be seen: new towns, national parks, new housing – modernity with economic prosperity. During the 1970s those very same fruits looked far less agreeable and for the last 20 years town planning has lost its popular, hopeful profile. Today it is an activity which occasions massive indifference to its claims, and attracts hostility when it is in association with development (which is currently perceived as bad). The benefits of a costly, highly regulative system, supported by an overmanned, self-protective bureaucracy, are called into question.

We observed in chapter 8 how town planning had been wounded by the onslaught of the critique from the social sciences. The criticisms have not abated, and the consequences of town planning and doubts about the 'value-addedness' of the statutory system have formed a ready target. One observer, Simmie (1993), lists six major criticisms which place 'planning at the crossroads'. Town planning, albeit unintentionally, has exacerbated the problem of urban poverty. The values underpinning town planning penalize the poorer classes. Town planning cannot deal with the complexity of cities; it interferes with the proper working of the market. Town planning limits wealth creation, innovation and experiment. It imposes unnecessary costs on development. Organized pressure groups use the planning system for their own ends. He observes:

> The remnants of the original vision and purpose of town planning could now be restated as the subsidization of unwanted agricultural activities and the maintenance of physical, residential apartheid. Meanwhile cities continue to de-urbanize and re-urbanize regardless of these major planning activities. Any consensus over such a vision has long since come to an end. It has become associated in the public mind with petty bureaucracy, nosey neighbours and timid, lowest-common-denominator

design solutions. Such support as it now receives comes mainly from the special and partial interest groups whose fragmented ends it serves. (p. 3)

Critiques such as these will hurt many of those in the professional ranks of town planning who (in particular) are discharging their duties as public servants in local authority offices. But it is necessary to repeat the criticisms, not in order to denigrate a profession or to belittle caring or conscientious staff, but to conduct a debate at corporate level.

The difficulty for town planning today is that intellectually it has ground to a halt. Its qualities of imagination for things that might be, and the inherent energy to achieve these things, are squeezed out of a system where other matters get in the way. The bread and butter job it has to do is, for much of the time, really rather limited – not by its own ambitions necessarily, but by the constraints put upon it. Town planners have become journeymen at one level, managerialists at the other. The maintenance of the process of town planning has become everything; the purpose behind it all is rather more obscure. The outlook of town planning is cautious, its practitioners power-brokers balancing the interests of elected members, community organizations and the ideology of their own profession.

It is often remarked that British town planning has one of the most sophisticated systems in the world. Perhaps this is so, but it was put in place to do a task envisaged 50 years ago; it is still in place but many of the assumptions behind the tasks have been removed.

References

Aalen, F. H. A. (1987) 'Public Housing in Ireland, 1880–1921', *Planning Perspectives*, 2(2), pp. 175–93.
—— (1989) 'Lord Meath, City Improvement and Social Imperialism', *Planning Perspectives*, 4(2), pp. 127–52.
Abercrombie, Patrick (1933) *Town and Country Planning*, Oxford University Press, Oxford.
—— (1945) *Greater London Plan*, HMSO, London.
Addison, Paul (1987a) 'The Road from 1945', in Peter Hennesey and Anthony Seldon (eds), *Ruling Performance: British Governments from Attlee to Thatcher*, Basil Blackwell, Oxford.
—— (1987b) 'Churchill in British Politics 1940–55', in J. M. W. Bean (ed.), *The Political Culture of Modern Britain*.
—— (1992) *Churchill on the Home Front 1900–55*, Jonathan Cape, London.
Aldridge, Mary (1979) *The British New Towns: a programme without a policy*, Routledge and Kegan Paul, London.
Ambrose, Peter (1986) *Whatever Happened to Planning*, Methuen, London.
—— and Colenutt, Bob (1975) *The Property Machine*, Penguin Books, Harmondsworth.
Ashworth, William (1954) *The Genesis of Modern British Town Planning: a study in economic and social history of the nineteenth and twentieth centuries*, Routledge and Kegan Paul, London.
Audit Commission (1995) *Calling the Tune: performance management in local government*, HMSO, London.
Audit Commission (1995) *Paying the Piper: people and pay management in local government*, HMSO, London.
Bacon, Roger and Eltis, Walter (1975) *Britain's Economic Problems: too few producers*, Macmillan, Basingstoke.
Barnett, Correlli (1972) *The Collapse of British Power*, Eyre, London.
—— (1986) *The Audit of War*, Macmillan, London.
—— (1995) *The Lost Victory*, Macmillan, London.
Beattie, Susan (1980) *A Revolution in London Housing: LCC architects and their work 1893–1914*, The Greater London Council/The Architectural Press, London.
Beer, Samuel H. (1982) *Britain Against Itself: the political contradictions of*

228   *References*

collectivism, Faber, London.

Beevers, Robert (1988) *The Garden City Utopia: a critical biography of Ebenezer Howard*, Macmillan, London.

Beveridge, Sir William (1942) *Social Insurance and Allied Services*, Cmd 6404, HMSO, London.

—— (1944) *Full Employment in a Free Society*, Allen and Unwin, London.

Birchall, Johnston (1995) 'Co-partnership Housing and the Garden City Movement', *Planning Perspectives*, 10(4), pp. 329–58.

Blackstone, Tessa and Plowden, William (1988) *Inside the Think Tank: advising the Cabinet 1971–1983*, William Heinemann, London.

Blair, Thomas L. (1973) *The Poverty of Planning: crisis in the urban environment*, Macdonald, London.

Blunden, John and Curry, Nigel (eds) (1990) *A People's Charter?*, HMSO, London.

Booth, Charles (1889–1903) *Life and Labour of the People of London* (17 vols), Macmillan, London.

Booth, William (1890) *In Darkest England and the Way Out*, 1970 edition, Charles Knight, London.

Bournville Village Trust (1941) *When We Build Again*, George Allen and Unwin, London.

Branson, Noreen (1985) *History of the Communist Party of Great Britain, 1927–1941*, Lawrence and Wishart, London.

Broady, Maurice (1968) *Planning for People: essays on the social context of planning*, Bedford Square Press, London.

Brownhill, Sue (1990) *Developing London's Docklands: another great planning disaster?*, Paul Chapman, London.

Bruce-Gardyne, Jock (1974) *Whatever Happened to the Quiet Revolution: the story of a brave experiment in government*, Charles Knight, London.

Brundtland, Gro Harlem (1987) *Our Common Future: Report of the World Commission on Environment and Development*, Oxford University Press, Oxford.

Buchanan Report (1963) *Traffic in Towns: Ministry of Transport*, HMSO, London.

Buchanan, C. D. (1958) *Mixed Blessing; the motor in Britain*, Leonard Hill, London.

Buckingham, James Silk (1849) *National Evils and Practical Remedies*, London.

Bullock, N. (1987) 'Plans for Post-war Housing in the UK: the case for mixed development and the flat', *Planning Perspectives*, 2(1), pp. 71–98.

Burnett, John (1978) *A Social History of Housing 1815–1970*, David and Charles, Newton Abbot.

Cadbury, George, Jnr (1915) *Town Planning: with special reference to the Birmingham schemes*, Longmans Green, London.

Calvocoressi, Peter (1978) *The British Experience 1945–75*, The Bodley Head, London.

Castells, Manuel (1977) *The Urban Question: a Marxist approach*, Edward Arnold, London.

Central Housing Advisory Committee (1961) *Homes for Today and Tomorrow*, HMSO, London.

Central Housing and Advisory Committee (1966) *Our Older Homes: a call for action*, HMSO, London.

Checkland, S. G. (1981) *The Upas Tree*, University of Glasgow Press, Glasgow.

Checkland, Sydney (1983) *British Public Policy 1776–1939: an economic, social and political perspective*, Cambridge University Press, Cambridge.

Cherry, Gordon E. (1970) *Town Planning in its Social Context*, Leonard Hill, London.

—— (1974) *The Evolution of British Town Planning*, Leonard Hill, Heath and Reach.

—— (1974) 'The Housing, Town Planning etc. Act, 1919', *The Planner*, 60(5), pp. 681–4.

—— (1975) *Environmental Planning, vol. II, National Parks and Recreation in the Countryside*, HMSO, London.

—— (1976) 'Aspects of Urban Renewal', in Tom Hancock (ed.), *Growth and Change in the Future City Region*, Leonard Hill, London, pp. 53–72.

—— (1980) 'The Place of Neville Chamberlain in British Town Planning', in (ed.), *Shaping an Urban World*, Mansell, London, pp. 161–79.

—— (1981) 'George Pepler, 1882–1959', in *Pioneers in British Planning*, The Architectural Press, pp. 131–49.

—— (1982) *The Politics of Town Planning*, Longman, Harlow.

—— (1988) *Cities and Plans: the shaping of urban Britain in the nineteenth and twentieth centuries*, Edward Arnold, London.

——, Jordon, Harriet, and Kafkoula, Kiki (1993) 'Gardens, Civic Art and Town Planning: the work of Thomas Mawson (1861–1933)', *Planning Perspectives*, 8(3), pp. 307–32.

—— (1994) *Birmingham: a study in geography, history and planning*, John Wiley, Chichester.

—— and Rogers, Alan W. (1996) *Rural Change and Planning: England and Wales in the twentieth century*, E. & F. N. Spon, London.

Cockett, Richard (1994) *Thinking the Unthinkable: think tanks and the economic counter-revolution, 1931–1983*, HarperCollins, London.

Coleman, Alice (1985) *Utopia on Trial: vision and reality in planned housing*, Hilary Shipman, London.

Committee on Land Utilisation in Rural Areas (1942) *Report*, Cmd 6378, HMSO, London.

Cox, Andrew (1984) *Adversary Politics and Land: the conflict over land and property policy in post-war Britain*, Cambridge University Press, Cambridge.

Crosland, C. A. R. (1956) *The Future of Socialism*, Cape, London.

Cullingworth, J. B. (1973) *Problems of an Urban Society* (3 vols), George Allen and Unwin, London.

—— (1975) *Environmental Planning, vol. I, Reconstruction and Land Use Planning 1939–1947*, HMSO, London.

—— (1979) *Environmental Planning, vol. III, New Towns Policy*, HMSO, London.

—— (1980) *Environmental Planning, vol. IV, Land Values, Compensation and Betterment*, HMSO, London.

Davies, J. G. (1972) *The Evangelistic Bureaucrat: a study of a planning exercise in Newcastle upon Tyne*, Tavistock, London.

Dennis, Norman (1970) *People and Planning*, Faber, London.

Department of the Environment (1973) *Greater London Development Plan: Report of the Panel of Inquiry*, HMSO, London.

Department of Health for Scotland (1947) *National Parks and the Conservation of Nature in Scotland*, Cmd 7235, HMSO, London.

Design of Dwellings Sub Committee of the Ministry of Health Central Housing Advisory Committee (1944) *The Design of Dwellings* (The Dudley Report), HMSO, London.

Donnison, David and Ungerson, Clare (1982) *Housing Policy*, Penguin, Harmondsworth.

Dower, John (1945) *National Parks in England and Wales*, Cmd 6628, HMSO, London.

Durbin, Elizabeth (1985) *New Jerusalems: the Labour Party and the economics of democratic socialism*, Routledge and Kegan Paul, London.

Dyos, H. J. and Aldcroft, D. H. (1969) *British Transport: an economic survey from the seventeenth century to the twentieth*, Leicester University Press. Pelican edition, Harmondsworth, 1974.

Eatwell, Roger (1979) *The 1945–1951 Labour Government*, Batsford Academic, London.

Eccleshall, Robert (1986) *British Liberalism: Liberal thought from the 1640s to the 1980s*, Longman, Harlow.

Elson, Martin J. (1986) *Green Belts: conflict and mediation in the urban fringe*, Heinemann, London.

Englander, D. (1983) *Landlord and Tenant in Urban Britain 1838–1918*, Oxford University Press, Oxford.

Eversley, David (1973) *The Planner in Society: the changing role of a profession*, Faber and Faber, London.

Expert Committee on Compensation and Betterment (1942) *Final Report*, Cmd 6386, HMSO, London.

Farnham, David and McVicar, Malcolm (1982) *Public Administration in the United Kingdom: an introduction*, Cassell, London.

Fishman, Robert (1977) *Urban Utopias in the Twentieth Century*, Basic Books,

New York.
Forrest, Ray and Murie, Alan (1988) *Selling the Welfare State: the privatization of public housing*, Routledge, London.
Forshaw, J. H. and Abercrombie, Patrick (1943) *County of London Plan*, Macmillan, London.
Fraser, Derek (1973) *The Evolution of the British Welfare State: a history of social policy since the Industrial Revolution*, Macmillan, Basingstoke.
Friend, J. K., Power, J. M., and Yewlett, C. J. L. (1974) *Public Planning: the inter-corporate dimension*, Tavistock, London.
Gans, Herbert J. (1968) *People and Plans: essays on urban problems and solutions*, Basic Books, New York.
Garside, Patricia L. (1988) '"Unhealthy Areas": town planning, eugenics and the slums, 1890–1945', *Planning Perspectives*, 3(1), pp. 24–46.
Gaskell, S. Martin (1983) *Building Control: national legislation and the introduction of local bye-laws in Victorian England*, Bedford Square Press, London.
George, Henry (1880) *Progress and Poverty*, New York. 1911 edition, Dent, London.
—— (1884) *Social Problems*, Kegan Paul, Trench, Trubner, London.
Glendinning, Miles and Muthesius, Stefan (1994) *Tower Block: modern public housing in England, Scotland, Wales and Northern Ireland*, Yale University Press.
Gray, John (1993) *Beyond the New Right: markets, government and the common environment*, Routledge, London.
Green, Brigid Grafton (1977) *Hampstead Garden Suburb 1907–1977*, Hampstead Garden Suburb Institute, London.
Greenleaf, W. H. (1983) *The British Political Tradition: vol. 1, The Rise of Collectivism*, Methuen, London.
—— (1983) *The British Political Tradition: vol. 2, The Ideological Heritage*, Methuen, London.
Hall, Peter et al. (1973) *The Containment of Urban England* (2 vols), George Allen and Unwin, London.
—— (1974) *Urban and Regional Planning*, Penguin Books, Harmondsworth.
—— (1980) *Great Planning Disasters*, Weidenfeld and Nicolson, London.
—— (ed.) (1981) *The Inner City in Context: the Final Report of the Social Science Research Council Inner Cities Working Party*, Heinemann, London.
Hall, Stewart and Schwarz, Bill (1985) 'State and Society 1880–1930', in Mary Langan and Bill Schwarz (eds), *Crises in the British State 1880–1930*, Hutchinson, London, pp. 7–32.
Harvey, David (1973) *Social Justice and the City*, Edward Arnold, London.
Hardy, Dennis (1979) *Alternative Communities in Nineteenth Century England*, Longman, London.
—— (1991a) *From Garden Cities to New Towns: campaigning for town and country planning, 1899–1946*, E. & F. N. Spon, London.

232   *References*

—— (1991b) *From New Towns to Green Politics: campaigning for town and country planning, 1946–1990*, E. & F. N. Spon, London.

—— and Ward, Colin (1984) *Arcadia for All: the legacy of a makeshift landscape*, Mansell, London.

Hayek, Friedrich A. (1944) *The Road to Serfdom*, University of Chicago Press, Chicago.

—— (1988) *The Fatal Conceit: the errors of socialism*, University of Chicago Press, Chicago.

Hennessy, Peter (1992) *Never Again: Britain, 1945–51*, Cape, London.

—— and Seldon, Anthony (eds) (1987) *Ruling Performance*, Basil Blackwell, Oxford.

Hill, Octavia (1883) *Homes of the London Poor*, Macmillan, London. 1970 edition, Frank Cass, London.

Hillman, Judy (1994) *The Bournville Hallmark: housing people for 100 years*, Brewin Books, Studley.

Holland, Milner *Report of the Committee on Housing in Greater London*, Cmnd 2605, HMSO, London.

Holden, C. H. and Holford, W. G. (1951) *The City of London: a record of destruction and survival*, The Architectural Press, London.

Holland, Stuart (1975) *The Challenge of Socialism*, Quartet, London.

Horsey, Miles (1988) 'Multi-storey Council Housing in Britain', *Planning Perspectives*, 3(2), pp. 167–96.

Horsfall, T. C. (1904) *The Improvement of the Dwellings and Surroundings of the People: the example of Germany*, Manchester University Press, Manchester.

Howard, Ebenezer (1898) *Tomorrow: a peaceful path to real reform*, Swan Sonnenschein, London.

—— (1902) *Garden Cities of Tomorrow*, Swan Sonnenschein, London.

Hubbard, Edward and Shippobottom, Michael (1988) *A Guide to Port Sunlight Village*, Liverpool University Press, Liverpool.

Hutton, Will (1995) *The state we're in: why Britain is in crisis and how to overcome it*, Cape, London.

Interim Report (1920) of the Committee appointed by the Minister of Health to consider and advise on the principles to be followed in dealing with unhealthy areas, HMSO, London.

Jackson, Frank (1985) *Sir Raymond Unwin: architect, planner and visionary*, Zwemmer, London.

Jenkins, Peter (1987) *Mrs Thatcher's Revolution: the ending of the socialist era*, Jonathan Cape, London.

Jewkes, John (1948) *Ordeal by Planning*, Macmillan, London.

Joad, C. E. M. (1946) *The Untutored Townsman's Invasion of the Country*, Faber and Faber, London.

Johnson, Paul (1980) *The Recovery of Freedom*, Basil Blackwell, Oxford.

Jones, Gareth Stedman (1971) *Outcast London: a study in the relationship between classes in Victorian society*, Oxford University Press, Oxford. 1976 edition, Peregrine, Harmondsworth.

Joseph, Sir Keith (1974) 'The Continuing Heritage', RIBA/Civic Trust Conference.

Kavanagh, Dennis (1987) *Thatcherism and British Politics: the end of consensus?*, Oxford University Press, Oxford.

—— and Morris, Peter (1989) *Consensus Politics from Attlee to Thatcher*, Blackwell, Oxford.

Langan, Mary (1985) 'Reorganizing the Labour Market: unemployment, the state and the labour movement, 1880–1914', in Mary Langan and Bill Schwarz (eds), *Crises in the British State 1880–1930*, Hutchinson, London, pp. 104–25.

Law, Christopher M. (1980) *British Regional Development since World War I*, David and Charles, Newton Abbot.

Lees, Andrew (1985) *Cities Perceived: urban society in European and American thought*, Manchester University Press, Manchester.

Letwin, Shirley Robin (1992) *The Anatomy of Thatcherism*, Fontana, London.

Leventhal, F. M. (1987) 'Seeing the Future: British left wing travellers to the Soviet Union, 1919–32', in J. M. W. Bean, *The Political Culture of Modern Britain*, Hamish Hamilton, London, pp. 209–27.

Local Government Board (1919) *Manual on the Preparation of State-Aided Housing Schemes*, HMSO, London.

London, Jack (1903) *The People and the Abyss*, Macmillan, New York. 1978 edition, Journeyman Press, London.

London County Council (1961) *The Building of a New Town*, Alec Tiranti, London.

MacEwen, Ann and Malcolm (1982) *National Parks: conservation or cosmetics?*, George Allen and Unwin, London.

Macfadyen, Dugald (1933) *Sir Ebenezer Howard and the Town Planning Movement*, Manchester University Press, Manchester.

Macintyre, Stuart (1980) *A Proletarian Science: Marxism in Britain, 1917–1933*, Lawrence and Wishart, London.

Mackenzie, Norman and Jeanne (1977) *The First Fabians*, Weidenfeld and Nicolson, London.

Marmaras, Emmanuel and Sutcliffe, Anthony (1994) 'Planning for Post-war London: the three independent plans, 1942–3', *Planning Perspectives*, 9(4), pp. 431–53.

Marquand, David (1987) 'British Politics 1945–1987, Four Perspectives', in Peter Hennessy and Anthony Seldon (eds), *Ruling Performance*, Basil Blackwell, Oxford, pp. 301–30.

Marr, T. R. (1904) *Housing Conditions in Manchester and Salford*, Manchester.

Marsh, David and Rhodes, R. A. W. (eds) (1992) *Implementing Thatcherite Policies: audit of an era*, Open University Press, Buckingham.

234   *References*

Marshall, Alfred (1884) 'The Housing of the London Poor: where to house them', *Contemporary Review*, 45.

Martin, Ray (1989) 'Deindustrialisation and State Intervention: Keynesianism, Thatcherism and the regions', in John Mohan, *The Political Geography of Contemporary Britain*, Macmillan, Basingstoke, pp. 87–112.

McCrone, Gavin (1969) *Regional Policy in Britain*, George Allen and Unwin, London.

McKay, David H. and Cox, Andrew W. (1979) *The Politics of Urban Change*, Croom Helm, London.

Meller, Helen (1990) *Patrick Geddes: social evolutionist and city planner*, Routledge, London.

—— (1995) 'Philanthropy and Public Enterprise: international exhibitions and the modern town planning movement, 1889–1913', *Planning Perspectives*, 10(3), pp. 295–310.

Middlemass, Keith (1980) *Politics in Industrial Society*, Deutsch, London.

—— (1986) *Power, Competition and the State: vol. I, Britain in Search of Balance, 1940–61*, Macmillan, Basingstoke.

Miller, Mervyn (1989) *Letchworth: the first garden city*, Phillimore, Chichester.

—— (1992) *Raymond Unwin: garden cities and town planning*, Leicester University Press, Leicester.

Ministry of Health, Departmental Committee (1935) *Report: Garden Cities and Satellite Towns*, HMSO, London.

—— *Housing Manual 1949*, HMSO, London.

Ministry of Housing and Local Government (1964) *The South East Study: 1961–1981*, HMSO, London.

Ministry of Town and Country Planning (1944) *The Control of Land Use*, Cmd 6537, HMSO, London.

—— (1946) *Interim Report of the New Towns Committee*, Cmd 6759, HMSO, London.

—— (1946) *Second Interim Report of the New Towns Committee*, Cmd 6794, HMSO, London.

—— (1946) *Final Report of the New Towns Committee*, Cmd 6876, HMSO, London.

—— (1947) *The Redevelopment of Central Areas*, HMSO, London.

—— (1947) *Report of the National Parks Committee*, Cmd 7121, HMSO, London.

—— (1947) *Footpaths and Access to the Countryside: Report of the Special Committee*, Cmd 7207, HMSO, London.

Ministry of War Transport (1946) *Design and Layout of Roads in Built-up Areas*, HMSO, London.

Moggridge, D. E. (1976) *Keynes*, Macmillan, London.

Montgomery, J. and Thornley, A. (eds) (1990) *Radical Planning Initiatives: new directions for urban planning in the 1990s*, Gower, Aldershot.

Morgan, Kenneth O. (1984) *Labour in Power 1945–1951*, Clarendon Press, Oxford.

—— (1987) 'The Rise and Fall of Public Ownership in Britain', in J. M. W. Bean, *The Political Culture of Modern Britain*, Hamish Hamilton, London, pp. 277–98.

Muchnick, David H. (1970) *Urban Renewal in Liverpool: a study of the politics of redevelopment*, Occasional Papers on Social Administration no. 33, G. Bell & Sons, London.

New Townsmen (1918) *New Towns After the War*, Dent, London.

Newman, Oscar (1972) *Defensible Space*, Macmillan, New York.

Nicholson, Max (1970) *The Environmental Revolution: a guide for the new masters of the world*, Hodder and Stoughton, London.

Nuffield Foundation (1986) *Town and Country Planning: Report of a Committee of Inquiry*, London.

Orbach, Laurence F. (1977) *Homes for Heroes: a study of the evolution of British public housing, 1915–1921*, Seeley, Service, London.

Pahl, R. E. (1970) *Whose City?*, Longman, London.

Parker, R. B. and Unwin, R. (1901) *The Act of Building a Home*, Longmans Green, London.

Parliamentary Papers (1917) *Report of the Royal Commission on the Housing of the Industrial Population of Scotland*, Cd 8731, HMSO, London.

—— (1918) *Report of the Committee – to consider questions of building construction in connection with the provision of dwellings for the working classes* (The Tudor Walters Report), Cd 9191, HMSO, London.

—— (1936) *Third Report of the Commissioner for the Special Areas (England and Wales)*, Cmd 5303, HMSO, London.

Parliamentary Paper (1944) *Employment Policy*, Cmd 6527, HMSO, London.

—— (1963) *London – Employment: Housing: Land*, Cmnd 1952, HMSO, London.

—— (1963) *The North-East 26/12/95: a programme for development and growth*, Cmnd 2006, HMSO, London.

—— (1963) *Central Scotland: a programme for development and growth*, Cmnd 2188, HMSO, London.

—— (1964) *South East England*, Cmnd 2308, HMSO, London.

—— (1966) *Leisure in the Countryside, England and Wales*, Cmnd 2928, HMSO, London.

—— (1971) *Local Government in England*, Cmnd 4584, HMSO, London.

—— (1971) *The Reorganization of Central Government*, Cmnd 4506, HMSO, London.

—— (1985) *Lifting the Burden*, Cmnd 9571, HMSO, London.

—— (1989) *The Future of Development Plans*, Cm 569, HMSO, London.

—— (1990) *This Common Inheritance: Britain's environmental strategy*, Cm 1200, HMSO, London.

Pearson, Lynn F. (1988) *The Architectural and Social History of Cooperative Living*, Macmillan, Basingstoke.

Perkin, Harold (1989) *The Rise of Professional Society: England since 1880*, Routledge, London.

Pimlott, Ben (1985) *Hugh Dalton*, Jonathan Cape, London.

Pinto-Duschinsky, Michael (1987) 'From Macmillan to Home, 1959–1964', in Peter Hennessey and Anthony Seldon (eds), *Ruling Performance*, Basil Blackwell, Oxford, pp. 150–85.

Planning Advisory Group (1965) *The Future of Development Plans*, HMSO, London.

Plowden, William (1973) *The Motor Car and Politics in Britain*, Pelican, Harmondsworth.

Poor Law Commissioners (1842) *Report on the Sanitary Condition of the Labouring Population of Great Britain*, HMSO, London.

Popper, Karl (1945) *The Open Society and its Enemies*, Routledge, London.

Preston, W. C. (1883) *The Bitter Cry of Outcast London*, London. 1969 edition, Cedric Chivers, Bath.

Pugh, Martin (1994) *State and Society: British political and social history 1870–1992*, Edward Arnold, London.

Ravetz, Alison (1974) *Model Estate: planned housing at Quarry Hill*, Croom Helm, London.

Redcliffe Maud, Sir John (1969) *Report of the Royal Commission on Local Government in England 1966–1969*, Cmnd 4040, HMSO, London.

Report of the Ministry of Housing and Local Government for the period 1950/51 to 1954, Cmd 9559, HMSO, London, August 1955.

Report of the Ministry of Housing and Local Government 1959, Cmnd 1027, HMSO, London, June 1960.

Reynolds, Jack (1976) *Saltaire: an introduction to the village of Sir Titus Salt*, Bradford Art Galleries and Museums, Bradford.

Richardson, Benjamin Ward (1876) *Hygeia, a City of Health*, Macmillan, London. 1985 edition, Garland Publishing, New York.

Robbins, Lionel (1937) *Economic Planning and International Order*, Macmillan, London.

Rowntree, B. Seebohm (1901) *Poverty: a study of town life*, Longmans, London.

Royal Commission on the Distribution of the Industrial Population (1940) *Report*, Cmd 6153, HMSO, London.

Rural Housing Sub Committee of the Central Housing Advisory Committee (1944) *Rural Housing, Third Report*, HMSO, London.

Sandford, Lord (1974) *Report of the National Park Review Committee*, HMSO, London.

Schaffer, Frank (1970) *The New Town Story*, MacGibbon and Kee, London.

Schneer, Jonathan (1987) 'The Labour Left and the General Election of 1945', in J. M. W. Bean (ed.), *The Political Culture of Modern Britain*, Hamilton, London, pp. 262–76.

Schumacher, F. (1973) *Small is Beautiful: economics as if people really mattered*, Abacus, London.

Schuster, Sir George (1950) *Report of the Committee on the Qualification of Planners*, Cmd 8059, HMSO, London.

Schwarz, Bill (1985) 'The Corporate Economy 1890–1929', in Mary Langan and Bill Schwarz (eds), *Crises in the British State 1880–1930*, Hutchinson, London, pp. 80–103.

Scottish Council (Development and Industry) (1961) *Report of the Committee of Inquiry into the Scottish Economy*.

Scottish National Parks Survey Committee (1945) *National Parks: a Scottish survey*, Cmd 6631, HMSO, London.

Seebohm Report (1968) *Report of the Committee on Local Authority and Allied Personal Services*, Cmnd 3703, HMSO, London.

Seldon, Anthony (1981) *Churchill's Indian Summer: the Conservative Government, 1951–55*, Hodder and Stoughton, London.

—— and Ball, Stuart (eds) (1994) *Conservative Century: the Conservative Party since 1900*, Oxford University Press, Oxford.

Shanks, Michael (1961) *The Stagnant Society*, Penguin, Harmondsworth.

Sharp, Thomas (1932) *Town and Countryside: some aspects of urban and rural development*, Faber and Faber, London.

—— (1940) *Town Planning*, Penguin Books, Harmondsworth.

Sheail, John (1975) *Nature in Trust: the history of nature conservation in Britain*, Blackie, Glasgow.

—— (1979) 'The Restriction of Ribbon Development Act: the character and perception of land use control in inter war Britain', *Regional Studies*, 13(6), pp. 501–12.

—— (1995) 'John Dower, National Parks and Town and Country Planning in Britain', *Planning Perspectives*, 10(1), pp. 1–16.

Shoard, Marion (1980) *The Theft of the Countryside*, Temple Smith, London.

Simmie, J. M. (1974) *Citizens in Conflict: the sociology of town planning*, Hutchinson, London.

Simon, E. D. (1929) *How to Abolish the Slums*, Longmans, Green, New York.

Simpson, Michael (1985) *Thomas Adams and the Modern Planning Movement: Britain, Canada and the United States, 1900–1940*, Mansell, London.

Skeffington, A. M., Committee on Public Participation in Planning (1969) *People and Planning*, HMSO, London.

Skidelsky, Robert (1967) *Politicians and the Slump: the Labour Government of 1929–1931*, Macmillan, London.

—— (1983) *John Maynard Keynes: Vol. 1, Hopes Betrayed, 1883–1920*, Macmillan, London.

—— (ed.) (1988) *Thatcherism*, Chatto and Windus, London.

—— (1992) *John Maynard Keynes: Vol. 2, The Economist as Saviour, 1920–1937*, Macmillan, London.

Skilleter, K. J. (1993) 'The Role of Public Utility Societies in Early British Town Planning and Housing Reform 1901–36', *Planning Perspectives*, 8(2), pp. 125–65.

Starkie, David (1982) *The Mororway Age: road and traffic policies in post-war Britain*, Pergamon, Oxford.

Stephenson, T. (1988) *Forbidden Land: the struggle for access to mountain and moorland*, Manchester University Press, Manchester.

Sutcliffe, Anthony (1981) *Towards the Planned City: Germany, Britain, the United States and France, 1780–1914*, Basil Blackwell, Oxford.

Tarn, J. N. (1973) *Five Per Cent Philanthropy: an account of housing in urban areas between 1840 and 1914*, Cambridge University Press, Cambridge.

Taylor, Nicholas (1973) *The Village in the City*, Temple Smith, London.

Taylor, Paul (1995) 'British Local Government and House Building during the Second World War', *Planning History*, 17(2), pp. 17–21.

Temple, William (1942) *Christianity and the Social Order*, Penguin, Harmondsworth.

The National Plan (1965), HMSO, London.

Thomas, Andrew D. (1986) *Housing and Urban Renewal*, George Allen and Unwin, London.

Thomas, David (1970) *London's Green Belt*, Faber and Faber, London.

Traffic in Towns (1963) Reports of the Steering Group and Working Group appointed by the Minister of Transport, HMSO, London.

Tripp, H. Alker (1942) *Town Planning and Road Traffic*, Edward Arnold, London.

Tudor Walters Committee (1918) *Report*, HMSO, London.

Unwin, Raymond (1909) *Town Planning in Practice: an introduction to the art of designing cities and suburbs*, Fisher Unwin, London.

—— (1921) 'Some Thoughts on the Development of London', in Sir Aston Webb (ed.), *London of the Future*, T. Fisher Unwin, London.

—— and Parker, R. Barry (1907) *The Art of Building a Home*, Longmans Green, London.

Vaizey, John (1983) *In Breach of Promise*, Weidenfeld and Nicolson, London.

Vine, J. R. Somers (1879) *English Municipal Institutions: their growth and development 1835–1879 statistically illustrated*, Waterlow, London. 1985 edition, Garland Publishing, New York.

Waller, P. J. (1983) *Town, City and Nation: England 1850–1914*, Oxford University Press, Oxford.

Wannop, Urlan and Cherry, Gordon E. (1994) 'The Development of Regional Planning in the United Kingdom', *Planning Perspectives*, 9(1), pp. 29–60.

Ward, Stephen (1974) The Town and Country Planning Act, 1932, *The Planner*,

60(5), pp. 685–9.

Ward, Stephen V. (ed.) (1992) *The Garden City: past, present and future*, E. & F. N. Spon, London.

—— (1994) *Planning and Urban Change*, Paul Chapman, London.

Wates, Nick (1976) *The Battle for Tolmers Square*, Routledge and Kegan Paul, London.

West Central Scotland Plan Team (1974) *West Central Scotland: a programme of action*, West Central Scotland Plan Steering Committee, Glasgow.

Williams-Ellis, Clough (1928) *England and the Octopus*, Portmeirion.

Wilson, Harold (1971) *The Labour Government 1964–70: a personal record*, Weidenfeld and Nicolson, Michael Joseph, London.

Wilson, William H. (1989) *The City Beautiful Movement*, Johns Hopkins University Press, Baltimore.

Wohl, Anthony S. (1983) *Endangered Lives: public health in Victorian Britain*, Dent, London. 1984 edition, Methuen, London.

Wolfe, Lawrence (1945) *The Reilly Plan: a new way of life*, Nicholson and Watson, London.

Wootton, Barbara (1945) *Freedom under Planning*, Allen and Unwin, London.

Wright, Myles (1982) *Lord Leverhulme's Unknown Venture: the Lever Chair and the beginnings of town and regional planning 1908–48*, Hutchinson Bentham, London.

Yelling, J. A. (1986) *Slums and Slum Clearance in Victorian London*, Allen and Unwin, London.

—— (1992) *Slums and Redevelopment: policy and practice in England, 1918–45*, UCL Press, London.

Young, Michael amd Willmott, Peter (1957) *Family and Kinship in East London*, Routledge and Kegan Paul, London.

Index

Chorley, 153
Chrysler, 176
churches, 2, 6
Churchill, Sir Winston, 49, 145
    Coalition government, 88, 93, 109
    loses election (1945), 110, 112
    Party Conference (1946), 117
    prime minister (1951–55), 135,
        138–9
    Unemployment Insurance Act, 118
Citizen's Charter, 196
City Challenge, 203
city competitions, 40, 42
City Corporation, 4
city grants, 203
city life *see* urban life
Civic Trust, 189
Civil Amenities Act (1967), 148
civil aviation, 115, 116
Civil Service, 88, 89, 190
Clark, Colin, 54
Clyde Valley, 100, 109, 123
Clydeside, 72, 92
Co-operative Building Society, 106
co-partnership schemes, 29–30
Co-partnership Tenants Housing
    Council, 29
Co-partnership Tenants Ltd., 30
coal mines
    attempts to reorganize (1920s), 62
    nationalization of, 51, 52, 115, 117
    protection of during First World
        War, 62
    safety in, 8
Coalition Government (1940–5), 213,
    216
    corporate state established, 88–92
    end of, 109–12
    housing, 204
    industry, 111–12
    land compensation, 102–3, 107–8
    national parks, 105–6
    planning ethos, 92–5
    regional economic planning, 109,
        112
    reports commissioned, 100–6, 112
    roads, 100
    town planning developments,
        95–100, 106–9
coastal development, 80
Cockett, Richard, 91, 137, 140, 171,

172, 177
Cole, G.D.H., 47, 54
Coleman, Alice, 206–7
Colenutt, Bob, 186–7
Collard, David, 138
communism, 55–6, 95
Communist Party, 56–7, 104
Community Development Programme,
    188
community involvement, 147, 183
Community Land Act (1975), 187, 198
Community Land Scheme, 187
consensus politics, 113–14, 117–18,
    134–8, 215–16, 217
    collapse of, 171–4, 191–5
Conservation Areas, 148
Conservative government (1951–64),
    133, 135–7, 138–41, 213–14, 217
    housing, 139, 157, 204
    land compensation, 146, 149–50
    national parks, 146, 154–5
    new towns, 140, 146, 151–3
    regional planning, 136, 140, 164–5,
        168
    roads, 160–4
Conservative government (1970–4),
    133, 135, 137, 143–5, 148, 149,
    217
    development gains tax, 187
    housing, 158, 159–60, 204
    inner cities, 188
    land compensation, 150
    national parks, 156
    nationalization, 144
    new towns, 153–4
    regional planning, 166–7, 168
Conservative government (post-1979),
    190, 191–7, 214, 217, 219, 220
    development land tax, 187
    environment, 208–10
    housing, 195, 196, 203–7
    nationalization, 193
    regional economic planning, 200,
        207–8
    town planning policy, 197–203
Conservatives
    caretaker government (1945), 109
    Conference (1963), 141
    consensus politics, 113, 135–8
    during Second World War, 94, 95
    electoral record, 219

see also education; housing
socialism, 219
  economic liberals attack on, 60–1,
    110, 119–20, 137, 172
  Fabian attraction to, 47–8
  see also Labour Party
Socialist Labour Party, 56
sociology, 179–83
Solihull, 148
Somerset Levels, 209
Sorel, Georges, 23
South Downs, 154, 209
South Woodham Ferrers, 201
Southampton, 92, 163
Southwark, 206
Soviet Union, 55–6
Special Areas, 64–5, 84, 109, 128
Special Areas Amendment Act (1937),
  64
Special Areas (Development and
  Improvement) Act (1934), 64
Special Development Areas, 207
Spencer, Herbert, 23
Stadtebau, 32, 34
Der Stadtebau, 34–5
Stalin, Joseph, 56
Stamp, Dudley, 103
Standing Committee on National
  Parks, 105
Standing Conference on London
  Regional Planning, 98–100
Stapleford, 121
Starkie, David, 131, 161
state intervention, 170, 211, 215–17
  Communists on, 56–7
  Conservative attack on (post-1979),
    190, 191–7, 217
  Conservatives on (pre-1939), 44,
    50–1, 69, 70
  Fabian justification for, 45–8, 50
  increase of during nineteenth
    century, 1–16, 43–5, 216
  increase of during First World War,
    52, 61–2, 66
  increase of during Second World
    War, 87–92
  inter-war period, 62–5, 216
  Labour Party Conference (1963),
    141
  Labour Party on (pre-1939), 50,
    51–6

  Liberals changed attitude to (pre-
    1939), 44, 48–50, 53, 61
  slum housing (nineteenth century),
    20
  see also central planning;
    Coalition government
    (1940–5); Conservative
    government (1951–64);
    Conservative government
    (1970–4); Labour govern-
    ment (1945–51); Labour
    government (1964–70); Labour
    government (1974–9); local
    government; Keynesian
    economics
state protection policy, 49
statutory planning
  inter-war developments in, 61, 66,
    67–72, 212
  pre-1914, 18, 35–8, 61
  for post-1945 see Town and Country
    Planning Acts
steel industry, 115, 116, 138, 142,
  144, 165
Stein, S., 83
Stenning, Sir Alexander, 38
Stephenson, T., 81
Stevenage, 121, 122, 123, 124, 160
Stoke, 30
Stone Bassett, 201
Stonehouse, 153, 187
Strachey, John, 114
Strathclyde, 167
structure plans, 147, 186, 200
Stuart, J., 151
suburban housing
  in Birmingham, 8, 35–6
  inter-war years, 74, 76, 78, 86
  in London, 7, 22–3, 29
  see also garden suburbs
Sunderland, 26, 159
Supply, Ministry of, 88, 89
Surrey, 71, 121
Sutcliffe, Anthony, 32, 96
Sutcliffe, G. Lister, 30
Swansea, 198

Tai Cymru, 205
Tamworth, 154
Tarn, J.N., 19
Tawney, R.H., 52, 54